# Wheelchair Sport

A complete guide for athletes, coaches, and teachers

**Vicky Goosey-Tolfrey, PhD**

*Loughborough University*

Ed

Human

D0025432

**Library of Congress Cataloging-in-Publication Data**

Wheelchair sport / Vicky Goosey-Tolfrey, [editor].
    p. cm.
  Includes bibliographical references and index.
  ISBN-13: 978-0-7360-8676-9 (soft cover)
  ISBN-10: 0-7360-8676-5 (soft cover)
  1.  Wheelchair sports.  I. Goosey-Tolfrey, Vicky, 1971-  II. Title.
  GV709.3.G66 2010
  790.196--dc22

                                    2009051856

ISBN-10: 0-7360-8676-5 (print)
ISBN-13: 978-0-7360-8676-9 (print)

The Web addresses cited in this text were current as of February 2010, unless otherwise noted.

**Acquisitions Editor:** John Dickinson, PhD; **Developmental Editor:** Jacqueline Eaton Blakley; **Assistant Editor:** Elizabeth Evans; **Copyeditor:** Alisha Jeddeloh; **Indexer:** Bobbi Swanson; **Permission Manager:** Dalene Reeder; **Graphic Designer:** Bob Reuther; **Graphic Artist:** Tara Welsch; **Cover Designer:** Bob Reuther; **Photographer (cover):** JULIEN CROSNIER/DPPI/Icon SMI; **Photo Asset Manager:** Laura Fitch; **Visual Production Assistant:** Joyce Brumfield; **Photo Production Manager:** Jason Allen; **Art Manager:** Kelly Hendren; **Associate Art Manager:** Alan L. Wilborn; **Printer:** Sheridan Books

Printed in the United States of America       10  9  8  7  6  5  4  3  2  1

The paper in this book is certified under a sustainable forestry program.

**Human Kinetics**
Web site: www.HumanKinetics.com

*United States:* Human Kinetics
P.O. Box 5076
Champaign, IL 61825-5076
800-747-4457
e-mail: humank@hkusa.com

*Canada:* Human Kinetics
475 Devonshire Road Unit 100
Windsor, ON N8Y 2L5
800-465-7301 (in Canada only)
e-mail: info@hkcanada.com

*Europe:* Human Kinetics
107 Bradford Road
Stanningley
Leeds LS28 6AT, United Kingdom
+44 (0) 113 255 5665
e-mail: hk@hkeurope.com

*Australia:* Human Kinetics
57A Price Avenue
Lower Mitcham, South Australia 5062
08 8372 0999
e-mail: info@hkaustralia.com

*New Zealand:* Human Kinetics
P.O. Box 80
Torrens Park, South Australia 5062
0800 222 062

                          E4941

# Contents

## PART I          Understanding Wheelchair Sport

## CHAPTER 10  Wheelchair Rugby . . . . . . . . . . . . . . . . . . . . . . . . . . 151

*Kevin Orr and Laurie A. Malone*

## CHAPTER 11  Wheelchair Tennis . . . . . . . . . . . . . . . . . . . . . . . 167

*Dawn Newbery, Geraint Richards, Stephanie Trill,
and Martyn Whait*

# foreword

All people need to maintain healthy, active lifestyles. Sport can play a large part in such a lifestyle; for those who use a wheelchair, many sports are available. The International Paralympic Committee strives to ensure that sport is accessible to all potential Paralympic athletes. We encourage all participants to be the best they can be, whether that involves making small personal gains in weekly local competitions or working towards becoming a Paralympic champion.

*Wheelchair Sport* has everything you need for optimal performance. You will also find that the sport-specific chapters provide plenty of advice on excelling in wheelchair rugby, basketball, racing, handcycling, and tennis.

What most impresses me about *Wheelchair Sport* are the insights from the world's leading athletes, sport scientists, and coaches in the field. Their thoughts on training and preparing for competition will benefit all readers looking to gain an edge in their sports.

I have known Dr. Vicky Goosey-Tolfrey and her team of contributors for many years, and I have always been impressed by their knowledge and the way in which they communicate their ideas to their athletes, coaches, and support staff. *Wheelchair Sport* superbly reflects these levels of expertise; you will benefit from the advice of Dr. Goosey-Tolfrey and the contributors.

I look forward to seeing the future wheelchair sport stars being inspired by the information contained in these pages.

Sir Philip Craven, MBE

# Preface

Each year thousands of men and women become disabled due to an accident or illness and thereafter use a wheelchair for locomotion. The statistics tell us that there are approximately 1 to 2 million wheelchair users in the United States and approximately 1 to 2 million wheelchair users in Europe. This means that approximately 1 in every 200 people in the United States and Europe are in wheelchairs.

In 1948, Sir Ludwig Guttman, a neurologist who was working with World War II veterans with spinal injuries at Stoke Mandeville Hospital, Aylesbury, in the United Kingdom, began using sport as part of the rehabilitation programmes for his patients. Since that time, participation in wheelchair sport has grown beyond a method to improve wheelchair users' physical capacity. Wheelchair sport can increase confidence and self-esteem, and it may provide people with a positive outlook on life. There is a wheelchair sport for almost everyone who wants to participate and for any level of expertise, from novice through to Paralympic competition.

High-performance athletes are high performance whether they have a disability or not. However, the journey to this level of sporting excellence is dramatically different for wheelchair sport. Wheelchair athletes need sporting opportunities that nurture, recruit, and develop them through to the national level. They need access to sporting facilities and the community, as well as effective disability sport organizations. Access and support are just some of the challenges that wheelchair athletes and nondisabled athletes do not share.

Although the unique challenges of wheelchair sport participation can present obstacles, there are more opportunities than ever before to compete at any level. Advances in wheelchairs, understanding of the classification system, training methods, pushing techniques, and psychological aspects of wheelchair sport should help people with disabilities to achieve their sporting dreams. At the highest level, wheelchair sports have a dominating presence at the Paralympic Games, and while the science, engineering, and sporting classification systems evolve we rely on evidence practice through scientific communities to keep up. *Wheelchair Sport* bridges the gap between sporting excellence to wheelchair sport at a grassroots level. *Wheelchair Sport* is an educational resource for coaches, physical trainers, sport scientists, rehabilitation practitioners, wheelchair users, and all those with an interest in the field of wheelchair sport.

The development and implementation of safe and effective exercise and technical training programmes for wheelchair athletes may be based on theory for nondisabled athletes. After appreciating the many differences between nondisabled and wheelchair athletes, the book highlights the practical application of conventional strength and conditioning principles, nutritional considerations, and aspects of travel in relation to the needs of athletes who use a wheelchair for sport or for daily locomotion. Many questions may be asked by coaches, athletes, and practitioners, such as, "Do I need to adapt my coaching techniques to suit athletes with disabilities?", "How should I set up my sport wheelchair?", and "What are the energy requirements of the wheelchair athlete?" There are obviously going to be differences to the conventional theories regarding nondisabled athletes; however, even among wheelchair users there is likely to be a wide range of answers to these questions based on whether the athlete has a spinal cord injury, at what point the injury is sited, when the onset of the disability occurred, whether it is complete or incomplete, and whether the athlete uses a wheelchair for a different reason.

In order to answer some of these questions, *Wheelchair Sport* is divided into two parts. The contributors of part I have all made significant contributions to sport science education through involvement with national sporting governing bodies and national Paralympic associations. The structure of this text provides a balance between a general overview of and details about classification; psychological, mechanical, biomechanical, and physiological factors; strength and conditioning; nutrition and body composition; and the travel concerns that may be experienced when participating in wheelchair sport.

The first chapter introduces the sports that form the basis of this text and familiarizes the reader towards classification. This is followed by a chapter that describes the importance of wheelchair selection and propulsion technique. The third chapter demonstrates the importance of understanding the physiological differences between nondisabled and wheelchair athletes and the physiological adaptations that result from training. As a natural progression from this, chapter 4 introduces the concepts of strength and conditioning for wheelchair sport. Optimum nutritional strategies for health, training, and competition are discussed in chapter 5, along with assessment of body composition. Chapter 6 provides some practical advice to the wheelchair athlete who is travelling and competing abroad. Finally, chapter 7 describes principles and considerations that should be incorporated into the practice of those working with wheelchair athletes.

Part II is made up of sport-specific chapters and covers the five main sports (wheelchair basketball, racing, rugby, tennis, and handcycling). Although their experience lies in a number of wheelchair sports, the contributors of this section are united by their passion towards each sport, a respect of other coaches and athletes, and a desire to further the status that wheelchair sport deserves. All the contributors in this section have personally coached or been involved themselves as either an athlete or part of the support team at a very high level (including the Paralympics). These chapters provide a brief background of the sport, tactical advice in the form of drills, and playing and racing strategies. There is a truly international flavour to this section, with contributions from Belgium, Canada, Germany, the United Kingdom, and the United States.

The authors contributing to this book include coaches, applied sport scientists, and specialists in sports medicine and physical therapy working within Paralympic sport, as well as four high-performance wheelchair athletes whose stories can only have enhanced wheelchair sporting knowledge. It was a pleasure to incorporate these brief insights of life as a Paralympian by Mike Frogley; the Baroness Grey-Thompson; Peter Norfolk, OBE; and Randy Snow. This text is designed to help readers gain the necessary knowledge to enhance performance while at the same time allowing people with disabilities to realize what it may take to achieve their sporting dreams at any level.

# Acknowledgements

I am indebted to Professor Ian Campbell, Professor Lucas van der Woude, and the Baroness Grey-Thompson, whose scientific knowledge of and dedication to wheelchair sport has strengthened my desire to work in this field.

I also thank my parents, Marvin and Ruth; my sister, Helen; my husband, Keith; and my children, Owen and India. Without their love and support my journey so far would not have been possible.

I am grateful for the contributions of Professor Tom Reilly and Randy Snow, who both passed away prior to the publication of this book. I admire and am inspired by their international academic and sporting excellence. Those of us who have known them, worked with them, and learned from them know that their legacies have motivated many and will continue to do so.

## Randy Snow

I came from an active background. My family played tennis, participated in water activities, camped out, hunted and fished, and attended all kinds of camps. So when my accident occurred, thoughts of living my life from a wheelchair were daunting. For three years I tried to live as if I was still walking. I would not associate with anyone in a wheelchair because I believed I wasn't like them. It is said that when it becomes more painful to stay the same than it does to change, we are finally ready. That was my story.

While in college, I began playing wheelchair basketball informally with friends. We pushed and turned and shot baskets as we cut our teeth playing a sport that I had always loved. We purchased some sport chairs, named our team the High Rollers, and began travelling and playing in tournaments—and I was good. Suddenly, rather than focusing on the things that I couldn't do, basketball highlighted the things that I could do. In just three years I was selected to travel to Japan and represent the United States on a tour of six cities. The crowds, the emotion, the responsibility of fighting for my teammates in a cause that was bigger than anything I had ever experienced tapped a nerve, and from that point on I was never the same.

Unfortunately, the Paralympics is often regarded as either a watered-down form of admirable competition or a "feel-good" pacifier. It's considered good for *those people*. To a Paralympian, it's much more. For me, wheelchair sport created a pathway out of the condescending corner of being handicapped and guided me through the initial negativity of my injury.

When a person makes the decision to attempt to go to the Paralympics, he puts his life on hold. Winning a gold medal takes living a gold medal. It's a lifestyle: every decision made, every action taken, every bit of interaction with life on and off the court, awake or asleep.

Competing overseas challenged my perspective and gave me a unique view of the world. For years, wars, accidents, pandemics, and birth defects have caused physical challenges. The way in which people with disabilities are treated exposes a country's empathy, fear, and personality. To some societies, disability means failure, weakness, and undignified death. In other countries, like Holland and Australia, wheelchair athletes are accepted, respected, and revered.

There is no predetermined mold of acceptability at the Paralympics. Watching a quadruple amputee swim or a blind man run in the 1500-metre race or a dwarf slam on some table tennis teaches us lessons about adapting, persevering, and *using what we have* in order to achieve. These lessons aren't just for common folk. With each of my Paralympic competitions I have been able to see further.

# PART I

# Understanding Wheelchair Sport

# Introduction to Wheelchair Sport

Sean Tweedy and Nicholas Diaper

The aim of this chapter is to introduce wheelchair sport. It includes an overview of spinal cord injury, a review of the health benefits of wheelchair sport, descriptions of the sports covered in this text, and an introduction to the concept of classification. It is a common misconception that wheelchair sport is only for people with spinal cord injuries (SCI). In fact, wheelchair sport is appropriate for people with a range of disabilities, including those resulting from amputations, cerebral palsy, and spina bifida. However, the focus of this text is SCI because it is the condition that affects most wheelchair athletes.

Wheelchair sport has grown incredibly since 1948, when Sir Ludwig Guttmann organized the first international sport competition for wounded World War II veterans at Stoke Mandeville Hospital in England. What began as a rehabilitation exercise has evolved into one of the world's largest multisport events—the Paralympic Games. From a modest 400 athletes representing 23 countries at the first Paralympic Games in Rome in 1960, the modern summer Paralympic Games now boasts 4,000 athletes from 150 nations and an ever-increasing global television audience.

There are currently 10 Paralympic sports (summer and winter) that involve competition in a form of wheelchair (see table 1.1). These range from individual and team sports involving propulsion, such as wheelchair racing and wheelchair basketball, to nonpropulsion wheelchair sports, such as fencing and shooting. Some sports have even developed an equivalent to the wheelchair that is used for travelling on snow and ice, such as in sit skiing and ice sledge hockey whereby the wheels of the chair are replaced with skis or blades. However, these sports are beyond the scope of this text, which focuses on the following:

- Wheelchair basketball
- Wheelchair racing
- Wheelchair rugby
- Wheelchair tennis
- Handcycling

## Spinal Cord Anatomy, Functions, and Injury

The aim of this section is to introduce the effects of SCI. It covers the anatomy and functions of the spinal cord, followed by types of SCI.

### Anatomy of the Spinal Cord

The spine has two main components—the spinal column and the spinal cord. The spinal column comprises 33 vertebrae, which are positioned so that the vertebral foramen are aligned, making a single, continuous bony tube called the *spinal canal*. This structure of small, bony segments provides strong protection for the spinal cord, which lies in the canal, and allows a great variety of movement.

As indicated on the right side of figure 1.1 (page 6), the 33 vertebrae in the spinal column are divided into five types. There are 7 cervical, 12 thoracic, 5 lumbar, 5 sacral, and 4 coccygeal vertebrae. Each vertebra has a name that is derived from its type and its position relative to the others of that type. For example, the fifth cervical vertebra is called *C5*, and the first lumbar vertebra is called *L1*.

## TABLE 1.1

# Paralympic Sports With Wheelchairs or Open to People With SCI

| Sport | Wheelchair | Tetraplegic | Paraplegic |
|---|---|---|---|
| Alpine skiing | ○ | | ● |
| Archery | ✓ | ● | ● |
| Athletics: Track* | ✓ | ● | ● |
|        Field | ○ | ● | ● |
| Basketball* | ✓ | | ● |
| Boccia | ✓ | | |
| Curling | ✓ | | ● |
| Equestrian | | ● | ● |
| Fencing | ✓ | ● | ● |
| Football: Blind | | | |
|       Cerebral palsy | | | |
| Goalball | | | |
| Handcycling | ○ | ● | ● |
| Ice sledge hockey* | ○ | | ● |
| Judo | | | |
| Nordic skiing | ○ | | ● |
| Powerlifting | | | ● |
| Rowing | | | ● |
| Rugby* | ✓ | ● | ● |
| Sailing | | ● | ● |
| Shooting | ✓ | ● | ● |
| Swimming | | ● | ● |
| Table tennis | ✓ | ● | ● |
| Tennis* | ✓ | ● | ● |
| Volleyball | | | ● |

✓ Wheelchair sport

○ Assistive device or adapted version of a wheelchair is used, where wheels are replaced by skis or blades for travel on ice/snow.

● Open to individuals with SCI, separated into quadriplegic and paraplegic

\* Sports that require hand propulsion

The spinal cord comprises a large number of nerve fibres bound together as a single cord by a thin skin. The cord is approximately 2.5 centimetres in diameter and acts as a communication cable, carrying instructions from the brain to the muscles and organs of the body and also permitting the brain to receive sensory feedback from these structures. The cord doesn't fill the entire length of the spinal canal; it extends from the brain to the upper border of L2 (see figure 1.1).

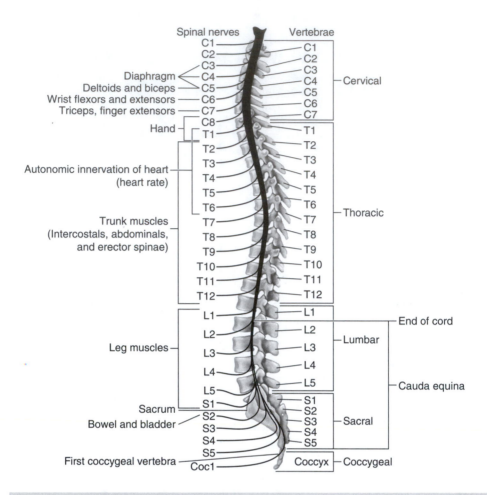

**Figure 1.1** Spinal column and cord.

The spinal canal below L2 is filled by a loose bundle of spinal nerves collectively known as the *cauda equina,* which literally means "horsetail".

The cord is organized into 31 spinal segments—8 cervical, 12 thoracic, 5 lumbar, 5 sacral, and 1 coccygeal. Each spinal segment has a pair of spinal nerves, one for the left side of the body, one for the right. The left side of figure 1.1 shows the spinal nerves that arise from each spinal segment, along with the main muscles that are innervated by the nerves.

## Functions of the Spinal Cord

The spinal cord serves three main functions.

**1. Voluntary motor functions.** The cord transmits signals from the brain that are required for voluntary contraction of skeletal muscle. Each spinal segment uses its pair of spinal nerves to control a specific group of skeletal muscles. Table 1.2 lists the spinal segments and the movements they contribute to. In general, the muscles of the arms and hands are innervated by the cervical segments, the trunk by the thoracic segments, and the legs and feet by the lumbar and sacral segments.

TABLE 1.2

## Segmental Innervation of Major Movements

| Segmental Innervation | Joint | Action |
|---|---|---|
| C5-C6 | Shoulder | Abduction |
| C5-C8 | | Adduction |
| C5-C7 | | Flexion |
| C6-C8 | | Extension |
| C5-c8 | | Internal rotation |
| C5-C6 | | External rotation |
| C5-C6 | Elbow | Flexion |
| C7-C8 | | Extension |
| C6-C8 | Wrist | Flexion |
| C6-C8 | | Extension |
| C7-T1 | Hand | Finger and thumb movements |
| T5-L1 | Trunk | Abdominal muscles |
| C1-L5 | | Spinal extensors |
| L1-L3 | Hip | Flexion |
| L5-S2 | | Extension |
| L4-S1 | | Abduction |
| L2-L4 | | Adduction |
| L2-L4 | Knee | Extension |
| L5-S2 | | Flexion |
| L4-S1 | Ankle | Dorsiflexion |
| S1-S2 | | Plantar flexion |

**2. Sensory functions.** A range of sensory information is transmitted from the periphery to the brain via the cord, including tactile (touch), proprioceptive (location of the body in space), and deep-pressure sensations. Each area of the body sends tactile information to the brain via a specific spinal segment, as presented in figure 1.2. In general, the head and arms send sensory information to the brain via the cervical segments, the trunk sends information via the thoracic segments, and the lower back and legs send information via the lumbar and sacral segments.

**3. Autonomic functions.** Autonomic functions are controlled by the autonomic nervous system (ANS). Autonomic functions include cardiovascular function (e.g., heart rate, blood pressure), respiration, digestion, excretion, and thermoregulation (i.e., maintaining a constant body temperature in hot or cold conditions). The ANS controls these functions automatically with relatively little conscious control; for example, heart rate increases automatically with exercise without requiring conscious thought.

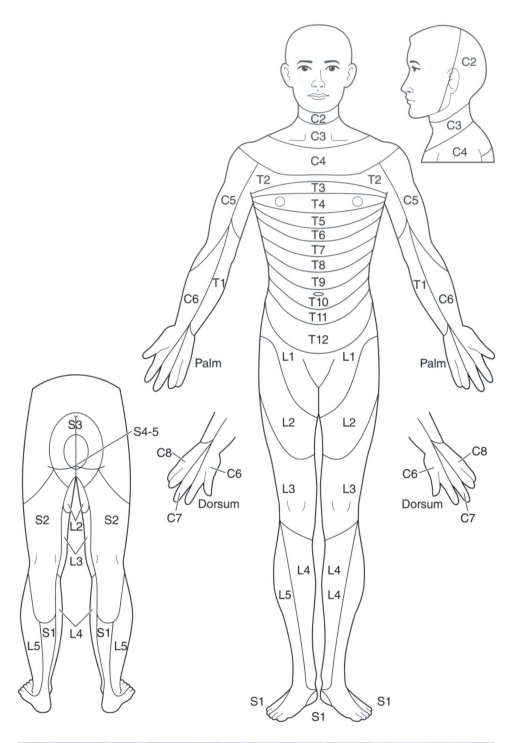

**Figure 1.2** Tactile areas are associated with each spinal segment.

America Spinal Injury Association: International Standards for Neurological Classification of Spinal Cord Injury, revised 2000; Atlanta, GA. Reprinted 2008.

## Injury to the Spinal Cord

The spinal cord can be damaged in a number of ways, including congenital malformation (e.g., spina bifida, which occurs during formation of the spine in the fetus), disease processes (e.g., poliomyelitis, cysts or tumours, meningitis), or injury. In Paralympic sport, most people with cord damage compete together regardless of cause. However, the majority of athletes competing in wheelchair sport have a damaged cord as a result of injury from events such as motor vehicle accidents, diving accidents, and high falls, and therefore SCI is the focus of this book.

Injury to the spinal cord can affect all three functions of the spinal cord—motor, sensory, and autonomic. The two factors that determine exactly which functions are affected and how much they are affected are the level and the completeness of the injury.

**Injury Level**   When the cord is injured, connections are broken between the brain and the segment of the cord that has been injured, as well as all the segments below the injury. However, the connections between the brain and segments above the injury remain intact. In other words, the lower the injury (i.e., the farther from the brain), the more function is preserved. The term *tetraplegia*—generally preferred to *quadriplegia*, which is also used in relation to other health conditions and can therefore be ambiguous—refers to people with an SCI at or above T1 because they have impaired movement or sensation in all four limbs as well as the trunk *(tetra* meaning "four"). *Paraplegia* refers to people with an injury at or below T2 because they have normal strength and sensation in their head, neck, and arms but impaired sensation or voluntary movement in their trunk and legs. The incidence of tetraplegia is quite high—between 40 and 70 percent of SCIs, depending on the country surveyed.

**Injury Completeness**   In about 50 percent of cases, cord injuries do not interrupt all the connections between the brain and the segments below the level of the lesion (Ackery, Tator, & Krassioukov, 2004). This is known as an *incomplete injury*. A person with an incomplete injury will retain some motor or sensory function below the level of the lesion. Exactly how much function is preserved is determined by how much of the cord is damaged and which parts of the cord are damaged. People with incomplete injuries have widely varying functional profiles—people with injuries that are almost complete may have a tiny amount of sensation below the level of their lesion, but when more of the cord is preserved, they may be able to move their legs a little, stand up, walk, or even run. The amount of movement and sensation that is retained depends on how many of the connections are broken.

Table 1.3 presents the main effects of SCI, the level of injury the effects are usually associated with, and the main implications for sport participation.

**revolutions**

This section provides a brief introduction to SCI and its effects. In reality, there is a tremendous amount of variation with cord injury. Consequently, when practitioners commence working with athletes with SCI for the first time, the most effective way to find out how the cord injury affects them is to ask them.

## TABLE 1.3

## Main Effects of SCI

| Effect | Associated with complete cord injury at or above | Implications in sport |
|--------|--------------------------------------------------|------------------------|
| Reduced or absent movement in the hands and fingers | T1 | Grasping and manipulating objects is difficult or impossible (e.g., picking up objects). |
| Reduced or absent sitting balance | L1 | Sitting without a backrest, reaching outside base of support, or using trunk to propel wheelchair is difficult or impossible. |
| Reduced or absent ability to walk | S2 | Use wheelchair for competitive sport. |
| Reduced or absent sensation | Any level (When cord injury is complete, sensation is usually absent below the level of the injury.) | When collisions or falls occur, assess the seriousness of the injury by means other than pain; when trying new activities, be careful of knocks and rubbing on areas with reduced sensation. |
| Spasms | Any level (excluding injury to the cauda equina) | When an athlete changes position (e.g., from sitting to lying on a bench), paralysed muscles below the level of the lesion may reflexively contract, causing movement that the athlete cannot control. Type, size, duration, and force of the contractions vary from athlete to athlete—some are not affected by spasms at all, whereas others have severe spasms. |
| Decreased maximal heart rate | T6 | Heart rate is not a good indicator of exercise intensity, and some athletes will have a lower physical work capacity. |
| Exertional hypotension (decrease in blood pressure in response to exercise—in people without SCI, blood pressure usually increases during exercise) | T6 | Care is needed when exercising. |
| Orthostatic hypotension (sudden drop in blood pressure when moving from lying to sitting or sitting to standing, especially if the movement is fast) | T6 | Care is needed when moving into and out of exercise positions, especially if the exercises are new or the athlete has a history of orthostatic hypotension. |
| Autonomic dysreflexia (rapid, often dangerous increase in blood pressure that occurs when a stimulus that would usually be painful is applied to an area where the athlete does not have sensation) | T6 | Some athletes deliberately induce this response to enhance performance, commonly referred to as boosting; however, its use is both dangerous and illegal in Paralympic sport. |

| Effect | Associated with complete cord injury at or above | Implications in sport |
|---|---|---|
| Reduced or absent sweat response | Any level (When cord injury is complete, the ability to sweat is usually absent below the level of the injury.) | Difficulty losing heat in hot weather. |
| Reduced or absent shivering response and piloerector response (goosebumps) | Any level (When cord injury is complete, the ability to shiver and get goosebumps is usually absent below the level of the injury.) | Difficulty retaining heat in cold weather. |
| Reduced or absent ability to void bladder or bowels | S4 | Usually minimal impact because most athletes have independent bowel and bladder management strategies. |

# Health-Related Effects of Wheelchair Sport

It is well established that people who are not physically active on a regular basis have a reduced life expectancy, as well as an increased risk of coronary heart disease, hypertension, ischemic stroke, type 2 diabetes, obesity, colon and breast cancers, and depression (Bauman & Owen, 1999; Haskell, 1998; U.S. Department of Health and Human Services, 2002). For good health, it is recommended that people participate in at least 30 minutes of moderate-intensity physical activity on most, preferably all, days of the week (World Health Organization, 2004). The physical activity can take many forms, including structured exercise programmes and competitive sport, as well as outdoor recreation and incidental activity (e.g., pushing or walking to shops). Unfortunately, many people in developed countries do not do enough activity to be healthy regardless of whether they have a disability or not.

Although many people are not sufficiently active, studies indicate that people with SCI are among the most inactive in society. For example, people with SCI have significantly lower aerobic capacity than nondisabled people of the same age and gender (Grange, Bougenot, Groslambert, Tordi, & Rouillon, 2002) and develop signs of cardiovascular disease such as high blood pressure and elevated blood lipids earlier in life (Bauman, Raza, Spungen, & Machac, 1994; Bauman et al., 1992). A large study of 145,000 people showed that wheelchair users were 2.5 times more likely to be obese than the general population. Obesity was more prevalent among wheelchair users than any other disability group, considerably more so than people who are deaf, vision impaired, or seriously mentally ill, as well as those who have upper-limb impairment (Bauman et al., 1994; Bauman et al., 1992; Weil et al., 2002).

The poor health and disease associated with a lack of physical activity is particularly detrimental for people with SCI because it compounds the loss of motor, sensory, and autonomic function caused by injury to the cord. For instance, one study found that nearly one in four otherwise healthy people with paraplegia were not sufficiently fit to perform many essential activities of daily living (Noreau, Shephard, Simard, Pare, & Pomerleau, 1993).

Sport is one of many ways that people with SCI can increase physical activity and improve health. It is particularly important in the SCI population because the people most frequently injured are those who are young and otherwise healthy (Ackery et al., 2004). Sir Ludwig Guttmann is credited with pioneering and popularizing the use of sport to enhance health-related outcomes in people with cord injuries. In 1944, he established the Spinal Injuries Centre at Stoke Mandeville Hospital, where he promoted sports participation as part of his innovative approach to management of paraplegia (Ackery et al., 2004; Guttmann, 1976). Guttmann indicated that his sport programme would have benefits in three main areas—physical rehabilitation and health, recreation and psychological well-being, and social reintegration (Ackery et al., 2004; Guttmann, 1976). Research that has been conducted in the 65 years since the Stoke Mandeville programme commenced indicates that Guttmann's summary of the benefits of sport was remarkably prescient.

The best established benefit of physical activity for people with SCI is improved cardiorespiratory fitness. A significant number of scientific studies have shown improvements in oxygen uptake ($\dot{V}O_2$max) between 10 and 60 percent, although the higher the level of the injury, the less capacity there is for improvement (Jacobs & Nash, 2004). It is also well established that muscular strength increases in response to sport participation, as well as conventional resistance training and circuit-type resistance training (Jacobs & Nash, 2004).

Studies indicate that people with SCI who have good levels of fitness are likely to accrue several additional health benefits, a selection of which is presented in table 1.4. Some of the benefits are the same as those seen in the nondisabled population; for example, people with SCI who are physically active have better levels of high-density lipoprotein (HDL) cholesterol. However, many other health benefits are specific to people with SCI, such as better respiratory function and better functioning in activities of daily living.

## Sport Classification

Classification is a feature of most modern sports. In many competitions, athletes are classified according to age, sex, or body mass. When competitors are classified in this way, it minimizes the impact of these attributes on the outcome of competition.

For example, if all the boys at a school athletics carnival competed together, the age of each child would have a huge impact on where he finished in the field—the top-placed children would likely be older, and the youngest would be among the last–placed children. This is because age is closely related to physical maturation, and the more physically mature children are, the faster they will be able to run. However, if the children were classified according to how old they were, then the impact of maturation on the order of finishing would be minimized and other factors, such as training and athletic talent, would have a much bigger effect.

From a social perspective, classification is a way of encouraging people to participate. One of the factors that motivates people to participate in sport is close competition (Vallerand & Rousseau, 2001), and classification is a way of increasing the prospects of close competition. If children weren't classified according to age and 6-year-old boys competed against 13-year-old boys at the school carnival, the prospects of close competition would be low and the 6-year-olds would have little motivation to participate. Classification according to age minimizes the impact of age on competition outcome, and this encourages participation.

TABLE 1.4

## Health-Related Benefits of Physical Activity

| Health parameter | Evidence for benefits of increased physical activity |
|---|---|
| HDL cholesterol | HDL cholesterol is the good cholesterol—it lowers the risk of coronary heart disease—and physical activity increases levels of HDL. Although many people with SCI have low levels of HDL, those who are active in sport or who have higher cardiorespiratory fitness or strength have much better levels of HCL (de Groot, Dallmeijer, Post, Angenot, & van der Woude, 2008; Jacobs & Nash, 2004). |
| Physical functioning and independence | Better cardiorespiratory fitness and muscular strength are associated with better physical functioning and independence—for example, the ability to transfer into or out of a wheelchair is improved (Dallmeijer & van der Woude, 2001; Noreau et al., 1993). |
| Shoulder pain | Manual wheelchair use increases the magnitude, frequency, and intensity of forces through the shoulder, and consequently many wheelchair users experience shoulder pain. However, evidence indicates that, compared with athletes, nonathletes are twice as likely to be affected by shoulder pain (Fullerton, Borckardt, & Alfano, 2003). Greater muscular strength is associated with less shoulder pain (van Drongelen et al., 2006), and in people with preexisting shoulder pain, specific strength training can reduce pain intensity (Nash, van de Ven, van Elk, & Johnson, 2007). |
| Respiratory function | People with injuries above T12 can have reduced capacity to breathe deeply and quickly due to impaired strength in the intercostal and abdominal muscles. A number of studies indicate that exercise can improve this capacity (Noreau & Shephard, 1995; Silva et al., 1998). |
| Psychological well-being | Compared with people with SCI who did not undertake an exercise program, people who exercised significantly improved their perceived health, satisfaction with function, and overall quality of life and decreased their stress (Hicks et al., 2003). Those who continued to exercise after completing the program maintained these benefits, while those who stopped exercising did not (Ditor et al., 2003). |

## Classification in Paralympic Sport

Paralympic classification systems are used to minimize the impact of impairments (e.g., muscle paralysis, amputation, lost range of movement, and loss of coordination) on the outcome of competition. If the effect of these impairments is minimized, then the athletes who succeed will be those who have the most favourable combination of physiology, anthropometry, and psychology and not simply those who are less disabled than the other competitors. This is the aim of classification in Paralympic sport (International Paralympic Committee [IPC], 2007).

Achieving this aim requires that athletes are placed into classes according to how much their impairment affects performance in their chosen sport. Consequently, each Paralympic sport has its own classification system that assesses how various impairments affect performance in that particular sport. This is called *sport-specific classification*. For example, consider an athlete who has had an arm amputated below the elbow—she would have a big disadvantage when swimming but a relatively minor disadvantage when running. Therefore, the athletics classification system places such athletes in one of the least disabled running classes, but the swimming system places them in a moderately disabled class. This example illustrates why classification systems that minimize the impact of impairment on the outcome of competition must be considerably more complex than ones that minimize the impact of age, sex, or body mass.

## Classification in Paralympic Wheelchair Sport

There is considerable variation in the approach to classification in each of the wheelchair sports. However, with relatively few exceptions the principles outlined next apply to all Paralympic sports.

When an athlete presents for classification, two questions are answered:

- Does the athlete have an eligible type of impairment?
- Is the impairment severe enough?

If the answer to these first two questions is *yes*, then a third question must be addressed:

- What class should the athlete compete in?

**1. Does the athlete have an eligible impairment?** Not everyone who competes in wheelchair sport has paralysis resulting from SCI, although many do. To compete in wheelchair sport, athletes need to have one of the following physical impairment types:
- Muscle weakness or paralysis, such as results from SCI, spina bifida, polio myelitis, or muscular dystrophy
- Movement or coordination disorders, such as spastic hypertonia, ataxia, or athetosis resulting from cerebral palsy, brain injury, stroke, or multiple sclerosis
- Limb loss, such as results from amputation or being born with limbs missing
- Loss of range of movement such as results from severe trauma to a joint
- Leg length difference

**2. Is the impairment severe enough?** In all Paralympic sports it is possible to have an eligible type of impairment that is not severe enough to meet eligibility criteria. For example, a person who has had a little toe amputated has an eligible type of impairment (amputation), but the level of amputation is not severe enough to meet eligibility criteria in any of the Paralympic sports. The criteria describing the severity of an impairment are called *minimum disability criteria,* and each Paralympic sport sets its own criteria. For example, to compete in wheelchair track racing, an amputee must lose at least half of the foot. A person who has lost only toes does not meet the minimum disability criteria.

**3. What class should the athlete compete in?** Once it has been determined that an athlete is eligible, the athlete is assessed and placed into a class. In most sports, a higher number indicates higher functioning (e.g., a 2-point player is more functional than a 1-point player, and class T54 is more functional than class T53). Once again, there is a great deal of variation in how the assessments are carried out, but usually the assessment is conducted by a team of two or three people, each of whom has expertise important for evaluating physical impairments and their impact on the sport. The teams may include medical doctors, physiotherapists, sports scientists, coaches, or ex-athletes. They usually assess an athlete's impairment in isolation (e.g., exactly which muscles are weak and how weak

**Classification ensures that athletes do not succeed simply because they are less disabled than their competitors.**

Photo courtesy of John Lenton.

they are) and then ask the athlete to perform a number of motor tasks in order to observe how the impairment affects functioning for the sport. The final step in the classification process is observing the athlete in competition to confirm that the decision was correct.

Systems of classification have evolved considerably since the commencement of Paralympic sport, and current sport-specific classification systems focus on assessing how much an impairment will affect a person's sport performance. However, the task of classifying is extremely challenging, and the International Paralympic Committee (IPC) is committed to improving classification systems through scientific research.

## Common Questions About Classification

Following are some of the questions that classifiers are frequently asked.

*Q: Why is so much attention paid to classification?*

**A:** The class to which an athlete is assigned will have a tremendous impact on the success he is likely to achieve—if an athlete is placed in a more disabled class, he will achieve considerably more success than if he is placed in a less disabled class. This will influence the peer and community recognition that is received, as well as the ability to attract sponsorship and other financial rewards. For coaches and sport scientists, knowledge of an athlete's class is crucial for correct interpretation of physical performance. For example, unless the class of an athlete with an incomplete SCI is known, there is no way of determining whether a 100-metre time of 18 seconds is outstanding or merely average.

*Q: Can athletes cheat the system?*

A: Classification incorporates assessment of function, and an accurate assessment obviously requires the athlete to cooperate—she must try as hard as she can to do the tests as well as possible. Intentional misrepresentation of functioning in classification is a serious offense in Paralympic sport and harsh penalties apply, including an automatic 2-year ban for a first offence and a lifetime ban for a repeat offence (IPC, 2007). Additionally, successful deceit is very rare. Athletes' in-competition performances are monitored not only by the classification team but also by other competitors and their coaches who have a vested interest in ensuring that people who cheat are brought to the attention of the authorities.

*Q: Can athletes change classes through training?*

A: Ideally this would never happen, and the reality is that it rarely does. In athletes with impairments that do not respond at all to training (e.g., amputees and people with complete SCI) and in elite athletes who are well trained, classification will not be influenced by training. Chances are highest with an athlete who is new to a sport or poorly conditioned and close to a borderline between classes. In such cases there are sometimes adjustments to class because there are subtle changes to the athlete's impairment. However, experienced, conservative classifiers can ensure that even in these cases, adjustments are rarely required.

*Q: How does an athlete get classified?*

A: To be classified, an athlete must be seen by a qualified classification team. Unfortunately, some people make the mistake of accessing a classification manual and then using it to self-classify or asking a medical friend or therapist to read it and provide an opinion. Such classifications are not recognised and the results can be frustrating and disappointing. The best way to get a class is to enquire through the closest disability sports club or contact the National Paralympic Committee (NPC).

# Sports for Wheelchair Athletes

This section provides an overview of the five wheelchair sports that are the focus of this book. In each instance, a brief introduction to the sport is followed by a description of the classification system, the rules of the sport, the physical demands, and a table summarizing the desirable characteristics for the sport.

## Wheelchair Basketball

One of the most popular and well-known wheelchair sports, wheelchair basketball originated in 1945 in the United States and made its first appearance at the Paralympic Games in 1960. It was created when American basketball players who were wounded during World War II adapted the running game so that they could play in their wheelchairs.

**Classification**   Classification rules and procedures for wheelchair basketball are described in the International Wheelchair Basketball Federation (IWBF) classification system (IWBF Player Classification Commission, 2004). The full system is available at www.iwbf.org. This section briefly describes the most important features.

To be eligible for wheelchair basketball, a player must

- be unable to run, pivot, or jump at a speed and with the control, safety, stability, and endurance of a nondisabled player; and
- have a permanent physical disability in the lower limb that can be objectively verified by acknowledged medical or paramedical investigations such as measurement, X-ray, CT, MRI, and so on.

The key element of classification is the observation of a player's volume of action, which is described as

the limit to which a player can move voluntarily in any direction and, with control, move to the upright seated position, without holding the wheelchair for support or to aid the movement. The volume of action includes all directions and describes the position of the ball when held in both hands (IWBF Player Classification Commission, 2004).

Factors that affect a player's volume of action include range of movement, strength, and coordination in the hands, arms, trunk, and legs. Players are observed in their competition wheelchairs, complete with all the strapping they will use, in a training situation before the tournament commences. Based on these observations, players are placed into one of eight classes—the higher the number, the more functional the athlete. A summary of the classes follows.

- **1-point player:** Little or no trunk movement in any plane. Balance in both forward and sideways directions is significantly impaired, and players rely on their arms to return them to the upright position when unbalanced. No active trunk rotation.
- **2-point player:** Some partially controlled trunk movement in the forward direction, but no controlled sideways movement. Has upper trunk rotation but poor lower trunk rotation.
- **3-point player:** Good trunk movement in the forward direction to the floor and up again without arm support. Has good trunk rotation but no controlled sideways movement.
- **4-point player:** Normal trunk movement but has difficulty with controlled sideways movement to one side, usually due to limitations in one lower limb.
- **4.5-point player:** Normal trunk movement in all directions and able to reach the side with no limitations.

There are situations where a player does not seem to fit exactly into one class, exhibiting characteristics of two or more classes. In such instances the classifier may assign the player a half-point, thus creating 1.5-, 2.5-, and 3.5-point players. This is usually done only when the player cannot be assigned a defined class and should not be regarded as the first option.

Only five players from each team are allowed on court at one time, and the total number of points for the five players on court must not exceed 14 (for example, two players in the 4-point class, two in the 3-point class, and one in the 2-point class would be illegal). This rule ensures that teams maintain a balance of players of high and low functional ability.

TABLE 1.5

## Desirable Characteristics for Wheelchair Basketball

| Physical | Skill/technical | Other |
|---|---|---|
| Acceleration | Chair skills (e.g., agility) | Decision making |
| Power | Ball skills (passing, catching, dribbling, shooting) | Tactical awareness |
| Aerobic endurance | Accuracy | Teamwork |
| Anaerobic capacity | Consistency | Pattern recognition |
| Strength | | |
| Speed | | |

**Rules**   Wheelchair basketball rules are similar to those of the running game, with the same court dimensions and basket height. Field baskets count for 2 points, baskets from beyond the 3-point line score 3 points, and free throws from the foul line score 1. Dribbling is performed by bouncing the ball and pushing the chair simultaneously or by placing the ball on the lap for a maximum of two pushes before bouncing it again. Only 5 players from each team can be on the court at any time, but up to 12 players can be on the team. Players are classified using a points system as outlined previously, and the total points for the five players on court at any time cannot exceed 14. Unlike wheelchair rugby, men and women compete separately.

**Physical Demands**   Wheelchair basketball is a physically demanding team sport that requires a high degree of skill, technical expertise, and teamwork. Desirable characteristics for wheelchair basketball are presented in table 1.5. Although contact between chairs is not permitted, it is not uncommon for players to tip over in their chairs because of the high speed and need for sharp changes in direction. Acceleration, speed, and agility are of particular importance since the game is often played at a fast pace, and excellent chair and ball skills are fundamental to the game.

International games are 40 minutes played in four quarters of 10 minutes, and therefore a high level of conditioning is required to maintain work intensity and to prevent injury. A high anaerobic capacity is also beneficial for repeated sprint efforts. As with any other team sport, players need to have good tactical awareness, be able to recognize patterns of play, and have great decision-making abilities.

## Wheelchair Racing

Wheelchair racing is a discipline within Paralympic athletics that comprises race distances ranging from 100 metres to the marathon (42.2 km). The first organized wheelchair racing competitions began in 1952 at Stoke Mandeville hospital in England as part of the games for soldiers injured in World War II. Racing was one of the sports at the first Paralympic Games in Rome, 1960. The sport has come a long way since then with advances in wheelchair design and technology. The modern racing chair is lightweight, aerodynamic, and capable of high speeds in the hands of a good athlete. Many of the major city running marathons such as London and New York now incorporate a wheelchair race, and elite wheelchair-racing finish times are substantially quicker than their nondisabled counterparts.

**Classification**   Classification rules and procedures for wheelchair racing are described in the *IPC Athletics Classification Handbook*. The full system is available at http://ipc-athletics.paralympic.org/Classification/. This section provides a brief overview of the most important features.

In IPC athletics, athletes with SCI compete in classes T51 through T54. A second group of classes—T31 through T34—is for athletes with movement disorders such as spastic hypertonia, ataxia, or athetosis resulting from cerebral palsy, brain injury, stroke, or multiple sclerosis. The focus of this section is classes T51 through T54.

To be eligible for classes from T51 to T54, an athlete must be affected by one or more of the following impairment types:

- Limb deficiency (e.g., amputees)
- Lost range of movement (e.g., from joint trauma)
- Muscle weakness or paralysis (e.g., resulting from SCI or spina bifida)
- Leg length difference

In addition, the impairment must be severe enough to alter the biomechanical execution of the running action in a way that is demonstrable and that will adversely affect performance.

The class profiles are as follows:

- **Class T51:** In general, equivalent activity limitation to person with complete cord injury at level C5 to C6, including normal elbow flexion and wrist dorsiflexion but weak pectoralis major and triceps.
- **Class T52:** Equivalent activity limitation to person with complete cord injury at cord level C7 to C8, including normal shoulder, elbow, and wrist muscle power; poor to normal finger flexors and extensors; and wasting of the intrinsic muscles of the hands.
- **Class T53:** Equivalent activity limitation to person with complete cord injury at cord level T1 to T7, including normal arm muscle power with no abdominal or lower spinal muscle activity.
- **Class T54:** Equivalent activity limitation to person with complete cord injury at cord level T8 to S4, including normal arm muscle power with a range of trunk muscle power extending from partial trunk control to normal trunk control. Athletes who compete in this group may have significant leg muscle power.

**Rules**   There are a number of technical rules related to wheelchair design and set-up that all athletes must adhere to, and all racing chairs are scrutinized by officials before and after races to ensure they meet the specifications. Competition rules are similar to those of nondisabled athletic events.

**Physical Demands**   Wheelchair racing is a linear sport with an objective performance measure. As a result, the main contributing factors to success are largely physiological and theoretically depend on the race distances involved and the technical ability to reach and hold high speeds across all distances. Sprint events such as 100 metres, 200 metres, and 400 metres rely on the ability to reach peak speed in a short amount of time and to maintain a high proportion of this speed for the duration of the race. Anaerobic capacity, power, and high power-to-weight ratio (to achieve rapid acceleration from low speed) therefore may be fundamental to success in these short events, although research has yet to fully confirm this (Bhambhani, 2002). Middle-distance races such as 800 metres and 1500 metres require a combination of speed and endurance to maintain high mean velocities for the duration of the race and high top speeds in the sprint finish. The long-distance events of 5000 metres, 10000 metres, and marathon and other road races may be more reliant on factors associated with oxygen uptake and delivery than those related to pure speed (Bhambhani, 2002). Pacing strategies, tactical aware-ness, and high top speeds for sprint finish, midrace accelerations, and downhill exploitation are important in the longer distances. Tables 1.6, 1.7, and 1.8 provide the desirable characteristics for wheelchair racing.

TABLE 1.6

### Desirable Characteristics for Wheelchair Racing: 100 m, 200 m, 400 m

| Physical | Skill/technical | Other |
|---|---|---|
| Speed | Technique | |
| Strength | Hand speed | |
| Power | | |
| Power-to-weight ratio | | |

TABLE 1.7

### Desirable Characteristics for Wheelchair Racing: 800 m, 1500 m

| Physical | Skill/technical | Other |
|---|---|---|
| Speed | Technique | Pacing |
| Strength | Hand speed | Tactical awareness |
| Power | Chair handling | |
| Aerobic endurance | | |
| Anaerobic capacity | | |

TABLE 1.8

### Desirable Characteristics for Wheelchair Racing: 5000 m to Marathon, Road Racing

| Physical | Skill/technical | Other |
|---|---|---|
| Speed | Technique | Pacing |
| Strength | Hand speed | Tactical awareness |
| Power | Chair handling | |
| Aerobic endurance | | |

## Wheelchair Rugby

Originally called *murderball,* wheelchair rugby began in Canada in 1977 when a group of tetraplegic athletes were looking for an alternative team sport to wheelchair basketball. Occasionally referred to as *quad rugby,* this sport is for athletes with severe disabilities affecting at least three limbs, and it is the only team sport for athletes with upper-limb impairments. As such, the majority of players are tetraplegics.

Wheelchair rugby was officially recognized as a Paralympic sport in 1994 and was included as a demonstration sport at the 1996 Paralympic Games. It was not until the 2000 Games that the first official Paralympic wheelchair rugby medal was contested.

**Classification**   Classification rules and procedures for wheelchair rugby are described in the *International Wheelchair Rugby Federation Classification Manual* (IWRF, 2008). The full system is available at www.iwrf.com. This section provides a brief overview of the most important features.

Elements of wheelchair rugby classification include a bench test where upper-extremity musculature, range of motion, tone, and sensation are examined; a functional trunk test, where musculature of the trunk and lower extremities is evaluated in all planes and situations; and functional movement tests, where players perform pushing, turning, stopping, and starting manoeuvres. Additionally, players are observed on court. Based on these assessments, players are placed into one of seven classes: 0.5, 1.0, 1.5, 2.0, 2.5, 3.0, and 3.5. The higher the number, the more functional the athlete.

Only four players from each team are allowed on court at one time, and the total number of points for the four players on court must not exceed 8 (for example, two players in the 3-point class and two players in the 2-point class would be illegal). This rule ensures that teams maintain a balance of players of high and low functional ability on court.

**Rules**   The game is played on a standard basketball court with key areas and goals at each end. The object of the game is to score by carrying the ball over the opponent's goal line. Only four players from each team are permitted on the court at any time. A regulation volleyball is used and players can pass it in any direction. Full contact between chairs is allowed, and it is one of the few wheelchair team sports where men and women can play on the same team.

**Physical Demands**   Wheelchair rugby is not for the fainthearted. Chair collisions are a major part of the game, and it is not uncommon to see players tipping over in their chairs as a result. This is a sport that requires a combination of physical fitness; excellent chair, ball, and decision-making skills; and the ability to play as a team and recognize and anticipate patterns of play.

International games are played over four quarters that are 8 minutes in duration, with tournaments taking place over a number of days. Physiologically, it is an intermittent sprint sport with periods of explosive effort superimposed on a background of aerobic activity (Goosey-Tolfrey, Castle, Webborn, & Abel, 2006). An excellent level of conditioning is therefore important not only to maintain work intensity over the course of a competition but also to withstand the physical nature of the sport and minimize the risk of injury. As with any team sport,

TABLE 1.9

## Desirable Characteristics for Wheelchair Rugby

| Physical | Skill/technical | Other |
| --- | --- | --- |
| Speed | Chair skills (e.g., agility) | Decision making |
| Power | Ball skills (e.g., passing) | Tactical awareness |
| Acceleration, deceleration | Blocking | Pattern recognition |
| Strength | Shadowing | Aggression |
| Aerobic endurance | | |
| Anaerobic capacity | | |

teamwork is critical to success. The same can be said for the tactical side of the game, which is generally split into offensive and defensive plays.

Players have different roles within the team depending on their classification, and thus there are subtle differences between the competitive profiles of each classification. However, the general desirable characteristics for elite performance are shown in table 1.9.

## Wheelchair Tennis

Initially developed as a recreational sport in 1976 by Jeff Minnenbraker and Brad Parks, wheelchair tennis is now one of the fastest growing wheelchair sports, boasting an international professional tour with more than 120 worldwide events. Wheelchair tennis became a full medal sport at the 1992 Paralympic Games, but it was not until the 2000 Games that separate medals were awarded for the tetraplegic classes. In 1998, wheelchair tennis became the first disabled sport to be fully integrated with a nondisabled world governing body, the International Tennis Federation (ITF). As a result, major wheelchair tennis tournaments take place together with the nondisabled events, such as Wimbledon and the Australian Open.

**Classification**  Classification rules and procedures for wheelchair tennis are described in the ITF's *Wheelchair Tennis Handbook* (ITF, 2009) . The full system is available at www.itftennis.com/wheelchair. This section provides a brief overview of the most important features.

To be eligible for wheelchair tennis, a player must have a medically diagnosed, permanent, mobility-related physical disability and meet one or more of the following criteria:

- Neurological deficit at the S1 level or proximal that is associated with loss of motor function
- Ankylosis, severe arthrosis, or joint replacement of the hip, knee, or upper ankle joints
- Amputation of any lower-extremity joint proximal to the metatarsophalangeal joint
- Functional disabilities in one or both lower extremities equivalent to the other criteria

TABLE 1.10

## Desirable Characteristics for Wheelchair Tennis

| Physical | Skill/technical | Other |
|---|---|---|
| Acceleration | Chair skills (e.g., agility) | Decision making |
| Power | Accuracy | Tactical awareness |
| Aerobic endurance | Consistency | Anticipation |
| Anaerobic capacity | Shot variety | Shot disguise |
| Strength | | Perception |
| Speed | | Eye–hand coordination |

Eligible athletes play in one of two classes:

- **Tetraplegic class:** These players meet the eligibility criteria but also have a permanent physical disability that affects one or both upper extremities and that has a substantial impact on one or more of the following activities:
  - Overhead service action
  - Forehand and backhand
  - Manoeuvring a manual wheelchair
  - Gripping the racket, necessitating taping or an assistive device in order to play
- **Open class:** These players meet eligibility criteria but do not meet the criteria for the quad class.

**Rules**  Wheelchair tennis is much like nondisabled tennis. The only exception is that the ball is allowed to bounce twice, and the second bounce does not have to be within the dimensions of the court.

**Physical Demands**  Wheelchair tennis is predominantly a skill-based sport, and as such, a high degree of skill and technical ability is critical for success in the modern game. A number of the current top-ranked players in the world were high-level tennis players before becoming wheelchair users, which shows that technical skills learned prior to injury can be effectively transferred to the wheelchair game. Desirable characteristics for wheelchair tennis are presented in table 1.10.

With the increasing competitiveness of the game, frequent travel, and long periods of play in hot environments, good conditioning is vital for performance and injury prevention. Also of importance are anticipatory and perceptual skills, along with good eye–hand coordination and fast reactions.

## Handcycling

In the Paralympic context, handcycling is a discipline within the sport of cycling, and it has been governed by the International Cycling Union (UCI) since 2007. It is for athletes who are wheelchair users and are unable to ride a standard racing bicycle or tricycle due to severe impairment of the lower limbs. A handcycle differs from a traditional wheelchair in that it is an upright or semirecumbent three-wheeled vehicle. It has a gearing system, and the cranks are positioned in front of the rider's chest.

There are two main events for handcyclists—the individual road race and the individual time trial. Road races can be anywhere from 35 to 70 kilometres for men and 20 to 60 kilometres for women, whereas time trials are generally between 5 and 30 kilometres for both men and women.

**Classification**   Classification rules and procedures for handcycling are described in the *IPC Cycling Rulebook* (IPC Cycling, 2002). The full system is available at http://www.uci.ch/templates/UCI/UCI5/layout.asp?MenuId = MTI2MzI&LangId = 1 This section provides a brief overview of the most important features.

Handcycling is for athletes who are unable to use a conventional bicycle or tricycle because of severe lower-limb disability. The classification process comprises medical documentation of the athlete's disability, functional tests, and observation in training and competition.

- **Class H1.1:** Tetraplegia with disabilities corresponding to a complete cervical lesion at C6 or above, including complete loss of trunk and lower limb function, limited elbow extensors, limited handgrip, thermoregulatory limitations, and impaired sympathetic nerve system
- **Class H1.2:** Tetraplegia with disabilities corresponding to a complete cervical lesion between C7 and C8 or above, including complete loss of trunk and lower limb function, limited handgrip, thermoregulatory limitations, and impaired sympathetic nerve system
- **Class H2.1:** Paraplegia with disabilities corresponding to a complete lesion from T1 to T3, including very limited trunk stability and impaired sympathetic nervous system
- **Class H2.2:** Paraplegia with disabilities corresponding to a complete lesion from T4 to T9 or T10, including limited trunk stability
- **Class H3:** Paraplegia with disabilities corresponding to a complete lesion at T11 or below including no lower limb function or limited function, normal or almost normal trunk stability but disabilities prevent safe use of the kneeling position in a handbike
- **Class H4:** Paraplegia with disabilities corresponding to a complete lesion at T11 or below including no lower limb function or limited function, normal or almost normal trunk stability but disabilities do not prevent use of the kneeling position. Includes double below-knee amputation, single above-knee or below-knee

**Rules**   Several rules cover the technical specifications of the handcycle itself as governed by the international governing body of the sport (UCI). However, the actual competition rules are similar to standard cycling. Road races begin with a bunched start and the first rider to complete the course is declared the winner, whereas time trials are seeded with staggered starts of 60-second intervals between riders. The winner of the time trial is the rider who completes the course in the shortest time.

Riders only compete against other riders in their class, but road races must start with a minimum of 2 minutes between classes in order to avoid the mixing of classes. In the event that mixing occurs, riders from one class are not permitted to follow, take pace, or draft from riders in another class.

TABLE 1.11

## Desirable Characteristics for Handcycling

| Physical | Skill/technical | Other |
|---|---|---|
| Aerobic endurance | Bike-handling skills | Tactical awareness |
| Strength | | |
| Power | | |

**Physical Demands**   Handcycling is a linear sport with a definite start and end point together with an objective performance criterion (i.e., time to complete the course). It therefore follows that the person who can maintain the highest mean velocity over the course of the race will be the winner. The ability to sustain high velocities for prolonged periods of time (in the region of 60 minutes for road races) is determined largely by physiological parameters related to oxygen transport to and utilization at the working muscles. Success in handcycling therefore depends on the ability to sustain high power outputs for prolonged periods of time, which in turn relies on a large aerobic capacity and high maximal power output. Desirable characteristics for handcycling are presented in table 1.11, and further details can be found in chapter 12. Good tactical awareness (e.g., pacing strategies) and excellent bike-handling skills are also advantageous.

## Using Sport Knowledge for Athlete Profiling

The sport-specific information presented in the preceding section—physical demands, classification system, and rules—can be used to assist with athlete profiling. Profiling, an important tool for increasing the chances of competitive success in sport, refers to the identification of an athlete's strengths and weaknesses in relation to the characteristics required for success in a given sport. A person's chances of success in a given sport are increased if that person has the desirable characteristics required of that sport. For this reason, some are better at certain sports than others; for example, a good wheelchair racer may not necessarily make a good wheelchair tennis player. Note that profile matching does not guarantee success, particularly in nonlinear sports such as wheelchair rugby and wheelchair basketball.

In Paralympic sport, classification brings an added dimension to profiling—being classified by an accredited classifier allows athletes to identify the performance standards needed for local, national, and international success in their class. A male class T54 athlete who pushes 100 metres in 30 seconds would have to improve a lot to be competitive, even at a local level; however, a T51 female who pushes 100 metres in the same time would be a world-record holder. Additionally, because of the classification systems used in some sports, people with certain types of impairments are at a significant disadvantage compared with others in the same class. For example, in wheelchair tennis, a single below-knee amputee with full trunk function competes in the same class as a person with a complete T4 SCI who has no leg function and severely limited trunk function. In this instance, athletes with high thoracic injuries have a considerable physical disadvantage compared with others in their class, and therefore the prospects of success are reduced commensurately.

## revolutions

**Key Questions to Consider When Choosing a Sport**

- Does the nature of the sport appeal to you (e.g., team sports versus individual sports, skill-based versus physiological)?
- How many of the desirable characteristics of the sport can you match?
- How important is body type and shape (e.g., endurance versus power events)?
- How important is disability type and severity?
- If you have an acquired disability, are you able to match your sporting background to a new sport?

It goes without saying that there are other aspects to consider when selecting the right sport. For example, the social dynamics and cultures of team sports are very different to individual sports, and some sports may not appeal to everyone, such as wheelchair rugby, which involves full contact between chairs.

For people with acquired disabilities who are looking to get back to competitive sport, the sporting background of the person prior to injury can play a significant role in selecting a sport that fits the person's profile. For instance, many of the game skills (such as tactical awareness and recognizing patterns of play) developed while playing nondisabled team sports such as rugby and football can be transferred to wheelchair team sports such as basketball and rugby. Likewise, people with a competitive tennis background prior to injury can easily transfer technical and game skills to the wheelchair game and make rapid progress. People with acquired disabilities should therefore consider their sporting background when selecting a wheelchair sport.

## Conclusion

This book focuses on athletes with SCI and their participation in five of the main wheelchair sports—wheelchair basketball, wheelchair racing, wheelchair rugby, wheelchair tennis, and handcycling. Injury to the spinal cord can affect voluntary motor function, sensory functions, and autonomic functions, and two factors determine the effects of a cord injury—the level of the injury and its completeness. Sport provides people with SCI with an effective, self-directed means of improving health and fitness, including cardiorespiratory fitness, muscular strength, cholesterol levels, and physical functioning. Classification in wheelchair sport minimizes the impact of impairment on the outcome of competition so that the athletes who succeed are those who are the most talented and best prepared, not simply those who are less disabled. The five wheelchair sports are then profiled in terms of their classification system, rules, physical demands, and desirable characteristics. This information can help athletes choose sports for which they are best suited.

Chapter acknowledgements: Sean Tweedy's work is supported by the Motor Accident Insurance Commission, Australia. His work on this manuscript was made possible through support from the Australian Research Council (grant LP0882187), the International Paralympic Committee, the Australian Sports Commission, and the Australian Paralympic Committee.

# References

Ackery, A., Tator, C., & Krassioukov, A. (2004). A global perspective on spinal cord injury epidemiology. *Journal of Neurotrauma,* 21(10), 1355-1370.

Bauman, A., & Owen, N. (1999). Physical activity of adult Australians: Epidemiological evidence and potential strategies for health gain. *Journal of Science in Medicine and Sport,* 2, 30-41.

Bauman, W.A., Raza, M., Spungen, A.M., & Machac, J. (1994). Cardiac stress testing with thallium-201 imaging reveals silent ischemia in individuals with paraplegia. *Archives of Physical Medicine and Rehabilitation,* 75(9), 946-950.

Bauman, W.A., Spungen, A.M., Raza, M., Rothstein, J., Zhang, R.L., Zhong, Y.G., et al. (1992). Coronary artery disease: Metabolic risk factors and latent disease in individuals with paraplegia. *Mt. Sinai Journal of Medicine,* 59(2), 163-168.

Bhambhani, Y. (2002). Physiology of wheelchair racing in athletes with spinal cord injury. *Sports Medicine,* 32(1), 23-51.

Dallmeijer, A.J., & van der Woude, L.H. (2001). Health-related functional status in men with spinal cord injury: Relationship with lesion level and endurance capacity. *Spinal Cord,* 39(11), 577-583.

de Groot, S., Dallmeijer, A.J., Post, M.W., Angenot, E.L., & van der Woude, L.H. (2008). The longitudinal relationship between lipid profile and physical capacity in persons with a recent spinal cord injury. *Spinal Cord,* 46(5), 344-351.

Ditor, D.S., Latimer, A.E., Martin Ginis, K.A., Arbour, K.P., McCartney, N., & Hicks, A.L. (2003). Maintenance of exercise participation in individuals with spinal cord injury: Effects on quality of life, stress and pain. *Spinal Cord,* 41(8), 446-450.

Fullerton, H.D., Borckardt, J.J., & Alfano, A.P. (2003). Shoulder pain: A comparison of wheelchair athletes and nonathletic wheelchair users. *Medicine and Science in Sports and Exercise,* 35(12), 1958-1961.

Goosey-Tolfrey, V., Castle, P., Webborn, N., & Abel, T. (2006). Aerobic capacity and peak power output of elite quadriplegic games players. *British Journal of Sports Medicine,* 40(8), 684-687.

Grange, C.C., Bougenot, M.P., Groslambert, A., Tordi, N., & Rouillon, J. D. (2002). Perceived exertion and rehabilitation with wheelchair ergometer: Comparison between patients with spinal cord injury and healthy subjects. *Spinal Cord,* 40(10), 513-518.

Guttmann, L. (1976). *Textbook of sport for the disabled.* St. Lucia, Australia: University of Queensland Press.

Haskell, W.L. (1998). The benefits of regular exercise. In D.C. Neiman (Ed.), *The exercise-health connection* (pp. 301-309). Champaign, IL: Human Kinetics.

Hicks, A.L., Martin, K.A., Ditor, D.S., Latimer, A.E., Craven, C., Bugaresti, J., et al. (2003). Long-term exercise training in persons with spinal cord injury: Effects on strength, arm ergometry performance and psychological well-being. *Spinal Cord,* 41(1), 34-43.

International Paralympic Committee (IPC). (2007). *IPC classification code and international standards.* Bonn: Author.

International Tennis Federation (ITF). (2009). *Wheelchair tennis handbook.* London: Author.

International Wheelchair Basketball Federation (IWBF) Player Classification Commission. (2004). *IWBF functional player classification system.* Bonn, Germany: Author.

International Wheelchair Rugby Federation (IWRF). (2008). *International wheelchair rugby federation classification manual.* Sheffield, UK: Author.

UCI Para-cycling. (2009). *IPC Cycling rule book.* Bonn: Author.

IPC Athletics. (2006). *IPC Athletics Classification Handbook.* Bonn: Author.

Jacobs, P.L., & Nash, M.S. (2004). Exercise recommendations for individuals with spinal cord injury. *Sports Medicine,* 34(11), 727-751.

Nash, M.S., van de Ven, I., van Elk, N., & Johnson, B.M. (2007). Effects of circuit resistance training on fitness attributes and upper-extremity pain in middle-aged men with paraplegia. *Archives of Physical Medicine and Rehabilitation,* 88(1), 70-75.

Noreau, L., & Shephard, R.J. (1995). Spinal cord injury, exercise and quality of life. *Sports Medicine,* 20(4), 226-250.

Noreau, L., Shephard, R.J., Simard, C., Pare, G., & Pomerleau, P. (1993). Relationship of impairment and functional ability to habitual activity and fitness following spinal cord injury. *International Journal of Rehabilitation Research,* 16(4), 265-275.

Silva, A.C., Neder, J.A., Chiurciu, M.V., Pasqualin, D.C., da Silva, R.C., Fernandez, A.C., et al. (1998). Effect of aerobic training on ventilatory muscle endurance of spinal cord injured men. *Spinal Cord,* 36(4), 240-245.

U.S. Department of Health and Human Services (USDHHS). (2002). *Physical activity fundamental to preventing disease.* Washington, DC: USDHHS, Office of the Assistant Secretary for Planning and Evaluation.

Vallerand, R.J., & Rousseau, F.L. (2001). Intrinsic and extrinsic motivation in sport and exercise. In R.N. Singer, H.A. Hausenblaus, & C.M. Janelle (Eds.), *Handbook of sport psychology* (2nd ed.). New York: Wiley.

van Drongelen, S., de Groot, S., Veeger, H.E., Angenot, E.L., Dallmeijer, A.J., Post, M.W., et al. (2006). Upper extremity musculoskeletal pain during and after rehabilitation in wheelchair-using persons with a spinal cord injury. *Spinal Cord,* 44(3), 152-159.

Weil, E., Wachterman, M., McCarthy, E.P., Davis, R.B., O'Day, B., Iezzoni, L.I., et al. (2002). Obesity among adults with disabling conditions. *Journal of the American Medical Association,* 288(10), 1265-1268.

World Health Organization. (2004). Chronic disease prevention—WHO global strategy on diet, physical activity and health. *Food and Nutrition Bulletin,* 25(3), 292-303.

# chapter 2

# Sport Chair Set-Up and Selection

Hsin-yi Liu, Ian M. Rice, Justin Z. Laferrier, Rosemarie Cooper, Mike Boninger, and Rory A. Cooper

Specialized equipment is often developed to augment athletes' performance in competitive sport. In addition to applying the latest technologies, customized equipment attempts to fit athletes precisely so that they may use the equipment as an extension of their body. Individual differences in body structure and physical ability are critical when designing sport equipment to gain maximal mechanical advantage and to prevent wasted energy. Athletes often use equipment intensely in training and competitions; consequently, failure to fit the equipment appropriately to the individual may result in poor performance and possibly injuries or accidents.

Athletes participating in wheelchair sport use their upper extremities for both locomotion and skill performance. Appropriate wheelchair selection and fitting optimizes performance in addition to protecting against injuries.

This chapter introduces principles for wheelchair selection, set-up, and training. General wheelchair configurations for basketball, rugby, and tennis are highlighted, followed by sport-specific sections for each sport. (Because handcycles and racing wheelchairs are different from other sport wheelchairs, their configurations are only discussed in the sport-specific sections.) Finally, recommendations for injury prevention are provided.

## Wheelchair Components and Accessories

Basketball, rugby, and tennis are common court wheelchair sports. The wheelchairs used for these sports have structures that are similar with everyday wheelchairs but are equipped with sport-specific features. Certain athletic characteristics among these sports are similar, such as speed, agility, and stability, and thus the wheelchairs for these sports share basic principles for equipment selection, set-up, and training.

### Frame

The frame is the key to the shape and dimensions of a wheelchair. Frames consist of various metals, designs, and components. The choice of materials, frame design, and components has a great effect on weight and strength.

**Weight**   Studies have shown that athletes prefer ultralight wheelchairs because they can push at higher speeds, travel longer distances, and propel using less force. In competitive sport, using a lighter wheelchair is essential because the chair has less inertia (resistance to acceleration) and therefore is easier to accelerate and turn. Lighter weight also makes it easier to lift a wheelchair into a vehicle. Thus, manual wheelchair users should use a wheelchair as light in weight as possible to help preserve upper-limb function (Consortium for Spinal Cord Medicine, 2005).

Manufacturers use materials with a high strength-to-weight ratio to build wheelchairs. Titanium, aluminum, and chromium-molybdenum steel are the most common materials used for sport wheelchairs.

**Strength**   International Organization for Standardization (ISO) standards (*American national standard for wheelchairs,* 1998) test impact, static, and fatigue strength to reveal the quality and durability of wheelchairs. However, manufacturers are not required to publish their test results. Studies from independent laboratories have shown that the quality of wheelchairs is not always as good as their manufacturers claim. Some models failed prematurely during fatigue tests. However, there are multiple design and manufacturing factors that can affect the strength and durability of a wheelchair, such as welding location and quality, frame and tubing geometry, screw locations, and caster sizes.

Wheelchairs designed specifically for sport use are not currently covered by the ISO standards, but the ISO test methods may still serve as a useful guide. Because sports can place high demands on a wheelchair, some people modify their chairs to meet their personal needs. Any modification to the frame may affect strength and durability. Many manufacturers offer customization services to meet this need. Rugby wheelchairs are known for their aggressive modifications to sustain heavy impacts and crashes during competitions. They usually have fully welded joints and axles and reinforced metal guards. Some wheelchair manufacturers sponsor elite athletes and build them customized chairs. Titanium and aluminum are commonly used in sport wheelchairs because of their high strength-to-weight ratios.

## Backrest

Rigid-shell backrests usually provide better support than soft, upholstered backrests, but their contours are less adjustable and they are more sensitive to individual fittings. Carbon fibre backrests are available and can provide light weight and good support. They are recommended for active people using lightweight or ultralightweight wheelchairs because their ultralightweight, ergonomic design helps distribute forces over the back and pelvis. Soft, upholstered backrests are standard components of conventional and most sport wheelchairs. Some soft backrests contain Velcro straps that can be tightened or loosened to adjust tension and create variable contours. Soft backrests change their shape when force is applied and allow more freedom for trunk movements. However, soft backrests may sag after use and cause pelvic instability, contributing to the users sitting in a slumped posture. Rigid-shell backrests provide better support, but users should find the backrest that best fits their needs.

**Soft backrests change shape when force is applied but may sag after use.**
Photo courtesy of R.A. Cooper.

## Cushion

A cushion is an essential seating and positioning device for any wheelchair user. Cushions provide seating comfort and pressure relief over users' weight-bearing areas. For active wheelchair users, appropriately adjusted and fitted cushions provide positional stability and further facilitate sport performance.

**Types of Cushions**   Contoured foam cushions, air-capsule cushions, air-foam cushions, viscoelastic-fluid cushions, and gel cushions are the most common wheelchair cushions. A contoured foam cushion is made from a piece of foam or a combination of foams with different densities. Its sitting area is shaped to the user's buttocks using either a vacuum-forming bead-bag system or a shape-measuring chair to determine the parameters of the contoured shape. To adjust the contoured shape, the maker either carves off more foam or glues in additional pieces of foam. Contoured foam cushions wear out faster than other types of cushion, but they are relatively inexpensive and provide good support.

Air-capsule cushions have a matrix of air-filled capsules. Air is allowed to move among the capsules. While the user is sitting on it, more air is pushed away from the capsules that are subjected to the higher pressure. Thus, the surface of the matrix conforms to the user's buttocks and provides pressure relief. The contour shape changes as the user shifts weight, which consequently compromises stability. Close attention to air flow and maintenance is required because capsules can be punctured and air leaks can occur even though they are made of heavy-duty rubber.

An air-foam cushion consists of a piece of foam wrapped tightly in an airtight and water-resistant cover. When the valve is open, the cushion self-inflates to resume its shape. When the user sits on it and opens the valve, air is released, allowing the user to sink into the cushion while the foam conforms to the user. After the valve is closed, the cushion keeps its shape. Air-foam cushions need daily regeneration through overnight inflation.

Viscoelastic and gel cushions distribute pressures via the transformation feature of the viscoelastic-fluid or gel-filled pouches. The pouches are often attached to a foam base to provide a stable base during sitting. Gel and viscoelastic cushions need daily kneading to mold and distribute the gel or viscoelastic fluid evenly to allow appropriate immersion and to prevent the cushion from bottoming out.

Additionally, hybrid cushions that incorporate the advantages of different cushions are available. For example, some consist of air-filled capsules embedded in a foam base, or gel or viscoelastic-fluid pouches attached on a foam base.

**Pressure Distribution**   Pressure-mapping systems are used to assess pressure distribution and calibrate cushions for appropriate fit. It is recommended that athletes try various cushions and conduct a clinical pressure-mapping assessment to ensure the most favorable pressure relief prior to final cushion selection. Air-capsule cushions have proven to be the most popular pressure-relief cushions (Collins, 2007; Defloor & Grypdonck, 2000). There are pressure-mapping systems that will fit into sport chairs, and the information can be useful for achieving a tight-fitting seat and minimizing high regions. Total or maximal contact is often a goal with sport seating.

Athletes positioned with knees higher than hips in sport chairs are at increased risk of developing pressure sores underneath the sacrum (tail bone) as body weight shifts backwards (Schaefer & Proffer, 1989). Rugby players may be at particularly high risk due to the extreme seat dump used and the reduced sensation among many people with tetraplegia. Basketball and tennis players typically do not sit with such a radical seat angle, but they often experience shear force over their buttocks, sacrum, and hips (Schaefer & Proffer, 1989). Using a proper pressure-relieving cushion and performing pressure relief manually are the main ways to prevent pressure sores.

**Pressure Sore Prevention**

Pressure sores are an important health concern for people with physical impairments. They are caused by multiple factors, such as prolonged pressure exposure, shear force, compromised soft tissue over bony prominences, excessive moisture over skin, high temperature at the seating surface, and impaired sensation. The development of pressure sores may be complicated by pain, infection, weight loss, immobilization, and negative emotions and result in hospitalization (Consortium for Spinal Cord Medicine, 2000). Athletes need to stay healthy to continue training programs and participate in competitions, but pressure sores interrupt training and competitions. Pressure ulcers also diminish performance capacity.

**Weight** Cushions should add minimal weight to the wheelchair. Excessive weight would reduce the advantage of using ultralightweight chair components. Gel, viscoelastic, and rubber air-capsule cushions may be too heavy for sport usage. Foam cushions are the most popular cushion because of their light weight. Honeycomb cushions are used frequently because they are extremely lightweight and provide good air flow throughout the cushion, but users should be aware that they provide limited pressure relief. Hybrid cushions that combine foam and local gel or viscoelastic pouches or air-filled capsules may be a good choice when attempting to balance weight and pressure distribution.

**Stability** Cushions with fixed contours provide a stable base of support for dynamic sitting. Contoured foam cushions seem to provide better stability than air-capsule cushions and gel or viscoelastic-fluid cushions (Aissaoui, Boucher, Bourbonnais, Lacoste, & Dansereau, 2001). Air-foam cushions may also be a good choice for sport because they provide the option of adjustable, custom-contoured shapes.

**Waterproof or Moisture-Wicking Cover** Waterproof covers provide moisture-resistant sheets, protecting the cushion from body fluid and moisture to promote hygiene and health. Covers made of moisture-wicking fibres help to quickly draw moisture away and keep the skin dry. Athletes should use either one or both covers to protect the skin and cushion. Additionally, the cover should be flexible enough to allow the cushion to contour for appropriate pressure distribution and relief.

## Wheels and Tyres

Lightweight wheels are recommended for decreasing the total weight of a wheelchair. The maximum wheel sizes are regulated by the official rules; 61-centimetre and 66-centimetre diameters are the common wheel sizes. High-pressure tyres are highly suggested for decreasing the strength demand for propelling a chair. Because high pressure makes tyres stiffer, wheels and tyres experience less deformation while rolling on the ground, resulting in less friction and rolling resistance.

## Hand Rims

Regular hand rims with smooth metal surfaces and a circular cross section require full grasp to achieve sufficient friction for propelling wheels. However, they allow a variety of hand positions for different propulsion tasks.

Various ergonomic hand rims have been developed to improve wrist kinematics during propulsion. Some manufacturers close the gap between the hand rim and wheel with soft rubber, and some have developed oval-shaped hand rims to decrease intensive finger flexion for gripping power. Natural-Fit is a commercialized hand rim that helps users feel less pain in the hands and wrists. People with full hand function would benefit most from this product. Wheelchair users who do not have full hand function often press the hypothenar eminence of their thumbs (the ball of the thumb) firmly against the hand rims to propel the wheels. Some people close the gap between the wheel and hand rim, and therefore the hand rim and tyre form a continuous surface that accommodates the limited propulsion pattern since high friction can be generated between the tyre and the hypothenar eminence.

## Casters

The front casters are mainly solid polyurethane and 5 centimetres in diameter. Smaller caster sizes allow the chair to be shorter while ensuring caster-foot clearance, and they make the chair more responsive. Stiffer tyres deform less and decrease rolling resistance.

## Anti-Tippers

Anti-tippers with swivel casters are necessary to prevent sport wheelchairs from tipping over. Wheelchair basketball has strict rules related to anti-tip devices. No more than two anti-tip casters may be attached to the underside or rear of the chair. Rear anti-tippers cannot extend past any part of the rear wheels. The distance between the lowest point of the anti-tip caster and the floor cannot exceed 2.5 centimetres. Wheelchair rugby has similar rules, but the number of anti-tip devices that a rugby chair can have is not limited. Each sport has official rules for the selection of anti-tip devices and mounting locations.

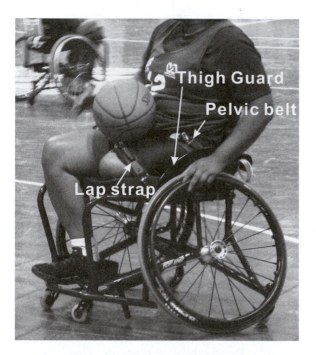

**Thigh guards and a pelvic belt provide pelvic stability, and a lap strap is applied around the athlete's thigh to stabilize lower-limb position.**

Photo courtesy of R.A. Cooper.

## Belts, Straps, and Thigh Guards

For wheelchair sports involving fast speed, quick turns, and potential impact, additional appliances are necessary to secure position and prevent falling. These include belts, straps, and thigh guards.

**Pelvic Control and Trunk Stability** Pelvic belts help athletes maintain sitting balance and avoid ejection from their chairs. Placement is important to provide stabilization. A belt that pulls the pelvis at 45 degrees sufficiently keeps the pelvis in position in most cases. A belt that pulls the pelvis at 90 degrees maintains the pelvic position for people with excessive hip extensor tone. Some people who have less strength in their trunk muscles may wear trunk or chest belts to maintain trunk stability, but upper-limb movements may be impeded when the belts are too high.

**Lower-Limb Positions**   Athletes are allowed to use straps to secure their feet onto the footrests to prevent dragging on the floor or trapping their chairs. Some athletes use lap straps to stabilize their knees to keep them from swaying. Solid and tight-fitting thigh guards also improve pelvic stability and control lower-limb position.

**Precautions**   To avoid excessive stress on the skin, belts and straps should not contact the skin directly. Excessive pressure from straps or belts may block blood circulation or even cause skin or muscle damage. Padding should be added to properly distribute the pressure. Using wider straps helps to prevent the tourni-quet effect and improve the pressure distribution applied to the skin and limbs. In addition, excessive pressure from the thigh guards may cause pressure sores on the greater trochanters (the bony prominences at the lateral sides of hip joints).

## Basic Wheelchair Set-Up

The goals of wheelchair set-up in all three court sports are similar, including

- increasing accessibility to the hand rims,
- improving sitting stability,
- making the wheelchair more responsive and faster, and
- making the entire user–wheelchair system more manoeuvrable yet stable.

Common adjustments of sport wheelchairs include

- camber,
- seat height,
- seat angle,
- horizontal rear-wheel axle position, and
- hyperflexed knee position.

All of these adjustments are elaborated next. However, to ensure safety and to maintain competition fairness, coaches and athletes must follow the official rules regulating wheelchair configurations as specified by each association of wheel-chair sport.

### Positive Camber

Camber is the orientation of the wheels in relation to the frame (see figure 2.1). Positive camber means that the tops of the wheels lean in. By improving accessibil-ity to the hand rims, positive camber may improve manoeuvrability and hand-rim comfort (Perdios, Sawatzky, & Sheel, 2007). Wheels with positive camber create a larger base of support and improve lateral stability. In addition, hands and fingers are protected by positive camber because the bottom of the wheel will be the first area of contact during side impacts.

**Figure 2.1** Wheels with 10 degrees positive camber (bottom) have more manoeuvrability than wheels with zero camber (top).

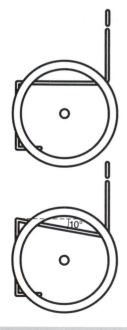

**Figure 2.2** The top seat is set at an angle of zero. The second seat is set at 10 degrees of seat dump.

Rolling resistance increases proportionally with positive camber because the contact area between the tyres and the ground becomes larger (Faupin, Campillo, Weissland, Gorce, & Thevenon, 2004). Athletes should find a balance between rolling resistance and accessibility to hand rims when adjusting camber angle. In addition, positive camber decreases the seat height and enlarges the footprint and turning radius of the chair. Some athletes may find this configuration unfavorable because they lose the height advantage and are blocked more easily. To achieve optimal performance, adjust camber to suit individual needs. This principle may be applied to all other categories of wheelchair set-up as well.

## Seat Height

Both front and rear seat heights should be considered for wheelchair set-up. The height is measured from the floor to the front and rear edge of the seat. The seat height can be elevated by increasing the vertical distance between the rear-wheel axles and the seat, adjusting caster position, using a thicker cushion, and using larger wheels and casters. Sitting on a higher seat may provide advantages in certain situations, such as playing as a forward in basketball and serving in tennis.

An elevated seat height raises the centre of gravity of the entire user–wheelchair system and thereby decreases both rearward and lateral stabilities. Users may have less accessibility to their hand rims as well.

## Seat Angle

The seat angle is the orientation of the seat plane with respect to level ground. When the front and rear seat heights are not equal, an angle is created. The preferred angle is created with the front edge of the seat higher than the rear edge of the seat. This is called the *seat dump* or *seat drop* (see figure 2.2). Seat dump greatly improves sitting stability by using gravity to hold the pelvis and lower back in the seat. This position also lowers the rear seat-to-floor height and thus provides greater accessibility to the hand rims. The wheelchair is more stable laterally because the centre of gravity of the user–wheelchair system is lower.

The seat dump decreases the overall height of the person in a sitting position. The shift of centre of gravity decreases rearward stability. The instability is more significant with decreased lower-limb weight or muscle mass.

## Horizontal Rear-Wheel Axle Position

Moving the horizontal position of rear wheels forward increases the push angle, therefore decreasing push frequency (Boninger, Baldwin, Cooper, Koontz, & Chan, 2000). The overall length of the chair is shorter, and the rider's centre of gravity is shifted backwards, allowing wheelchairs to be more responsive because of the smaller rotational inertia.

However, this position has drawbacks because the forward axle position decreases the stability of the wheelchair and may cause the chair to tip backwards when the athlete extends or rotates the trunk backwards to grab a ball, causing a quick rearward shift of centre of gravity. Athletes should be careful about adjusting their rear-wheel axle position, especially those who have had one or both lower extremities amputated or have lost significant weight in the lower limbs.

## Hyperflexed Knee Position

A hyperflexed knee position is when the knees are flexed more than 90 degrees, with zero degrees being full extension. This position can be achieved by increasing the seat-dump angle and moving the footrest back. A hyperflexed knee position can increase turning speed (MacPhee, Kirby, Bell, & MacLeod, 2001). By tucking the lower legs beneath the thighs, this position reduces the footprint of the user–wheelchair system, which in turn decreases the momentum of inertia and makes turning easier.

Nevertheless, this extreme knee position may cause muscle tightness and affect sitting stability and trunk movements. The athlete's physical condition and sport tasks are major factors to consider when setting a wheelchair with a hyperflexed knee position.

## Adjustment Summary

Adjustments in each category of wheelchair set-up may result in various changes in the performance of the wheelchair. Table 2.1 summarizes the adjustments and

### revolutions

**Basic Wheelchair Propulsion Training**

A propulsion pattern with long, smooth strokes in the push phase and the hand relaxing and moving below the hand rim during the recovery phase has been reported to improve efficiency and decrease repetition (a potential source of overuse injury) during wheelchair propulsion (Boninger et al., 2002). Although the pattern with long strokes is recommended, modifications may occur due to individual preferences and tasks. Proper wheelchair settings can increase hand-rim accessibility, which in turn facilitates efficiency in propulsion. Review table 2.1 for wheelchair set-up to improve hand-rim accessibility and to see how other aspects affect wheelchair performance.

Minimizing repetition and force during wheelchair activities can prevent repetitive strain injury. Common repetitive strain injuries for wheelchair users include muscle soreness or strains, tendinitis, and peripheral nerve disorders (such as carpal tunnel syndrome) in the upper limbs. Between 23 and 52 percent of wheelchair sport injuries may be due to overuse (Groah & Lanig, 2000), but wheelchair athletes do not appear to have a higher prevalence of upper-extremity pain compared with nonathletic wheelchair users (Finley & Rodgers, 2004; Fullerton, Borckardt, & Alfano, 2003). Experienced athletes may develop better wheelchair skills and knowledge of wheelchair selection and set-up; thus, they know how to manoeuvre their chairs more efficiently and select proper equipment, which may decrease risks of injury. It is essential to minimize repetitive strain injuries, because the pain, discomfort, and weakness resulting from these injuries interrupt daily activities as well as sport.

TABLE 2.1

## Wheelchair Adjustments and Their Effects in Sport Performance

| Wheelchair set-up | Seat height | Rearward stability | Lateral (sideways) stability | Sitting stability | Manoeuvr-ability | Accessibility to hand rims |
|---|---|---|---|---|---|---|
| Increase positive camber angles. | Decreased | — | Increased | — | Increased | Increased |
| Increase seat-dump angle. | Decreased | Decreased | Increased | Increased | Increased | Increased |
| Move rear-wheel axle forward. | — | Decreased | — | — | Increased | Increased |
| Increase vertical distance between rear-wheel axle and seat when seat is level. | Increased | Decreased | Decreased | Decreased | May decrease | Decreased |

Note: The correlation between each adjustment and its consequences can be reversed accordingly. For example, decreasing positive camber angles would increase seat height, decrease lateral stability, and so on.

their corresponding changes in sport performance. Certain adjustments may be advantageous for some athletes but not for others. To facilitate athletic performance, be aware of these relationships and find the best configuration to suit individual needs.

## Sport-Specific Wheelchair Set-Up

Besides the general rules for setting up a safe and efficient wheelchair, sport wheelchairs are set up specifically for the performance requirements of the sport and the position that the athlete plays in a team. Following are set-up details for basketball, rugby, tennis, handcycling, and racing.

### Wheelchair Basketball

A higher seat height can be beneficial in wheelchair basketball, but the seat height may differ according to the player's position on the team. Forwards usually set their seat as high as possible, but the official regulation limits the seat height to 53 centimetres or less, measured from the top of the side seat rails to the floor. To block opponents' attacks, guards want chairs to be faster, more manoeuvrable, and more stable so that seat height may be sacrificed to set the chairs with these features.

Basketball players tend to have fewer functional limitations and need to move their upper limbs with large ranges of motion. They commonly choose backrests as low as possible to allow upper limbs and trunk to move freely. Some chairs are equipped with forward bumpers on the footrest to reduce the risk of forward falls and foot injuries due to front impacts.

Exposed wheel spokes may allow opponents to illegally ram to disrupt play. Spoke guards made of high-impact plastic covering the rear-wheel spokes not only prevent wheel damage but also protect players' hands and fingers from being trapped in the spokes. Spoke guards allow basketball players to pick up the ball from the floor by pushing it against the spoke guard and rolling it onto the lap. Detailed equipment requirements can be located in the rules of wheelchair basketball outlined by the National Wheelchair Basketball Association (NWBA, 2007).

## Wheelchair Rugby

Wheelchair rugby is a combination of team handball and rugby that was developed for people with physical limitations involving both upper and lower extremities. Most of the players have tetraplegia due to cervical-level SCI. Wheelchair contact is legal for both defensive and offensive players during games.

A rugby chair needs to provide the player with highly stable, supportive seating. The rear wheels are radically cambered to approximately 15 degrees to create a larger base of support. Aluminum frames are preferred because they are lightweight. Metal guards covering lower frames and wheel spokes protect the player and the chair from impact, and they improve stability by lowering the centre of gravity of the chair. The

**Wheelchairs for basketball players should allow the trunk and upper limbs to move freely.**
Photo courtesy of the Department of Veterans Affairs.

**Wheelchair rugby players wear gloves or tape to protect their hands.**
Photo courtesy of the Department of Veterans Affairs.

seat dump may be set at an angle of 20 degrees to provide maximum pelvic stability.

Straps are used heavily to stabilize the lower extremities and trunk. Players limit knee position to a level that allows the ball to stay on their laps. Knee pads or braces are allowed for lower-limb protection.

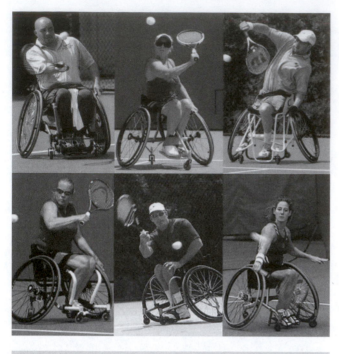

**Wheelchairs used in tennis must be fast and responsive.**
Photos courtesy of Wheelchair Sports Federation. Photographer Curt Beamer.

Scratches, abrasions, and friction blisters on hands and arms are frequent injuries in wheelchair rugby, and players wear gloves or tape to protect from these injuries. Players are allowed to put sticky glue on their gloves or tape to help catch the ball.

## Wheelchair Tennis

Wheelchair tennis is played at a fast tempo, even with the two-bounce rule. Because players have to do their best to cover the entire court, it is important that the wheelchair is fast and responsive. To hit the ball, the player has to swing the racket and push or turn the chair with one hand. Drive wheels are cambered to allow the player to cover a larger range on the hand rims and thus to manoeuvre the chair agilely. Lower backrests are preferred in tennis for trunk and upper-limb movements. Some players modify their chairs to have a single front caster or even a single anti-tip caster to make the chair more responsive in turns. However, this decreases stability in the diagonal directions.

## Handcycling

Handcycling is becoming increasingly popular for recreation and sport. Studies have shown that handcycling is more mechanically efficient than propelling a hand-rim wheelchair system because the handcycling system provides for more continuous arm motion and power transfer. Physical demands are decreased as larger and more muscles are used in the upper extremities. Cranking a handcycle typically results in higher speeds or longer durations than propelling a manual wheelchair. Handcycles can be grouped into three types according to the user's sitting position: upright handcycles, recumbent handcycles, and kneeling handcycles (U.S. Handcycling Federation, 2008).

Upright handcycling is for recreation only. It is relatively slow because the upright sitting position creates greater wind resistance (drag) and lower mechanical efficiency. These handcycles have a higher risk of tipping compared with the other types of handcycles because their centre of gravity is higher. However, upright handcycling is a good first step to learn the synchronized propelling pattern for handcycling. Steering and getting in and out of the upright handcycle are more manageable. Add-on handcycle units are available that clamp onto everyday wheelchairs. Add-on handcycling systems are less efficient than standalone handcycles due to the additional weight from the everyday chair and the components of the attachment mechanism. Often the add-on handcycles lift the front casters between 25 and 50 millimetres, which leads to scrubbing of the rear wheels when camber is used. Generally, the cranking system should be set up below the shoulder height of the rider to allow gravity to assist with propulsion, but not so low that the pedals and the steering system get in the way of transfers or the rider's legs.

Recumbent handcycles can be propelled fast enough for racing and are used in the Paralympics. Users lie back in a highly reclined position with the legs forward. The seat position is lower than that of upright handcycles, with the seat just a few centimetres off of the ground. The cranks are brought close to the trunk to make greater use of the pectoral muscles, which provides better ergonomics in cranking movement. Similar to upright handcycles, a lower-positioned cranking system provides gravity assist with propulsion.

There are two types of recumbent handcycles. A fork-steering handcycle turns via rotation of a shaft connected to the fork holding the front wheel and the cranking system. A lean-steering handcycle has the steering axis in the middle of the frame, and turning is accomplished by the user shifting body weight, resulting in the seat frame swinging from one side to the other (Zipfel, Olson, Puhlman, & Cooper, 2008). It may take longer to learn how to operate a lean-steering handcycle than a fork-steering handcycle. The lean-steering system is more efficient and smoother in turning compared with the fork-steering system because hand–body orientation is kept the same. This type of cycling is similar to monoskiing, in which athletes lean their bodies to shift the centre of gravity to turn. However, the lean-steering system is less stable at high speeds and requires better trunk control and balance to manoeuvre the chair.

Kneeling handcycles are essentially for racing. The rider assumes a position where the legs are tucked under a small

**Upright handcycling is for recreation only.**
Photo courtesy of the Department of Veterans Affairs.

**Recumbent handcycles can be used for racing.**
Photo courtesy of the Department of Veterans Affairs.

**Kneeling is most efficient for hill-climbing.**
Photo courtesy of Thomas Abel.

seat. This positioning is similar to that used in racing wheelchairs. The rider leans forward to turn the cranks, allowing the rider to use body weight as well as upper-body strength to propel the handcycle. Some racers use the cranks asynchronously whereas other use them synchronously. The choice is largely based on personal preference. For racers with good trunk function, a kneeling handcycle with asynchronous cranks may be fastest. The centre of the cranks should be about at the middle of the abdomen to allow the rider to use the anterior prime movers to push the cranks forward and then use the shoulder muscles and biceps to pull the cranks.

## Wheelchair Racing

The seat of a racing chair is composed of a cage and a sling. The cage is the metal frame of the seat, and the sling is the structure supporting the rider. Riders' knees are bent underneath the trunk into kneeling buckets or cages. People who are not used to the kneeling position and have good trunk control can use upright cages. When athletes are in the full down position, shoulder joints should align with the front of the hand rims, and athletes should be able to easily reach the bottom of the hand rims. Elite athletes prefer to fit in the seat slings tightly to obtain the most stable position possible.

Athletes tend to lean forward in racing chairs to use trunk muscle and weight to generate powerful strokes. Wheelchair racers should focus on propelling to increase speed but not waste energy and attention on maintaining balance. When riding in a racing chair, the anterior upper areas of the lower legs and posterior distal areas of the thighs are weight-bearing areas. The seat should be padded carefully in these areas to relieve excessive pressure and shear force. Athletes should check their skin in these areas at least daily to monitor skin integrity.

Hand rims of racing chairs are smaller than those on standard wheelchairs for increasing the accessible portion of the rims during propulsion. Smaller hand rims require more strength to propel the chair, but higher speeds can be achieved. Typically, hand-rim diameters range from 35 to 48 centimetres. They may be coated with rubber, plastic, or high-density foam for greater friction with gloves. The rear wheels are usually cambered 2 to 15 degrees so that the athlete can reach the bottom of the hand rims without hitting the top of the wheels. Some elite racers use carbon fibre disc wheels instead of traditional spoke wheels because disc wheels are light and rigid and have a lower rotating inertia.

To achieve the greatest mechanical efficiency, the frames are rigid and built with lightweight material. Adjustable joints of wheelchair frames consume power during force transmission. Thus, racing wheelchairs are usually handcrafted with welded joints to fit each athlete's anatomy and special needs.

**Wheelchair racing.**
Photo courtesy of Ian Thompson.

Many skilful wheelchair users do not have brakes on their everyday chairs, but brakes are required in most wheelchair racing competitions due to high racing speeds. Brakes should be adjusted appropriately so that the brake levers are long enough and angled properly for the athlete to be able to apply sufficient leverage to stop the chair. This issue is more critical for athletes with tetraplegia because they have less upper-limb strength.

# Injury Prevention

While pursuing supreme performance, athletes should also prepare to prevent injuries during sporting events. Proper protections should be applied to decrease risks of injuries from impacts, falling, and manoeuvring and propelling wheelchairs.

## Helmets

Athletes may propel racing chairs with speeds in excess of 30 kilometres per hour on flat ground and 80 kilometres per hour downhill. High speeds and the potential for accidents necessitate the use of helmets during wheelchair racing events. Aerodynamic helmets are designed to decrease drag and allow sufficient airflow to the head. The shape of a helmet and the airflow direction affect aerodynamics. The racing speed may increase when an aerodynamic helmet fits the athlete properly. There are no rules for wheelchair rugby and tennis requiring headgear or helmets during competitions. Headgear is not permitted in wheelchair basketball games. Novices should wear helmets because of the potential for chairs to tip over or crash.

## Gloves and Braces

Bruises, blisters, and scratches are frequent injuries in wheelchair sport. Proper protection to avoid these minor injuries can preserve athletes from being distracted by discomfort. Although these injuries seem to be small problems, they can become complicated by serious medical problems. For example, open wounds may become infected. Bruises may indicate hematoma or be associated with fractures or internal bleeding that need professional care.

Wearing protective braces or equipment on joints is legal in formal competitions if the equipment is properly covered or padded and does not pose a danger to other players. Gloves are necessary to prevent scratches or blisters on hands due to grinding from stopping or turning chairs.

## Skin Checks and Proper Padding

People who are at high risk of developing pressure sores (those who have a history of pressure sores, have lost or have impaired sensation over weight-bearing areas, are extremely thin, or have uneven weight bearing) should perform a weight shift once every hour for 1 to 2 minutes or full pressure relief once every 15 to 30 minutes for 30 to 60 seconds. Vigorous movements during hours and hours of training apply repetitive friction and shear forces on the skin, and damp clothing may macerate and weaken the skin. Because athletes subject their skin to a highly stressful environment, they should check their skin condition carefully at least daily and wear clean, moisture-absorbing clothing (Lai, Stanish, & Stanish, 2000).

The back is another location that could develop pressure sores. Players may be required to lean firmly against the backrest to gain sufficient counterforce for upper-limb movement; meanwhile, they have to move the upper trunk to increase the range that the upper limbs can cover. Caution must be taken because large shear forces may occur along the edges of the backrest, especially the tops of backrest posts. Proper padding should cover these edges to distribute forces, and players should have someone check the skin of the back frequently.

## Maintain a Proper Body Weight

Reducing the weight of the user–wheelchair system lessens the strength and endurance demands on the upper extremities to propel the chair. According to a study by Boninger and colleagues, body weight is correlated with deteriorated median nerve function and an increase in propulsion force (Boninger, Cooper, Baldwin, Shimada, & Koontz, 1999). Maintaining a proper body weight helps prevent or delay the onset of overuse injuries and preserve upper-limb functions.

# Conclusion

A sport wheelchair should be configured in a way that minimizes rolling resistance, maximizes manoeuvrability, provides adequate stability of the user and the wheelchair, increases hand-rim accessibility, and prevents injuries. Optimal wheelchair set-ups vary from sport to sport, but wheel camber, seat dump, forward axle position, and hyperflexed knee position are common configurations. Long, smooth strokes are generally the best propulsion pattern in terms of injury prevention; however, this type of stroke may not be practical or indicated in all sporting situations, particularly where quick accelerations are required. Furthermore, many principles of hand-rim propulsion do not translate to handcycles and racing chairs because they have unique set-ups and designs. The prevention of skin breakdown is fairly universal across all sports, though. To prevent pressure sores, athletes should check the skin condition of the buttocks, sacrum, hips, back, and any other areas subjected to pressure and shear force. Athletes should wear proper protective gear to prevent bruises, blisters, and scratches. Maintaining proper body weight also can lessen the forces experienced through the upper extremities during propulsion.

# References

Aissaoui, R., Boucher, C., Bourbonnais, D., Lacoste, M., & Dansereau, J. (2001). Effect of seat cushion on dynamic stability in sitting during a reaching task in wheelchair users with paraplegia. *Archives of Physical Medicine & Rehabilitation, 82*(2), 274-281.

*American national standard for wheelchairs: Vol. 1.* (1998). American National Standards Institute/ Rehabilitation Engineering and Assistive Technology Society of North America.

Boninger, M.L., Baldwin, M., Cooper, R.A., Koontz, A., & Chan, L. (2000). Manual wheelchair pushrim biomechanics and axle position. *Archives of Physical Medicine & Rehabilitation, 81*(5), 608-613.

Boninger, M.L., Cooper, R.A., Baldwin, M.A., Shimada, S.D., & Koontz, A. (1999). Wheelchair pushrim kinetics: Body weight and median nerve function. *Archives of Physical Medicine & Rehabilitation, 80*(8), 910-915.

Boninger, M.L., Souza, A.L., Cooper, R.A., Fitzgerald, S.G., Koontz, A.M., & Fay, B.T. (2002). Propulsion patterns and pushrim biomechanics in manual wheelchair propulsion. *Archives of Physical Medicine & Rehabilitation, 83*(5), 718-723.

Collins, F. (2007). A practical guide to wheelchair cushions. *International Journal of Therapy and Reha-bilitation,* 14(12), 557-561.

Consortium for Spinal Cord Medicine. (2000). *Pressure ulcer prevention and treatment following spinal cord injury: A clinical practice guideline for health-care professionals.* Washington, DC: Paralyzed Veterans of America.

Consortium for Spinal Cord Medicine. (2005). *Preservation of upper limb function following spinal cord injury: A clinical practice guideline for health-care professionals.* Washington, DC: Paralyzed Veterans of America.

Defloor, T., & Grypdonck, M.H.F. (2000). Do pressure relief cushions really relieve pressure? *Western Journal of Nursing Research,* 22(3), 335-350.

Faupin, A., Campillo, P., Weissland, T., Gorce, P., & Thevenon, A. (2004). The effects of rear-wheel camber on the mechanical parameters produced during the wheelchair sprinting of handibasketball athletes. *Journal of Rehabilitation Research & Development,* 41(3B), 421-428.

Finley, M.A., & Rodgers, M.M. (2004). Prevalence and identification of shoulder pathology in athletic and nonathletic wheelchair users with shoulder pain: A pilot study. *Journal of Rehabilitation Research & Development,* 41(3B), 395-402.

Fullerton, H.D., Borckardt, J.J., & Alfano, A.P. (2003). Shoulder pain: A comparison of wheelchair athletes and nonathletic wheelchair users. *Medicine & Science in Sports & Exercise,* 35(12), 1958-1961.

Groah, S.L., & Lanig, I.S. (2000). Neuromusculoskeletal syndromes in wheelchair athletes. *Seminars in Neurology,* 20(2), 201-208.

Lai, A.M., Stanish, W.D., & Stanish, H.I. (2000). The young athlete with physical challenges. *Clinics in Sports Medicine,* 19(4), 793-819.

MacPhee, A.H., Kirby, R.L., Bell, A.C., & MacLeod, D.A. (2001). The effect of knee-flexion angle on wheelchair turning. *Medical Engineering & Physics,* 23(4), 275-283.

National Wheelchair Basketball Association (NWBA). (2007). *National Wheelchair Basketball Association Official Rules and Case Book, 2007-2008.* www.nwba.org/index.php?option = com_content&view = article&id = 14&Itemid = 121.

Perdios, A., Sawatzky, B.J., & Sheel, W. (2007). Effects of camber on wheeling efficiency in the experienced and inexperienced wheelchair user. *Journal of Rehabilitation Research & Development,* 44(3), 459-466.

Schaefer, R.S., & Proffer, D.S. (1989). Sports medicine for wheelchair athletes. *American Family Physician,* 39(5), 239-245.

U.S. Handcycling Federation. (2008). *Handcycling basics.* www.ushandcycling.org/hc101.html.

Zipfel, E., Olson, J., Puhlman, J., & Cooper, R.A. (2008). Design of a custom racing hand-cycle: Review and analysis. *Disability & Rehabilitation: Assistive Technology,* 1(10).

# Mike Frogley

I began my Paralympic journey as a player with the Canadian men's national wheelchair basketball team at the 1992 Games in Barcelona. In 1996 in Atlanta, I took the next step when I served as assistant coach for Tim Frick and the Canadian women's team. I spent my past three Paralympics as the head coach of the Canadian men's team with Paul Bowes and Jerry Tonello as assistant coaches. I feel privileged to have been part of successful teams (a record of 5-3 as a player and 28-1 as a coach) and to have won three gold medals and one silver medal. Although winning has been fun, what I take most from the Paralympics are the lessons. Here, I share those lessons so that you might enjoy the success I had.

First, sort out the distractions. What makes the Paralympics more challenging than other competitions is the magnitude of the Games and the distractions that come with it. Your success depends on your ability to sort through the distractions, both good and bad. Everyone at the Paralympics is a great athlete. What separates the gold medalists from the rest is the ability to stay focused. If you don't play in the moment, you will make mistakes. The distractions are varied: A bus will be late. You will have to speak to the media. You'll have equipment problems, or somebody will not speak your language. You can gain a competitive edge by learning how to deal with the distractions.

Second, focus on improving with each game or event. Athletes and teams tend to look past the immediate game and dream of a gold medal. Each game and each day is an opportunity to improve. At the Games, a team is together for 10 days. Use that time to work toward a peak because you are playing against the best in the world.

Third, see the breadth of the Games. At each Paralympics I saw something and learned something that had nothing to do with sport. After losing in the quarterfinals of my first Paralympics and finishing fourth, I had time on my hands as the other teams prepared for the gold-medal game. My goal had been to win a gold medal. But I realized that there must be more to the Paralympics and the training than simply winning a gold medal. I realized that I was part of an experience that not many people get. At the closing ceremonies, I saw people from all over the world on the field—people trading uniforms and laughing and talking. There were no fights. I thought to myself, *If we can get along for these four hours, then why not four days? Why not four weeks? Why not four years? And why not forever?*

Photo courtesy of the University of Illinois, photographer Josh Birnbaum.

# chapter 3

# Physiology of Wheelchair Sport

Vicky Goosey-Tolfrey and Mike Price

Wheelchair sport performance depends on three factors: the athlete, the wheelchair, and the interaction between the athlete and the wheelchair. Like any other athlete, participants in wheelchair sport are looking for new ways to train and analyse their technique so that they may improve their performance. In spite of the advanced technical features of sport wheelchairs, racing times and the increase in pace of game play are also partly due to an improvement in our understanding and application of physical conditioning programmes designed especially for wheelchair participants.

Physical training programmes for wheelchair athletes should incorporate the same training principles as for nondisabled athletes, yet it is important to understand how the exercise responses differ in wheelchair athletes when compared with nondisabled athletes. It is obvious that wheelchair athletes rely upon the upper body for exercise, but their physical ability to exercise (functional capacity) depends on the level of SCI. This in turn determines the amount of muscle that can be used and the amount of sympathetic nervous system that is available. To develop and implement safe, effective training programmes, it is necessary to have a basic understanding of how levels of SCI affect exercise responses. This chapter builds on chapter 1, which describes the levels of SCI, and focuses on the physiological responses of SCI, training considerations, and fitness measurement.

# Physiological Responses

This section describes key components of the cardiorespiratory system and why they are important for training. The adaptations that occur to these components through training are fundamental to improving performance, especially endurance performance. By monitoring components such as heart rate, it is possible to determine training intensities and how well athletes are adapting to training.

## Heart Rate

During exercise, heart rate increases due to reduced activity of the vagus nerve (which normally restrains heart rate) and increased activity of the sympathetic nervous system (which normally accelerates heart rate). Nondisabled athletes are able to increase their heart rate to a value of approximately 220 minus their age, although this is lower for arm exercise (200 minus age). All sympathetic nerves originate from the thoracic and lumbar sections of the spinal cord. The nerves that allow the heart rate to increase exit from the spinal cord between the first and the fourth thoracic vertebrae (T1 and T4). Therefore, as with muscle innervation, athletes with spinal cord lesions within this area most likely will not be able to increase their heart rate to those levels expected for nondisabled athletes. Furthermore, athletes with injuries above this level will not be able to increase their heart rate much above the natural rhythm of the heart, which is approximately 100 beats per minute. This means that for tetraplegics, heart rate may not be the best indicator of training intensity.

## Stroke Volume and Cardiac Output

Stroke volume is the amount of blood ejected from the left ventricle with each heart beat, whereas cardiac output is the amount of blood ejected from the heart via the left ventricle in 1 minute. In nondisabled athletes, stroke volume is a key adaptation to endurance training and generally increases with training. For example,

Goodman, Liu, and Green (2005) showed that stroke volume during exercise can increase by 7 to 10 percent after only 6 days of endurance training. During exercise of gradually increasing intensity (incremental exercise), stroke volume initially increases with exercise intensity up until 40 to 50 percent of maximum exercise capacity due to more blood being returned to the heart from the venous circulation and more forceful contraction of each heartbeat (Hopman, 1994). This allows more oxygenated blood to be delivered to the exercising muscles. As the size of the left ventricle increases with endurance training, maximal cardiac output also increases.

Maximal values for stroke volume and cardiac output are reduced in athletes with SCI when compared with nondisabled athletes. Stroke volume is often reduced because the loss of sympathetic nervous system activity below the level of injury does not allow blood to be redirected as effectively from nonexercising areas. This means that less blood can return to the heart with each beat. The reduction in cardiac output may be from this alone or in combination with a reduction in the maximum heart rate obtainable.

## Aerobic Fitness

During incremental aerobic exercise, oxygen consumption for nondisabled athletes increases with exercise intensity until a maximum value is attained. The classic response shown in most exercise physiology textbooks is that with any further increase in exercise intensity from this point, there will be no further increase in oxygen uptake, resulting in the term *maximal oxygen uptake* or $\dot{V}O_2max$. During upper-body exercise or modes of exercise where local fatigue occurs before central cardiorespiratory fatigue, such a plateau is not achieved as often and the term *peak oxygen uptake* or $\dot{V}O_2peak$, although it still represents a maximal effort. $\dot{V}O_2peak$ is determined by many factors, especially the amount of muscle mass that can be exercised, maximal cardiac output, and amount of oxygen that can be delivered, extracted, and used by the body.

## Anaerobic Fitness

Just as aerobic parameters increase with lower levels of SCI, peak anaerobic parameters show a similar response. As peak anaerobic power relates to sprint activities, values are greater than for incremental aerobic exercise tests and are again greater where more muscle can be recruited for power production. As a result, blood lactate values are also greater after a sprint test where greater peak

### revolutions

If $\dot{V}O_2peak$ increases due to training, it is most likely that power output will also increase. This is known as *peak aerobic power.* For wheelchair athletes, peak aerobic power can be measured in a number of ways. Ideally, the athletes should exercise in their sport wheelchair. This can be done on treadmills or on wheelchair roller systems to determine peak physiological responses just as nondisabled athletes would do on a treadmill or cycle ergometer. These modes of exercise can give specific pushing speeds that athletes can relate to in their training, especially track and endurance athletes. However, where these techniques are not available, the coach could conduct field-based testing in the athlete's sporting environment, as described later. As we may expect based on the physiological responses noted already, athletes with lower levels of SCI can usually produce greater peak aerobic power outputs and greater wheelchair pushing speeds.

anaerobic power outputs are achieved. A standard lab-based exercise test to determine peak anaerobic power production is the Wingate anaerobic test, which can easily be adapted for wheelchair exercise or arm cycling. This test involves a load being suddenly applied to an arm-crank ergometer or wheelchair roller system with the athlete exercising as hard and as fast as possible for 30 seconds.

Figure 3.1 shows typical results for a wheelchair sprinter during an arm-crank Wingate test and highlights the key performance parameters obtained. Power increases rapidly until it reaches a peak and then begins to tail off as the athlete fatigues. The shape of this power curve is similar for most athletes; however, higher peak power values are evident for sprinters when compared with endurance athletes. On the other hand, endurance-trained athletes tend to demonstrate lower levels of fatigue. In general, if we compare the profile of a nondisabled athlete with a wheelchair athlete, greater differences occur as less functional muscle mass becomes available (figure 3.2).

## Training Considerations

It is imperative to develop and maintain the components of fitness. Certainly the training principles used with nondisabled athletes apply with some modifications. There is strong evidence to suggest that wheelchair athletes gain similar training adaptations to nondisabled athletes through aerobic and anaerobic conditioning (Goosey-Tolfrey, 2005). However, the degree of improvement following a training programme differs considerably among athletes. This is because of differences in SCI characteristics described earlier, the athlete's previous training history, and to a certain extent, the athlete's trainability, which is determined by the available active muscle mass.

It may appear at first glance that people who use wheelchairs are more restricted with their choice of exercise mode than their nondisabled counterparts. However,

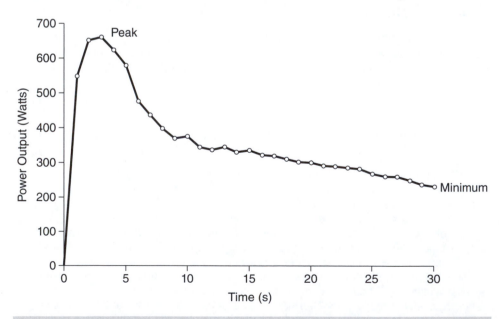

**Figure 3.1** Profile of the Wingate anaerobic arm-crank test in a T54 male sprint athlete with SCI.

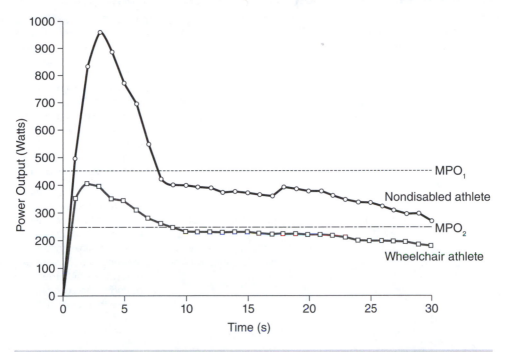

**Figure 3.2** Comparison between the Wingate anaerobic arm-crank test profile from a nondisabled athlete (upper-body sprint trained) and a male endurance athlete with SCI (T11 complete lesion). Mean power output (MPO) for nondisabled (1) and wheelchair (2) athletes.

with a little imagination several training types can be used, including wheelchair propulsion on rollers, swimming, wheelchair sports, seated aerobics, and electrical stimulation of the lower body combined with arm cranking. Recommended types of exercise for wheelchair participants are summarized in table 3.1. The main choice will depend on availability but should be specific to the chosen sport. For example, wheelchair athletes should focus training efforts on wheelchair-based exercises. However, to prevent the upper body from becoming overused, consider building the following key elements into a training programme: Vary the exercise types on a weekly basis, strengthen the muscles of the upper back and shoulders (e.g., pushing backwards or performing rowing actions), and stretch the muscles in the front of the shoulder and chest.

## revolutions

- The athlete and trainer should discuss the athlete's trunk stability or balance prior to participating in any new drills or skills. Generally, the higher the level of SCI, the less balance the athlete has.
- Experiment with different types and positions of strapping to improve trunk stability.
- For a weak grip, consider using gripping aids such as strapped gloves to help perform arm cranking.
- In addition to wheelchair pushing, it is important to include other forms of exercise in a training programme, such as handcycling and swimming, to reduce the likelihood of shoulder injuries from overuse.

TABLE 3.1

# Recommended Types of Exercise for Wheelchair Participants

| Type of exercise | Advantages | Disadvantages | Adaptations and tips |
|---|---|---|---|
| Arm crank ergometer | Found in most gyms. Inexpensive. | Lack of specificity to wheelchair propulsion. | People with limited grip can use flexion mitts of straps. Maintain a good pedal rate (60 to 90 rpm), although speed play sessions could be employed. Do not remain seated for long durations on a hard surface. |
| Circuits | Can be interspersed with high-revolution arm cranking. | Requires good wheelchair access throughout the gym's floor area. Lack of specificity to wheelchair propulsion. | Several exercise stations can be used. Alternate muscle groups when possible. Incorporate either a set number of reps or a set time period in the session. Rest either after each activity or when the circuit is completed. |
| Electrical stimulation leg cycle ergometry, with or without arm cranking | Has been shown to be more effective than arm cranking alone. | High cost of equipment and personnel required. Risk of burns and fractures of the lower extremities and increases in spasticity. | Seek qualified advice. |
| Handcycling | Relatively efficient form of locomotion with gearing system to accommodate difficult terrain. Is directly specific to those who handcycle. | Can be expensive if it's a competition hand bike. Transportation and storage are problematic. | An arm-crank attachment can be used on an everyday wheelchair at minimal cost. Maintain a good pedal rate (60 to 90 rpm), although speed play sessions could be employed. Alternate crank positioning for different modes (asynchronous or synchronous). |
| Lower-body positive pressure suits | Enhances exercise capacity by decreasing venous pooling in legs and increasing circulating blood volumes during exercise. | Unknown. | Seek qualified advice. |

| Type of exercise | Advantages | Disadvantages | Adaptations and tips |
|---|---|---|---|
| Pilates | Improved postural alignment.<br>Increased abdominal activation and low back strength.<br>Increased pelvic stability and muscle balance in larger muscle groups. | Unknown | Quality of movement is emphasized over quantity. Those with inadequate grip can use straps or gloves. Wedges and pads can be used to support the spine to assist in maintaining proper alignment. A supervised session is essential for proper instructions. |
| Rowing | Good all-round conditioning. For wheelchair participants, uses reverse muscle groups that are used during propelling of the chair. | Back strain may result unless advice from club instructors is sought. It should be remembered that rowing is not a direct substitute for the chair fitness required for wheelchair sports. | A stationary seat can be incorporated into the Concept Rower enabling the use by SCI. Ensure good posture. |
| Seated aerobics | Cheap and can be performed at home. | Unknown | Therabands can be incorporated into the routine. Needs to include a warm-up, stretching, and cool-down. Please check that your instructor has an understanding of your balance needs. |
| Swimming and aquatic exercise | Good cross-training. Good substitute for training of injured athletes. Water supports body weight, so good substitute for wheelchair athletes because it reduces the stress on joints. | Casual recreational ambling up and down the pool is worthless. It should be remembered that swimming is not a direct substitute for the chair fitness required for wheelchair sports. | Swim continuous lengths at own pace depending on physical conditioning and technique.<br>A swim-jogger buoyancy vest for running in the water can also be used. |
| Tai chi | Improves balance, posture, flexibility, and breathing patterns. | Unknown | Please check that your instructor has an understanding of your balance needs. |

(continued)

**TABLE 3.1** *(continued)*

| Type of exercise | Advantages | Disadvantages | Adaptations and tips |
|---|---|---|---|
| Wheelchair pushing: road, track, roller, or treadmill | Specificity training. | Not commercially available in all gyms, although freewheeling (pushing outdoors) is an option for all. Need wide treadmill belts to accommodate sport wheelchairs. Mechanical efficiency is lower than arm cranking. Overuse injuries: Increases stress to the shoulder region. Expensive. | Ideally a hybrid day chair or sport wheelchair should be used, and the correct choice of tyres depends on terrain. Treadmill: A safety tracking system is required, or a harness can prevent lateral movements of the chair. Rollers: Ramps for easy access on and off the device. Freewheeling: Push on a track or over ground for 20 to 40 min. at a moderate intensity (talking pace). Settle for a pace you can maintain consistently for whole duration of the push. If you have a circuit, you can monitor any improvements. As the pushing becomes easier, increase the distance. |
| Wheelchair sports | Good cross-training or specific training for a given sport. Variety. | Risk of collisions and injury with contact sports. | When performing new activities, use strapping for stability in the wheelchair. |

## Components of Fitness

Physical fitness is most easily understood by examining its components. All components need attention and should be carefully developed within an exercise programme, although some may have more emphasis than others depending on the sport and training goals. Each component is detailed next.

- **Cardiorespiratory endurance** is the ability to deliver oxygen and nutrients to tissues and to remove waste products over sustained periods of time.
- **Muscular strength** is the ability of a muscle to exert force for a brief period of time.
- **Muscular endurance** is the ability of a muscle or a group of muscles to sustain repeated contractions or to continue applying force against a fixed object.
- **Flexibility** is the ability to move joints and use muscles through their full range of motion.

- **Body composition** is often considered a component of fitness. It refers to the makeup of the body in terms of lean mass (muscle, bone, vital tissue, and organs) and fat mass. (More detail is provided in chapter 5.)

Both coaches and athletes must realize that high-performance wheelchair sport demands fitness levels that cannot be achieved by playing the game alone. Although physical training can be integrated into squad-based training sessions, there is no doubt that sport-specific training is essential so that participants can train at an appropriate level of intensity to provide the necessary overload for improved fitness. Many types of training methods could be included in a training programme, some of which are discussed later in this chapter and others in the chapters focusing on sport-specific training methods. However, the following section summarizes the key elements of a training programme and the principles of training.

## Overload

As with any athlete, training the wheelchair athlete is based on the overload principle. Evidence suggests that for this population, a positive stimulus is around 70 to 80 percent of peak heart rate. However, there is a small margin between an effective stimulus and overtraining. Because repetitive upper-limb movements are associated with shoulder complaints and degeneration, careful planning of recovery sessions within the training schedule is crucial.

Overload can be achieved by exposing the body to one or more of the following:

- Harder training (intensity)
- Longer training (duration)
- More frequent training (frequency)

Usually, training will improve by altering all three components in some way (i.e., increasing intensity, duration, and frequency). As with nondisabled participants, an active lifestyle should involve a minimum of five 30-minute sessions of aerobic activity per week. To achieve further gains in fitness, one must train harder. This produces the overload that is essential for adaptation—unless the body is overloaded, fitness cannot improve. The body must also reach a certain threshold for improvement to come about. Some people will adapt to a load more rapidly than others and may progress faster than others. If the load is too easy and the athlete has been training at the same level for a long time, then little or no adaptation will occur and performance will plateau. If athletes do not train hard enough, their fitness level will drop. This is known as the *detraining load,* and it commonly happens after an injury when an athlete has been unable to train at their normal level. For example, athletes can increase strength by improving their ability to use available muscle groups, maximize overall strength for functional independence (e.g., performing transfers in and out of the car), and make pushing their wheelchair easier by aiming for the following:

- **Intensity:** 50 to 80 percent peak heart rate
- **Frequency:** 3 to 5 days per week
- **Duration:** 20 to 60 minutes per session

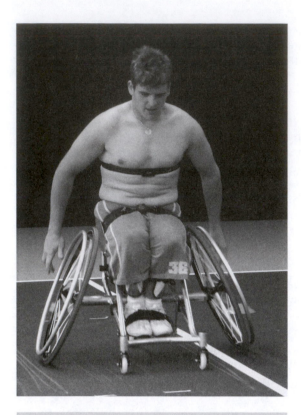

**Heart rate monitors are common in wheelchair sport training.**

Photo taken by John Lenton.

## Monitoring Training Intensity

A number of methods are available for monitoring training intensity. The most common are using heart rate, blood lactate, and ratings of perceived exertion. In the past, the term *top speed* was used to refer to wheelchair athletes training at varying percentages of their top speed for a given training session. However, heart rate monitors are now common in wheelchair sport training.

Although heart rate training principles may be similar across wheelchair sports, recommendations employed by nondisabled athletes may not be directly transferable because some wheelchair athletes have a unique heart rate response. As a result, more subjective measures may be more appropriate. For example, the subjective degree of training stress placed on the athlete during exercise can be used to prescribe aerobic training. The Borg Scale for rating of perceived exertion, referred to as *RPE*, is a numerical scale ranging from 6 (no exertion) to 20 (maximal exertion). In between these points are descriptors for exercise termed *light* (11), *somewhat hard* (13), *hard* (15), and *very hard* (17). For nondisabled athletes, each value of RPE is generally related to increases in exercise intensity such as blood lactate and especially heart rate. Whether a person is trained or untrained, RPE values remain related to physiological variables and thus are excellent for exercise prescription and monitoring the intensity of training. For example, exercising at lactate threshold consistently elicits RPE values of 10 to 11, exercising at a 2-millimole level of blood lactate elicits RPE values of 13 to 14, and exercising at a blood lactate level of 4 millimoles elicits an RPE of 16 or so. These intensities are useful for athletes who do not have access to laboratory testing to determine their specific lactate values (see page 59).

## Peripheral Versus Central Fatigue

Where upper-body exercise is concerned, athletes' arms may fatigue before their cardiorespiratory system does, resulting in what is referred to as *local fatigue*. As a result, it is possible to use RPE to determine either local fatigue (that of the working muscles) or general fatigue (that of the cardiorespiratory system). As fitness improves, a given pushing speed will elicit a lower RPE value as a result of adaptations to training. Although for nondisabled athletes RPE is closely related to heart rate, for wheelchair athletes it is also related to factors such as pushing speed and power output. Therefore, athletes who don't show a large increase in heart rate during exercise can use RPE to indicate training intensity.

# Types of Training

The wheelchair sports covered within this book all involve activities of an intermittent nature—in other words, there are changes in pace throughout the activity. This is also true if we consider the discontinuous nature of pushing a wheelchair in many daily activities. For both scenarios, a high level of anaerobic fitness is required. As with nondisabled training, speed should be trained through methods that are aimed at the development of fast arm speeds and strength. Speed play and hand speed are still important aspects to be included in training. One common training method for wheelchair athletes is downhill pushing, which focuses on hand speed at an easy resistance. This method helps develop power and strength, but it is often overlooked by athletes working on uphill sprints. Skill and tactical work (matches and club training) will always be paramount, but they offer limited opportunity for physical overload. Although specific to the muscles and movements involved, generally the intensity of this type of training is too low to provide sufficient overload.

Interval training is a common method used by many athletes. The greater the intensity of exercise, the less time athletes can exercise before they start to slow down. Interval training involves bouts of exercise separated by lower-intensity exercise or rest. This type of training therefore allows the athlete to undertake a greater amount of quality training than if the intensity were undertaken with no recovery. Interval training at a low intensity may also be a good start for people who are just starting to train and may not be able to exercise for long durations. The intensity and duration of each effort as well as the recovery period can vary greatly depending on what adaptations the athlete is trying to achieve. A coach will be able to develop interval training to suit an athlete's needs.

Traditionally, wheelchair athletes have placed a strong emphasis on high-volume training, the idea being that they could then compete in a range of events from 100 metres to the marathon. However, increased participation numbers and improved coaching mean that track events are becoming more competitive and athletes are becoming more specific in the events they regularly compete in. More recently, speed training programmes have switched to concentrate on low-volume, high-intensity training and long recoveries between repetitions with a major emphasis on quality work. This is of particular importance for developing speed as the competitive season draws near. (See table 3.2 on page 59 for types of training.) Examples of interval training for wheelchair racing are given next.

## revolutions

- Interval training at low exercise intensities may be useful for athletes who are new to training and cannot maintain exercise for a long time without a rest.

- Playing is not enough—individual off-court training is essential to optimize physical fitness in wheelchair sport.

- People with tetraplegia may have problems with muscular endurance. Thus, it may be necessary to reduce the number of repetitions and ensure additional recovery.

- It is advisable to keep a training diary so that you can track your training. For example, when you have a good performance, you can review what your training had involved leading up to that competition.

### Short Intervals

High-quality session: 60 metres, 80 metres, 100 metres, 120 metres, 140 metres, 160 metres (with 5 minutes recovery between repetitions)

Lactate tolerance session: 150 metres (220 m work recovery), 180 metres (190 m work recovery), 210 metres (160 m work recovery), 240 metres (130 m work recovery), 270 metres (100 m work recovery), 300 metres

### Tempo Training

Set 1: 130 metres, 120 metres, 40 metres slow wheel-back recoveries

Set 2: 80 metres, 30 metres, 60 metres slow wheel back recoveries

Set 3: 30 metres, 50 metres, 110 metres slow wheel back recoveries

### Tyre Pulling

Set 1: 150 metres, 90 metres, 60 metres

Set 2: 30 metres (with tyre), 30 metres, 40 metres (with tyre)

Set 3: 40 metres, 30 metres (with tyre), 60 metres

Circuit training is another type of training that can be beneficial. Research has found that 12 weeks of circuit training improves both cardiorespiratory endurance and muscular endurance. For example, $\dot{V}O_2$peak increases by up to 30 percent, which is greater than improvements noted for aerobic capacity using arm-cranking or wheelchair exercise programmes alone. A sample circuit programme might include 12 weeks of resistance training performed three times a week on non-consecutive days. Each session should be 40 to 45 minutes and employ resistance (weightlifting) and endurance activities (arm cranking) interspersed with periods of incomplete recovery (i.e., heart rate not falling below baseline). Exercises might include the military press, horizontal rows, pec dec, preacher curls, wide-grip lat pull-downs, and seated dips. For further information on circuit training, see Jacobs and Nash (2004).

Another type of training to consider is respiratory fitness training. Wheelchair athletes may improve their fitness levels through breathing training. Breathing is significantly impaired in tetraplegia due to paralysis of the intercostal and abdominal muscles and reduced movement of the diaphragm. Respiratory fitness programmes should be beneficial to wheelchair athletes of any competitive level and have been shown to have a positive effect on the quality of life of people with SCI. There are several respiratory training options:

- Muscle training devices
- Glossopharyngeal breathing and hyperinflation therapy, which can be performed with guidance from respiratory therapists
- Yoga and Pilates
- Blow darts
- Singing and shrugging exercises

## Measuring Exercise Intensity and Fitness

Monitoring skill and fitness levels should be a built-in component of any training programme. Results will provide both the coach and athlete with valuable

## TABLE 3.2

## Types of Training

| Aerobic training | |
|---|---|
| Continuous training | Involves performing an exercise or activity without stopping for a given period or a given distance. |
| Varied-pace training | Known as speed play. Exercise is continuous but includes changes of pace at various intervals. |
| Interval training | Improves strength, endurance, pace, and rhythm. Intervals are periods of time or distance over which the exercise is performed; these periods of exercise are separated by relative rest intervals. Four factors need to be considered: distance to be timed, distance covered, number of repetitions, and time between repetitions. |
| **Speed training** | |
| Short intervals | Involves repetitions over various distances with either active or passive rest between repetitions. During high-quality speed training, long passive rests (5 minutes) promote full recovery. During a lactate-tolerance session, recovery is normally over set distances. |
| Tempo training | Repetitions arranged into sets with each set comprising various distances. This training helps avoid overpacing during longer pushes, mixing speed work with overdistance work. Long recoveries between sets promote full recovery. |
| Tyre pulling | Performed over 20, 30, and occasionally 40 m to help develop strength and power for the initial parts of the race. Could be used with tempo training and mixed repetition with and without the tyres in the same set. |
| Overspeed training | Allows the athlete to work at very high intensities at speeds slightly above maximum with less maximum power output. This is achieved by performing pushes downhill on a slight incline and performing sprints off a rolling start. This type of session may also incorporate power starts and stops with an emphasis on hand speed. |

feedback on the training progress and the effectiveness of a particular training programme. Since laboratory tests require the use of specialized and expensive equipment that is not accessible to everyone, efforts have been made towards developing appropriate field tests, or tests that are undertaken in a sport-specific environment. Field testing is therefore a testing method that anyone could take part in and will be discussed later in this chapter.

First, an assessment in the laboratory enables control over the environment for determining an athlete's unique physiology and how it responds to exercise. Endurance and sprint tests in the laboratory help the athlete and coach determine exercise intensities. These can be obtained by either an incremental exercise test to determine heart rate training zones or maximal speed tests and sprint profiling to allow tracking of fitness progressions.

The incremental exercise test is based on aerobic and lactate thresholds, and the intensities where these occur are used to guide training with the use of heart rate monitors or RPE. It involves the athlete exercising for 4-minute periods at gradually increasing speeds. During the last minute of each bout, expired gas samples are collected to determine the amount of oxygen being used by the athlete to perform the exercise. A small blood sample is taken to determine the level of lactate, and heart rate is also recorded during each stage. After completing five to

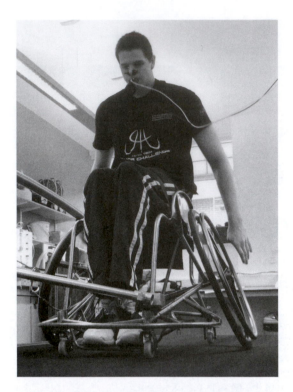

**During an incremental exercise test, expired gas samples are obtained to determine the amount of oxygen an athlete is using.**
Photo taken by John Lenton.

seven stages of the test, the athlete may rest for a short while before performing a further session of increment exercise (8-14 minutes) until exhaustion to determine $\dot{V}O_2$peak.

Each training zone (defined by heart rate and speed) has a specific physiological purpose. The zones are as follows:

- **Easy training.** The heart rate guidelines at this level will seem easy. This type of training allows the body to recover and is termed the *recovery* or *moderate activity.* It is important to build sufficient recovery into the training programme. Sessions at this level can be 30 to 60 minutes at an RPE of 6 to 9.

- **Steady training.** This is the level that most people train at. It has a positive training effect and can be maintained for steady-state pushing. These sessions can last for 30 to 60 minutes at an RPE of 10 to 12.

- **Tempo training.** It is essential for training to take place at this level so that the body becomes accustomed to pushing while lactate is building up and causing muscle fatigue. Take care, however, because too much training at this level can result in overtraining. At first, athletes may find this kind of session difficult. If so, they should combine the session with interval work (described next) until they feel comfortable sustaining a steady pace for 30 minutes, with interval sessions ranging from 5 to 30 minutes at an RPE of 15. When they are used to the training regime, they should aim for one to two sessions of tempo training per week.

- **Interval training.** This type of training is when the intensity is approaching peak heart rate. Sessions should include short, fast pushes with a short recovery. Training at this level will improve both aerobic and anaerobic fitness. To maintain or improve maximum endurance capacity, include speed training, which involves work duration of 3 to 5 minutes at an RPE of 16 to 18 with a recovery of the same duration as the workout.

Figure 3.3 demonstrates how heart rate and blood lactate increase with each exercise stage and how they relate to each training zone.

Maximal exercise intensity can be tested with sprints using a wheelchair roller system or arm-crank ergometer. To avoid arm frequency being the limiting factor of this test, a suitable resistance level must be applied. The tests can either be performed for a set test time (e.g., 30 seconds) or a series of multiple sprints (e.g., 6 to 10 sprints, with 10-second sprints and 30-second recoveries after each sprint).

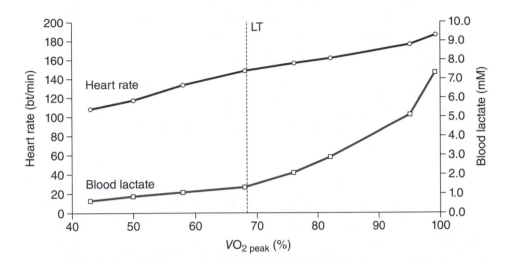

**Figure 3.3** Relationship between blood lactate concentration and heart rate for a highly trained female wheelchair athlete (aged 28) during a graded exercise test on a motorized treadmill. Lactate threshold (LT) occurred at 68 percent of $\dot{V}O_2$peak.

The aim is for the athlete to sprint as fast as possible for the entire test. From this it is possible to determine the athlete's sprint profile.

For anaerobic testing, see the earlier section relating to peak anaerobic power and the Wingate anaerobic test (page 49).

Since laboratory tests require the use of equipment that is not accessible to everyone, efforts have been made to develop field tests to help monitor improvements in fitness. An obvious advantage of field testing is that large groups of athletes can be tested in less time. A few studies have assessed the validity of field tests for wheelchair populations. For aerobic capacity, these have included a 12-minute push test and 20-metre to 25-metre straight multi-stage shuttle tests with varied turns. Note that there are some concerns with these field tests, such as effective pacing strategies and whether or not the severity of the turn means that the test reflects other components of physical fitness rather than just the aerobic capacity of the participant.

Maximum speed and acceleration may be tested like so:

- **Maximum speed.** The object is to cover 20 metres as fast as possible from a flying start, as could be obtained from a 30-metre set-up that involves timing gates positioned at 0, 10, and 30 metres.

- **Acceleration.** The object is to cover the distance as fast as possible from a stationary start; distances of 20 metres and 60 metres are commonly reported.

Aerobic capacity can be measured by two tests:

- **12-minute run or push.** The objective of this test is to go as far as possible in 12 minutes. The distance covered in the 12 minutes is recorded. It is important to note the weather conditions and surface used.

- **Multi-Stage Fitness Test (MSFT).** A 20-metre shuttle test performed in a gym or on a 400-metre athletics track can be used to measure endurance fitness. Athletes have to keep to a set pace determined by an audio track. Each time the track beeps, the athletes have to be at the set cone. After each minute, the time between the beeps decreases, and therefore the pushing speed has to increase in order for the athlete to maintain pace. Athletes have to exercise until they can no longer keep up with the speed of the soundtrack. The point in the test at which each athlete drops out is recorded. If a turn is required during the test, then wheelchair configuration and participants' chair skills can influence the outcome. Sport-specific field drills will be covered in part II.

## revolutions

To measure the effectiveness of training, the following must be controlled as much as possible:

- Tyre pressure is at its usual competitive level and noted.
- Any changes in wheelchair configurations are noted.
- Body mass of the participant is measured (to see if the rolling resistance may have altered).
- Any changes in training are noted.

## Conclusion

This chapter has shown that physiological differences exist between athletes with different levels of SCI and nondisabled athletes. However, although athletes with different levels of injury differ in their maximal exercise responses, the principles of training are the same as for nondisabled athletes. Furthermore, similar training responses can generally be observed. Standard exercise tests can be successfully adapted for wheelchair or arm-crank exercise in order to provide the same information for monitoring and developing training programmes. As athletes progress with training, they should discuss their training needs with a coach to produce a yearly plan (periodization). This will help to maximize performance and prevent overtraining.

## References

Goodman, J.M., Liu, P.P., & Green, H.J. (2005). Left ventricular adaptations following short-term endurance training. *Journal of Applied Physiology, 98*(2), 454-460.

Goosey-Tolfrey, V.L. (2005). Physiological profiles of elite wheelchair basketball players in preparation for the 2000 Paralympic Games. *Adapted Physical Activity Quarterly, 22,* 57-66.

Hopman, M.T. (1994). Circulatory responses during arm exercise in individuals with paraplegia. *International Journal of Sports Medicine, 15*(3), 126-131.

Jacobs, P.L., & Nash, M.S. (2004). Exercise recommendations for individuals with spinal cord injury. *Sports Medicine, 34*(11): 727-751.

For further information on field testing, please refer to the following:

Goosey-Tolfrey, V.L., & Tolfrey, K. (2008). The Multi-Stage Fitness Test as a predictor of endurance fitness in wheelchair athletes. *Journal of Sports Sciences, 26*(5), 511-517.

# chapter 4

# Strength and Conditioning for Wheelchair Sport

Andy Allford and Linda Mitchell-Norfolk

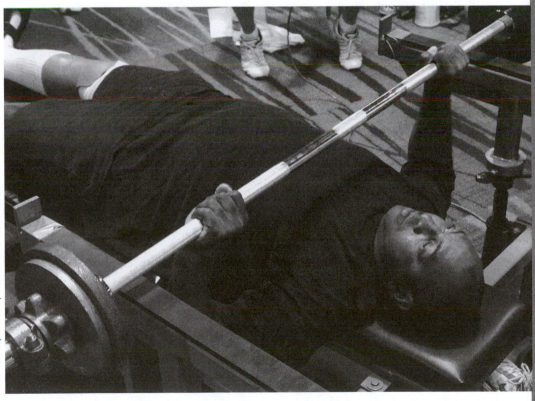

The focus of this chapter is the practical application of conventional strength and conditioning principles to the needs of athletes who use wheelchairs for sport or for daily locomotion. Many of the ideas expressed here are based on the experiences of the authors; there is little research available to guide practice. A foundational knowledge of strength and conditioning theory is assumed, along with a good understanding of how the body functions and how it adapts to physical fitness.

# Unique Strength Training Needs of Wheelchair Athletes

All athletes express the desire to be in optimal condition for competition; however, there are some fundamental differences between athletes with and without disabilities that should be borne in mind when designing a strength and conditioning programme. This may seem an unnecessary statement to make; however, differences are often overlooked by professionals when working with wheelchair athletes, leading to less effective interventions.

Athletes with disabilities should be treated in the same way as their nondisabled counterparts—that is, they want to be managed comprehensively and to achieve the best condition possible. However, using a wheelchair for ambulation means that the upper body is used for locomotion as opposed to the lower body. In a nondisabled athlete, the upper body is rarely used in strength activities in daily life, whereas the wheelchair user is dependent on upper-limb function for transfers to and from the wheelchair, in and out of bed, and in and out of the car, as well as every manoeuvre of the wheelchair. The consequences for the ability of the upper limbs to bear weight need to be remembered, especially regarding joint preservation for later life. The wheelchair athlete will have more extensively developed musculature in the upper limbs because of the extra daily loads and therefore is likely to be capable of better endurance using these extremities compared with a nondisabled athlete.

Posture and level of disability may also have an impact, and this can often be seen as a muscle imbalance, especially between the anterior and posterior muscle groups of the shoulders. Additionally, wheelchair users are not a homogenous group; individuals have varied underlying pathologies with vastly differing impacts on function. They also may vary greatly in their abilities to perform exercises and functional activities even when disabilities are similar.

Methods of propulsion and the muscles used therein must be considered in assessing the strength training needs of a wheelchair athlete. Methods and muscles vary according to level of disability and ability to grip the wheel rims to generate power but also according to wheelchair set-up and direction of propulsion.

In an everyday wheelchair (camber of 0-4 degrees), where the athlete is seated in an upright position and propelling at walking speed, an economic push action would use the anterior shoulder flexors and biceps to start the chair rolling, and then elbow extension and triceps would complete the push forward. Some wrist flexion would initiate the roll and wrist extension might complete it. A more aggressive, forceful push would recruit more muscle activity. If the level of disability meant that the forearm musculature was weakened, there would be increased activity in the anterior shoulder muscles to start the roll, and postural changes would be more evident.

In a sport wheelchair (camber approximately 16-20 degrees) where a more streamlined or extreme sitting position is used, muscle activity and push action may be markedly different. It is worth observing the push action of athletes in their everyday chair and in their sport chair to learn more about their individual technique and ability to produce power. Not all athletes have good technique or are making the most of their ability. Strength and conditioning work can obviously have an impact in this area and develop performance so long as the rudiments of muscle balance and good posture are remembered.

Further issues to consider in designing strength training programmes for wheelchair athletes include the following:

■ **Exercise selection.** Because the anterior muscles of the shoulder may be well developed, there may be less need to work them. Often these muscles are overworked and tight, and they benefit from stretching, relaxation, and release techniques rather than further development. Posterior shoulder muscles are often relatively underdeveloped and therefore require attention to improve muscle balance.

The athlete's functional ability also influences exercise selection, especially in relation to balancing ability. An athlete may have limited trunk control, which will have an impact on the ability to use both arms at once or to perform exercises above the head or away from the body. Additionally, reduced hand function may exclude safe use of some exercise equipment.

■ **Volume of programme.** Conventional gym programmes for the nondisabled tend to be standardized in length, and frequently programmes for wheelchair users follow similar formats. Content, however, needs to be varied according to the athlete's needs. Don't be afraid to reduce exercise volume if requirements are met. Quality and specificity of an exercise are most important. Simply adding in exercises to fit a so-called normal exercise time frame could well be counterproductive.

■ **Injury prevention.** A major focus of any programme should be injury prevention, especially in relation to the muscle imbalance that can occur from using wheelchairs or mobility aids (e.g., elbow crutches). Shoulder impingement pathologies are more likely in wheelchair athletes.

■ **Fatigue.** Some disabilities affect the athlete's ability to sustain exercise, resulting in early fatigue. High-level SCI can affect respiratory function and heart rate, leading to early fatigue and reduced exercise capacity.

■ **Impact of physical disability on functional ability.** The type of disability greatly influences the functional ability of athletes; however, a like diagnosis does not mean that every athlete is affected in the same way. Functional ability varies widely within the same pathology even when the condition is similar, so practitioners should never assume that they know what the athlete can do. Instead, they should always ask what the athlete can achieve. Table 4.1 shows how sensation and motor function might be affected in athletes according to SCI level.

## Needs Analysis

A good strength and conditioning programme needs to consider four areas: the athlete's health, keeping the athlete free from injury, and fitness work, which in turn forms the base for performance-enhancement work. The needs analysis

## TABLE 4.1

## Impact of spinal cord injury on motor and sensory function

| Level of lesion | Motor function | Sensation |
|---|---|---|
| L4-S2 paraplegia with complete lesion * | Gluts and hamstrings are affected but quadriceps unaffected | Absent or altered below knee and in groin area |
| T11-L3 paraplegia complete * | Ilio-psoas, quadratus lumborum, lower parts of erector spinae, and quadriceps are affected in addition to L4-S2 effects | Absent or altered in lower-limb and pelvic region |
| T6-T10 paraplegia complete * | Low intercostals and erector spinae are affected in addition to T11-L3 effects | Additional changes across trunk |
| T2-T5 paraplegia complete (effect is variable and individual if incomplete) | Abdominal muscles affected in addition to T6-T10 effects | Absent or altered up to chest level |
| C7-T1 tetraplegia complete * | Upper-limb function (especially grip) and triceps are affected in addition to T2-T5 effects | Additional changes in hands, especially middle, ring, and little fingers |
| C4-C6 tetraplegia * | Biceps, deltoid, rhomboids, and rotator cuff are affected in addition to C7-T1 effects | Absence or alteration in hand, wrist, and forearm in addition to previous changes |

*If incomplete lesion, the effect is variable and individualised.

of the athlete and sport should indicate how much emphasis to place each area within the strength and conditioning priority continuum (see figure 4.1). Priority is given to the general health of athletes, without which they are unable to train or perform, and the same is true of trying to keep them free from injury. The next two areas, basic fitness work and performance enhancement, need to be considered carefully in terms of each athlete's training status and the demands of the sport. Care should be taken not to base a programme too quickly on performance enhancement without addressing the health and injury status of an athlete. Priorities for each area might be described as follows:

- **Health:** Select volume and intensity in relation to additional cumulative demands on the athlete (mental and physical).
- **Injury prevention:** Aim for muscle balance and avoidance of tissue breakdown.
- **Base fitness:** Develop good foundation fitness before moving onto more complex work.

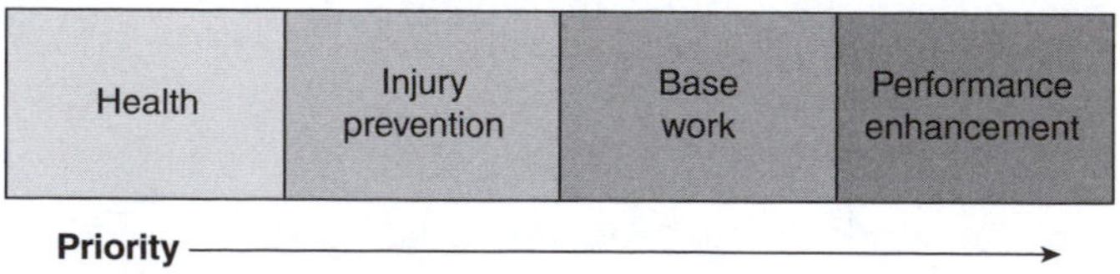

| Health | Injury prevention | Base work | Performance enhancement |

Priority ——————————————————→

**Figure 4.1** Strength and conditioning priority continuum.

● **Performance enhancement:** Develop strength and power that can translate directly into sport performance.

As an athlete develops, the emphasis within the strength and conditioning priority continuum will alter. The emphasis in each area is determined by an initial evaluation, which should be reviewed after each training cycle. It is important to work on laying a solid fitness foundation so that when the time comes to move on to the more demanding fitness components, such as power development, anaerobic work, and speed development, there is a good platform on which to build.

A needs analysis must be completed to look at the physical demands of the sport, the athlete's injury history, and how daily living affects the athlete's capacity to train. As part of this process, it is advisable to use fitness testing to get baseline data on the athlete's current physical condition in order to enable evaluation of the strength and conditioning programme. It is imperative to address areas of importance in developing the programme since this will have a huge effect on the type of training stimulus that is chosen.

### Questions to Ask the Athlete
● Do you need a great deal of strength within your sport?
● Do you need a great deal of speed? If so, what type? Initial acceleration? Maximum speed? Deceleration?
● Does your sport require agility? If so, for what types of movement?
● How do people beat you? (It is useful to ask this question, although not always nice!)

Once some of these questions have been answered, it's possible to periodize the work plan to accommodate the work that needs to be done and select the training stimulus that is needed for those specific areas.

The latter part of this chapter gives guidance on training for specific fitness components. As stated earlier, it is important to constantly evaluate training to ensure that adequate gains are being made.

## Guidelines for Safe and Effective Training

It is necessary to ensure safety specific to the concerns of wheelchair users. In addition, good posture and a warm-up and cool-down are necessary.

### Safety

Safety must be a primary concern for those participating in sport and those instructing exercise. The following should be addressed before beginning an exercise programme:

■ Any medical limitations to performance of exercise should be considered, such as respiratory or cardiac restrictions, epilepsy, limited range of motion around a joint, or hypermobility. These will not necessarily exclude an athlete from undertaking an exercise, but they may require caution, adaptation, or additional advice.

■ Exercises do not have to be undertaken from the wheelchair; in fact, part of the programme should take place outside the chair. A risk assessment (as recommended by current health and safety rules for the facility and personnel where the training is taking place) may need to be undertaken to evaluate the manual handling requirements for the athlete transferring to or from the wheelchair. Many athletes will be independent in transferring, whereas others may require some help. Instructors should ask athletes what help they need and for their opinion on the best way to assist or execute a transfer.

■ Many exercises may be undertaken in either the sport-specific wheelchair or the everyday wheelchair. There are advantages and disadvantages to using either depending on the exercise prescribed and the sport for which the wheelchair is set up. For example, a basketball wheelchair is designed for speed and mobility in all directions, whereas a shooting wheelchair is designed to be stable and solid. A shooting wheelchair therefore would not be ideal for speed work.

Many sport wheelchairs do not have brakes and therefore need external stabilization to stop movement during a static exercise. This can be accomplished by wedging an object (such as a sandbag) at the front and back of the rear wheels. However, the extra camber on a sport wheelchair and the additional anti-tip wheel used in some sports may help provide extra stability over an everyday chair, which is set up to assist everyday ambulation.

■ Try to gain an understanding of how the components of the wheelchair work (e.g., backrest angle and upholstery tightness, seat cushion firmness, and shoulder position over the rear-wheel axle) and how they contribute to balance, posture, and consequently power production. An athlete sitting in his wheelchair is able to correct posture (or slump) and alter position, although this can be challenging to some. Resting posture and sometimes active posture are influenced by wheelchair set-up, and therefore modifications to the set-up can affect the ability to perform.

## Posture

Before starting any exercise, poor posture needs to be corrected by encouraging a good starting posture and setting the shoulders, which consists of depressing and

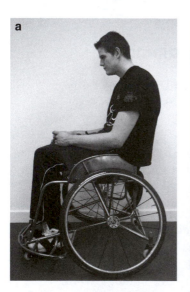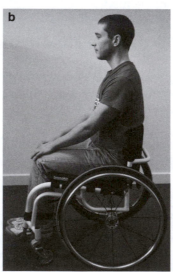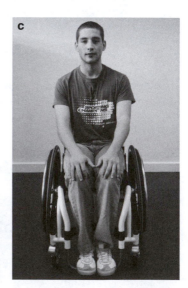

**Poor posture (a) and good posture (b and c).**
Photos courtesy of John Lenton.

retracting the shoulders while gently tucking the chin in. This postural control should be maintained throughout all exercise if possible. If the set position is lost, the aim should be to restore it as soon as possible.

## Warm-Up

An effective warm-up improves performance and reduces risk of injury. The warm-up should gradually prepare the body, physically and mentally, for the stress that will be placed on it while undertaking the more strenuous activities that are scheduled to follow. A warm-up consists of three components:

- An activity to increase heart rate and breathing rate, as well as increasing core temperature of the body by approximately 1 degree Celsius
- Stretching exercises for the limbs and trunk, either dynamic or passive
- Sport-specific skills rehearsal

These principles apply to people who use wheelchairs for sport, although creativity may be required to achieve a comprehensive warm-up for each athlete.

## Cool-Down

A cool-down should be performed following any exercise session to help the body gradually slow down from an active working state to a resting state. A cool-down can be part of an active recovery plan, assisting readiness for the next bout of exercise.

A cool-down usually consists of an activity, such as a gentle, steady push in the wheelchair, that gradually decreases the work of large muscle groups and therefore gradually reduces the demand on the heart. Stretching exercises for the upper limbs and trunk are also included.

Passive techniques, such as massage, can be used to assist recovery. They may be beneficial for athletes who fatigue easily or those who have difficulty exercising sufficiently to remove metabolic by-products from the preceding intense activity.

# Guidelines for Exercise Prescription

Building on the four areas of the strength and conditioning priority continuum the following section will expand on some of the key considerations for the exercise prescription for wheelchair athletes. It is not a definitive guide but should help you in developing individual programs based on your athletes needs.

## Health

In addition to ensuring the right balance of exercise volume and intensity as stated in chapter 1, developing cardiorespiratory fitness is integral to the wheelchair athlete's health. It is beyond the scope of this chapter to give specific advice on developing this aspect of fitness; however, chapter 3 provides ideas for types of exercises and guidelines that may be used.

## Injury Prevention

A common cause of neck, back, and shoulder pain is postural stress, which can arise from poor sitting, standing, or lying positions. A wheelchair athlete is at risk of developing postural stress from sitting for long amounts of time, using the upper limbs for propulsion of the wheelchair, or using walking aids for everyday ambulation. Poor postural habits can lead to changes in the natural curves of the spine and the position of the shoulder joints. Holding or resting in any position for a prolonged time will cause overload and undue strain on supporting joints, ligaments, and muscles, resulting in overstretching and eventual pain and injury. An athlete is at particular postural injury risk following exercise because it is easiest to relax in a poor position when fatigued, stressing and overstretching tired tissues and damaging otherwise healthy structures.

Small, regular adjustments to posture can counteract a slouched position. These adjustments increase tone in the postural muscles by encouraging them to be active, thus reducing the load on the underlying static ligaments that become the main structural support when muscle tone decreases. Good upper-body posture along with good range of motion in the shoulder joint are essential to long-term shoulder health and help to minimize the risk of shoulder impingement.

## revolutions

The musculature that is already heavily used during daily living should not be continually taxed in training, too. The balance of training for performance gains and training for injury prevention is so important with wheelchair athletes that it should always be in the thoughts of the practitioner.

Wheelchair users should also spend some time each day out of their wheelchairs in either a standing or lying position in order to prevent tightness in the hips. Lying prone for 10 minutes daily or standing in a standing frame each day can help stretch out the hip flexors, which can become tight due to prolonged sitting. Regular attention to flexibility and posture may also help to control the adverse effects of spasticity.

Regularly setting the shoulders as a postural check throughout the day and in preparation for strength and conditioning exercises can be a valuable tool in the prevention of postural and shoulder impingements. In addition, wheelchair users need to be vigilant about achieving a good sitting posture. They are strongly advised to undertake regular exercises to improve the strength of the shoulder extensors, depressors, and retractors, as well as flexibility and relaxation exercises to reduce tightness of the shoulder flexors, protractors, and elevators. This potentially creates a conflict of interest since a lot of the musculature that needs to be developed for performance enhancement is the very musculature that becomes overdeveloped in relation to other muscles, setting up the risk of an imbalance. Therefore as a rule of thumb, for every one exercise used to improve the flexor or anterior aspect of the shoulder (e.g., bench press to develop pectorals), add two exercises for the extensor or posterior shoulder muscles to reduce the imbalance (e.g., back pull and lat pulldown to develop the latissimus dorsi and rhomboids).

### Base Work

Completing a phase of base or foundation strength training is important in preparing the body for the performance-enhancement phases of developing speed, power, and maximum strength. The type of strength work completed at this time would involve hypertrophy.

Contrary to popular belief, hypertrophy (training to increase the size of the muscle) occurs at a training stimulus of 8 to 12 reps and not at lower repetitions (4-8 reps). The main difference occurs at a neurological level. At the higher repetition range, the actual muscles start to fatigue, which leads to muscle damage. During rest, the muscles repair themselves, and theory suggests that as they repair, they get stronger and bigger. Training at lower repetitions stimulates the nervous system to recruit as many muscle fibres as possible in order to lift maximally. This process takes time, which is why maximal lifts are often slower. Hypertrophy training is a useful way to train in early stages to get the body used to strength training and to prepare for more advanced forms of training. This is not to say that hypertrophy training will turn athletes into the next Arnold Schwarzenegger; putting on muscle mass is extremely difficult (especially for females), and lifestyle changes would also have to be made. It is also important to note that those with a great muscle mass are not necessarily the most powerful.

Normally, this type of weight training involves 8 to 12 reps to muscle fatigue. It can be done by alternating body parts or using various combinations of sets and reps to work muscles to fatigue

## Performance Enhancement

Training for strength and power can be quite complex. Most sports use several strength and power characteristics, so a needs analysis can help in deciding what characteristics need the most attention. The following is an example from wheelchair basketball.

There are times in a basketball game when strength is the predominant characteristic (e.g., holding an opponent off to get a dominant position). There are also times when a player needs to accelerate quickly from a static start position. The athlete then needs a combination of both strength to overcome the dead weight from a static position and speed to accelerate quickly. The speed component will be used predominantly once maximum speed is achieved. If the characteristics needed to slow down and change direction quickly are added, it can get quite complicated. Table 4.2 shows some benefits associated with repetition.

**Maximum Strength**   Training for maximum strength uses low repetitions and heavy weight. Here the athlete is trying to exert as much force as possible with no time limit. A good example of this is the bench press in disability powerlifting, where the predominant characteristic is maximal strength as a high force (the bar with weight on it) is overcome over a fairly long time frame. This is still thought

### TABLE 4.2

### Benefits Associated With Repetitions

|  | Rep range | Sets | Typical number of exercises |
|---|---|---|---|
| Maximum strength | 1-5 | 4-6 | 3-5 |
| Strength speed | 1-5 | 3-5 | 3-5 |
| Speed strength | 4-8 | 3-5 | 6-10 |
| Hypertrophy | 8-14 | 4-6 | 8-12* |
| Strength endurance | >15 | 1-4 | 10-15 |

*Indicates exercises can be done using a split programme.

to be a useful way to train for power because although the movement velocity is low, the athlete is still trying to recruit the most powerful muscle fibres. As long as the lift is performed with explosive intent, then the athlete is still trying to accelerate the mass as quickly as possible.

**Power**   Power is the ability to exert force at great speeds (or in more mathematical terms, force × velocity). Powerlifting in itself is not a powerful movement because of the slow speeds involved, although many lifters do have the characteristics of powerful athletes.

In simple terms, training for power can be subdivided into two sections—training for strength speed and training for speed strength. As stated, power is the combination of force times velocity, and these two areas change the balance of this relationship.

- *Strength speed* refers to overcoming a higher force with quick velocity. In sporting terms, this can be characterized by an acceleration start where the athlete is trying to overcome a fairly high force (e.g., the body and the wheelchair) as fast as possible. A good example in wheelchair sport is the initial acceleration from a static start position.

Lifts that mimic sport-specific movements are useful in this training so that there is transfer to the sport. An example is the bench press, which uses similar musculature to that of wheelchair pushing (chest and triceps). However, if an athlete does not have proficient pushing technique, then the transfer of strength from any exercise into a functional movement pattern will be limited. A good variation for this type of training therefore could be using heavy weights in similar movement patterns to that of wheelchair pushing, followed by free pushing to try to get that direct transfer.

- *Speed strength* occurs when velocity or speed is the predominant factor over force or strength. An example in wheelchair sport would be the contact time on

## revolutions

### Specificity

Specificity is an important concept in strength training programmes. There are two schools of thought on specificity training (also known as *functional training*). According to one school of thought, only exercises that mimic the movements needed within the sport are useful in training. The second school of thought suggests that gains in performance are still possible by training the musculature in a less specific way. Either way, specificity refers to the transfer of exercises from the gym to the specifics of a sport.

There is probably some benefit in both schools of thought; simply replicating exact sporting movements may interfere with the skill of those movements, and performing exercises that make muscles stronger will not transfer to the sport. Our personal view is that exercises can be nonspecific as long as there is a concerted effort to transfer those extra strength gains into a specific movement. A good example would be a bench press for improving strength in wheelchair pushing. Although the musculature used is similar, it is not the exact movement, so it would be important to add contrast work that transfers extra strength gains into the exact movement. Also, if athletes are not skilled in the art of wheelchair propulsion, it does not matter how strong they are because technique will always be the limiting factor. It is therefore important to understand which muscles are working in a specific movement and how they work.

the wheel in sprint wheelchair racing, where the speed of movement is more important than expressing high forces.

Using medicine balls is a good example of speed strength exercise. Medicine balls can also be useful for replicating sporting movements (e.g., a chest pass in basketball or rotational movements used in tennis).

**Strength Endurance**   Strength endurance is characterized by the body's need to replicate high forces repeatedly over long periods of time. Most sports have an element of strength endurance, although this type of training is typically done in the playing environment.

Strength endurance is predominantly trained by completing high repetitions (15 or more) with fairly light loads. In sports such as swimming, where the resistance of water must be overcome, this type of training can be useful in improving strength endurance at certain stages of a stroke.

## Free Weights Versus Fixed Resistance Machines

Although general opinion rates free weights above machines because of the greater recruitment of muscle fibres and greater skill involved with free weights, prescribing them for wheelchair athletes is not that simple. If trunk control is poor, then machines may be the preferred option because they remove the need to stabilize through the midsection, but it also depends on whether the machines have been designed with wheelchairs users in mind, especially if the user cannot transfer. The fact that most weight machines are bilateral also helps with balance. If the athlete has good functional ability, then free weights are the preferred choice.

## Sample Training Programmes

Tables 4.3, 4.4, and 4.5 show examples of programmes that can be used for wheelchair athletes of varying experience and skill. As stated earlier, wheelchair athletes are not a homogenous group, and therefore the programmes should be seen as a rough guide.

There is no Holy Grail of exercises for a wheelchair athlete's training programme. Many programmes that work for individual athletes have been developed

TABLE 4.3

### Training Programme for Novice Athletes or Those With Limited Trunk Control

| Exercise | Sets | Reps | Rest |
|---|---|---|---|
| Fixed resistance chest press | 3 | 12 | 60 sec |
| Lat pulldown (if good trunk control) | 3 | 12 | 60 sec |
| Seated row | 3 | 12 | 60 sec |
| Lat raise | 3 | 12 | 60 sec |
| Cable triceps extension | 3 | 12 | 60 sec |
| Cable biceps curl | 3 | 12 | 60 sec |
| Reverse fly | 3 | 12 | 60 sec |

TABLE 4.4

## Training Programme for Intermediate Athletes

| Exercise | Sets | Reps | Rest |
|---|---|---|---|
| Alternate dumbbell chest press | 3 | 8-10 | 2 min |
| Lat pulldown (if good trunk control) | 3 | 10 | 60 sec |
| Alternate dumbbell bench pull | 4 | 8 | 60 sec |
| Lat raise | 3 | 10 | 60 sec |
| Alternate dumbbell French curl | 3 | 10 | 60 sec |
| Hammer curl | 3 | 10 | 60 sec |
| Rear raise | 3 | 12 | 60 sec |

TABLE 4.5

## Training Programme for Advanced Athletes

| Exercise | Sets | Reps | Rest |
|---|---|---|---|
| Free-weight bench press | 5 | 5 | 3 min |
| Lat pulldown | 4 | 10, 8, 6, 4 | 2 min |
| Bench pull | 4 | 8 | 2 min |
| Shoulder press | 4 | 6 | 2 min |
| French curl | 3 | 10 | 60 sec |
| Biceps curl | 3 | 10 | 60 sec |
| Medicine ball abdominal throws (if good trunk control) | 3 | 8 | 2 min |
| Medicine ball rotations (if good trunk control) | 3 | 8 | 2 min |

over several years, and through trial and error they have ended up with something that what works best for them. The human body is an amazing machine, and we all adapt differently. In wheelchair sport, this is more evident than ever.

# Conclusion

Throughout this chapter we have tried to get across the uniqueness of training for wheelchair athletes. Athletes have different functional abilities, and because they use the upper body for ambulation, it is imperative to consider exercise selection, volume, and intensity when designing a strength and conditioning programme. With this in mind, the needs analysis for the athlete is extremely important. There is a fine balance between keeping the athlete healthy and training to improve performance in the sport. That is the challenge of working with athletes with disabilities.

# References

Allford, A., & Mitchell, L. (2005). *Balls and bands: Exercises to assist functional training for wheelchair athletes.* London, British Paralympic Association.

# chapter 5

# Nutrition and Body Composition

Thomas Reilly and Jeanette Crosland

The science of sports nutrition is well established, and it is now accepted that food and hydration can have a major impact on sport performance. Research has established guidelines for specific nutrient intakes for sport; however, this research is still lacking in the field of wheelchair sport. The specific requirements of wheelchair athletes are currently being investigated, and it is hoped that in the future, more evidence-based guidelines will be available.

The principles of nutrition for sport do apply to wheelchair athletes, and the information produced with nondisabled athletes in mind should form the basis of sound nutrition for wheelchair athletes. It is outside the scope of this book to present detailed information about nutrition for sport, but many books are available, some of which are listed at the end of this chapter. There are also a number of websites, some offering much more reliable, science-based information than others. Again, examples of good sites are given at the end of the chapter.

Key points for the wheelchair athlete include ensuring optimal nutritional strategies for health, training, and competition while accounting for any specific requirements or adaptations due to medical issues or the use of a wheelchair for sport.

## Eating to Train

The daily diet of an athlete is vital in providing the best support for health and training. To achieve this goal, the athlete needs a well-balanced, varied diet providing adequate fuel and hydration to support training and recovery. The diet needs to help the body maintain the immune system, and all this needs to be done in a way that maintains the best possible body weight and physique for the sport.

Several aspects of diet can be considered keys to success. These aspects include intakes of energy, carbohydrate, and protein, as well as fluids, minerals, and vitamins.

### Carbohydrate

There has been discussion about the role of individual nutrients as a source of energy for wheelchair sport, but the principles of energy provision are no different in wheelchair sport than in nondisabled sport. Carbohydrate is the major source of fuel for working muscle; during sport it is converted to glycogen and then broken down further to provide energy in the form of glucose. When considering the amount of carbohydrate needed to fuel participation in wheelchair sport, the athlete needs to consider the following:

- The amount of working muscle that will use energy during sport
- The intensity and volume of training
- Body weight and whether there is a need to reduce excess body fat

Wheelchair athletes take part in a variety of sports, and the energy required varies widely. However, when considering nutritional advice for sport, it is likely that the wheelchair athlete will need to reduce the suggested carbohydrate requirements due to a lower expenditure of energy and carbohydrate. Most wheelchair athletes should presume that requirements will be below the figures normally suggested for sport (see table 5.1). Carbohydrate intakes as low as half the expected intake for

TABLE 5.1

## Suggested Carbohydrate Requirements for Athletes Without Disabilities

| Training type | Carbohydrate g/kg body weight each day |
|---|---|
| Regular activity | 4-5 |
| Moderate duration, low intensity | 5-7 |
| Moderate to heavy endurance training | 7-12 |
| Extreme exercise programmes | 10-12 |

*Immediately after exercise (for the first 4 hours), it is often suggested that 1.0 to 1.2 grams of carbohydrate per kilogram body weight are needed per hour.

nondisabled athletes have been recorded in wheelchair athletes and have proved sufficient to fuel training. To find precise figures, the advice of a registered sports dietitian or registered sports nutritionist may be helpful.

Suggested carbohydrate requirements after training are often quoted as 1.0 to 1.2 grams of carbohydrate per kilogram of body weight as often as every hour following training. After the first hour, it is likely that the carbohydrate will become part of a meal. According to the suggested requirements, snacks should contain 60 to 100 grams of carbohydrate. Although this amount may be realistic if an actual meal is eaten immediately after training, snacks of this size are unlikely to be needed by most wheelchair athletes. An amount of 100 grams represents more than six slices of bread or up to five cereal bars. Many wheelchair athletes find that a snack of 20 or 30 grams may well be adequate, though sport participants undertaking heavy or long training sessions may need more. Table 5.2 outlines the carbohydrate content of some common foods to put this recommendation in context.

TABLE 5.2

## Carbohydrate Content of Common Foods

| Food | Portion size | Carbohydrate (g) per portion |
|---|---|---|
| Apple | 1 medium | 10-15 |
| Banana, peeled | 100 g (medium) | 25 |
| Raisins | 100 g | 70 |
| Jacket potato | 180 g (medium) | 60 |
| Yogurt, low fat | 150 g (one pot) | 10-15 |
| Bagel | 70 g (one) | 40 |
| Fruit scone | 50 g (one medium) | 25 |
| Cereal bar | 20-30 g (one bar) | 20-30 |
| Isotonic sports drink | 500 ml | 30 |
| Orange juice | 200 ml | 20 |

*Figures are rounded to nearest 5 grams and are designed to give a simple comparison only.

## Protein

Protein intake is important particularly to support muscle development and repair. Though extra protein intake is required to help carry out these functions, the normal diet of an athlete often contains more than the suggested intake (see table 5.3). Again, wheelchair athletes with reduced working muscle mass may need to consider a slightly lower protein requirement, and athletes with kidney impairment should consult their doctor and dietitian with regard to protein intake. There is gathering evidence that the timing of protein intake may be important, particularly for those undertaking intense resistance-based training, when the inclusion of protein in the posttraining snack might be useful. People who aim to reduce or maintain body weight may be more at risk of having a protein intake lower than needed.

## Fluid Intake

Appropriate fluid intake is necessary to support training, and this is covered in detail in chapter 6. In wheelchair sport, fluid strategies must be personalized. Fluid requirements will vary, and if the athlete uses a catheter and bag or intermittent catheterization, the normal routine may be affected by the volume of fluid consumed at one time and the frequency of drinking. People who are prone to autonomic dysreflexia should be particularly aware of the need to practise their drinking routine and have strategies for different conditions.

## Vitamins and Minerals

The final group of nutrients highlighted as vital for sport includes vitamins and minerals. Here the requirements for wheelchair athletes are *believed to be* the same as for nondisabled athletes. Athletes should ensure that their diet contains sufficient variety to ensure an adequate intake of all minerals and vitamins.

Here are key points to remember about a training diet:

- The principles of nutrition for sport should be applied to wheelchair sport, but individual requirements must be considered.
- Carbohydrate is important as a fuel for working muscle and should be included in meals (e.g., bread, rice, pasta, potatoes, fruit) and posttraining snacks (e.g., fruit, bread, cereal bars, yogurt, low-fat milkshakes).
- The energy requirements for wheelchair athletes may be lower than those for nondisabled athletes due to the lower mass of working muscle.

TABLE 5.3

## Suggested Protein Requirements for Athletes Without Disabilities

| Training type | Protein g/kg body weight each day |
|---|---|
| Sedentary to low levels of activity | 0.75 |
| More than 1 hour per day | 1.0-1.2 |
| Seriously training endurance athletes | 1.2-1.6 |
| Seriously training strength or speed athletes | 1.2-1.7 |

- The required quantity of carbohydrate may be lower than would be expected for nondisabled sports; however, the physically active wheelchair sports obviously require much higher energy intakes than the skill-based sports. Portion sizes must be tailored to individual requirements.

- Good hydration is vital to sport, and wheelchair athletes are likely to have very individual needs in terms of intakes and strategies for provision.

## Eating to Win

The athlete's training diet is a cornerstone to good health and performance, but eating to win is also important. Athletes need to prepare for competition by ensuring that they arrive with a store of energy appropriate to their sport, that they are well hydrated, and that they have achieved any body-weight targets (especially for weight-category sports). For longer competitions, it will be necessary to top up energy stores and replace fluid losses during performance. For all athletes, refuelling and recovering after events is vital, particularly when there are multiple events with short recovery time.

Athletes should also prepare for the practicalities of competition by carrying appropriate foods and drinks for the day or days of competition. For some wheelchair users, there may be issues of access to food and drink—for example, tennis players who strap their rackets to their hands—and athletes should make sure that support is available to allow them to have food and drinks when needed. Simple preparation such as removing wrappers and storing food in plastic boxes can increase accessibility, and drinking bottles with good drinking spouts and hand grips and possibly camel back–style drinking bags may all improve ease of access.

During longer competitions, sports drinks (containing carbohydrate and salt) may be needed to provide some energy and aid hydration. Those who perform in sports with lower energy demands may use drinks with lower energy content, but where sweat loss is an issue, a drink containing salt is advantageous.

Athletes must ensure that they eat at appropriate times for performance just as they would for training. This can be harder to achieve given timetables for competition, food provision, transport, and so on. The time needed for the transport to venues may be longer when wheelchairs have to be transported, which can affect eating plans. A suitable gap is needed after a meal and before training; for many this is around 2 hours or more, but if the gap reaches 3 hours or more, a small snack may be needed to top up. Good planning and packing strategies should help ensure that athletes can eat an appropriate amount of food at appropriate times for the competition, refuelling using foods available combined with snacks

## revolutions

- Consider carefully the demands of the sport.
- Training and competition may require different intakes.
- Plan in advance for possible issues in terms of accessing food and drink.
- Pack any snacks that may be needed and keep snacks to a realistic level—sufficient but not excessive.

carried by the athlete. Table 5.2 (page 77) indicates the carbohydrate content of some common foods.

In terms of nutrition for competition, planning, preparation, and packing are the keys to success.

## Body Composition

Maintaining a balanced body mass requires that energy intake and energy expenditure are equal. In wheelchair athletes, excess mass stored as body fat results in an added load for antigravity muscles and hence constitutes unwanted extra weight. This excess weight may result in increased rolling resistance of the wheelchair–user configuration, and for some wheelchair athletes, it may predispose them to pressure sores and other skin and soft tissue damage. Therefore, like any athlete, wheelchair athletes need to avoid excess body fat in order to maximize performance.

When considering body composition in wheelchair athletes versus nondisabled athletes, there is likely to be a difference in the distribution of muscle mass and fat mass due to atrophy and inactivity in the lower-limb muscles. Power output requirements for activity are met by upper-body muscles as these tissues develop with training and the sport concerned. Nutrition and exercise interact to affect body composition, and monitoring changes in body composition will provide information to help to tailor diet and training to assist in maintaining ideal body mass in terms of muscle and fat. But what is meant by body composition analysis, and what means are currently available for wheelchair athletes?

## Body Compartments

When talking about body composition in sport, we are generally interested in the muscle and fat content of the body. The only true way to divide the body into its constituent compartments (i.e., muscle, adipose tissue, water) is through dissection—a process that cannot be undertaken for obvious reasons. We therefore have to rely on methods that make assumptions about the individual body being considered and use formulas to calculate the expected composition of that body. A number of methods have been tested on nondisabled athletes, and some of these may give more accurate results than others. There is a much smaller knowledge base in this field when it comes to wheelchair athletes, and yet there are more confounding issues to consider.

There is also a question about how many compartments the body may be divided into. In many instances, a two-compartmental model is sufficient, the body being deemed to consist of a fat mass and a fat-free mass. Measuring one of these unknowns means that the other can then be calculated. In this model, the total amount of body fat is shown as a single value, usually expressed as a percent of body mass, irrespective of function or location. An example is the calculation of the fat-free and the fat mass values from densitometry (see the following section), assuming the density of these components is constant. The alternative is a multi-component model that allows for bone mineral mass and fat-free, bone mineral–free mass as well as fat mass. Adding measurements of total body water and bone mineral density to whole-body densitometry accommodates variations in mineral and hydration status.

Body fatness may be described as adiposity since lipid (fat) stores are held mainly within adipose tissue. The deposition of adipose tissue varies with body site, and this variation is known as *fat patterning*. Visceral adipose tissue (normally seen as an extending waistline) is a stronger indicator of risk to health than are skinfold thicknesses.

Essential lipids are contained in cell membranes and in nervous tissue. Although overall stores are relatively small, they are included in the fat mass as indicated by densitometry. The term *lean body mass* includes the essential nonadipose lipids and therefore should not be used interchangeably with *fat-free mass.*

# Assessment Methods

Over the years there have been many comparisons of methods for body-fat assessment. As previously explained, true figures can only be obtained by dissection, so indirect methods have to be used. Underwater weighing, or densitometry, is usually accepted as the gold standard; however, this method is described as indirect because it has to make some assumptions about the body. Techniques such as skinfold measurements and bioelectrical impedance are described as double indirect because they rely on even more assumptions. The major methods are now briefly described.

## Underwater Weighing (Densitometry)

Hydrostatic or underwater weighing has long been used as the classical reference standard for body composition assessment. It operates from Archimedes' principle that a solid heavier than a fluid will descend to the bottom of the fluid, and when weighed in the fluid, the solid will be lighter than its true weight by the weight of the fluid displaced. Instead of measuring the spilled water, the body is weighed in air and again underwater in a tank. The person is suspended in a sling attached to a scale and remains underwater long enough for the measurement to be recorded. The subject exhales before being immersed and holds her breath while underwater, emptying the lungs as far as possible. A series of immersions, maybe up to 10, is required for accurate data recording. The amount of air remaining in the lungs is known as *residual volume* (RV), and this function is measured in advance using standard physiological procedures.

Once body density has been calculated, this figure can be translated into a body-fat value using an equation. There are many such equa-

**An athlete may use underwater weighing as a method of body-fat assessment.**
Photo courtesy of Thomas Reilly.

tions in the literature, such as Siri's (1956) equation used for calculating percent body fat from the whole-body density.

Underwater weighing is feasible for some wheelchair athletes, although the assumptions for the density of the two compartments examined may not be correct. Moreover, since the technique requires multiple immersions, it may not be well tolerated by everyone.

## Air Displacement

Body volume can be measured using Archimedes' principle to record the amount of air or water that the body displaces. Equipment for measurement of air displacement consists of a test chamber large enough to hold an adult. The test chamber is separated from a reference chamber by a diaphragm. Pressure changes allow the test-chamber volume to be determined first with and then without the subject. The recordings allow body volume to be calculated, from which density is computed and then body fat is estimated using equations from the scientific literature.

Measurement using air displacement is employed by commercial systems such as the BodPod device, which are purchased by some professional sport clubs. The inaccuracy of current systems is a strike against their wider acceptance. This method is subject to assumptions about the constancy of fat-free mass and other factors, and the large errors that result make its use questionable for wheelchair athletes.

## Bioelectric Impedance Analysis

Bioelectric impedance analysis (BIA) employs the principle that lean tissue and body water conduct electricity better than fat does. The instrumentation is small enough to be portable—two electrodes are placed on the right foot and two on the right hand. The current at 50 Hz passes through the body and the resistance to it is recorded. This value is then used along with measures of frame size and other anthropometric details to estimate percent body fat. The portable systems are linked to a computer whose software is determined by the supplier. The resistance should be related to the square of body stature to take account of the length of the body through which the signal travels. The square of body stature is just the height measurement squared, as used to calculate BMI, for example.

BIA is sometimes employed for routine assessment of body fat, provided the measurement conditions are controlled. The requirements include a normal state of hydration, and so results are affected by exercise prior to observation. Emptying the bladder in between measurements can cause a change in estimated body fat of up to 2.5 percent body weight. Measurements are best taken early in the day, with the bladder emptied. The method correlates reasonably well with others, but agreement is not sufficiently strong to merit its use when small changes in body composition are being examined (Reilly & Sutton, 2008). There is still work to be done on the most appropriate anthropometric corrections to the conductivity (or resistance) values, and though widely available for coaches and athletes, BIA is too prone to error to be anything other than a crude approach.

## Near-Infrared Interactance

Near-infrared machines were developed commercially with the express purpose of assessing body fat. The principle of this approach is the differential absorption and reflection of light by the various layers of body tissue. A portable, low-cost instrument gathers data using a fibre optic probe over the belly of a muscle. The most common system selects the biceps muscle site for placement of the probe. Its simplicity is attractive to athletes and coaches, but its validity is doubtful. Moreover, the problems inherent in this method for wheelchair athletes may be magnified because of the unusual fat and muscle distribution that results from SCI. Thus, we need to explore other methods that examine the various segments of the body, such as dual-energy X-ray absorptiometry.

## Dual-Energy X-Ray Absorptiometry

Bone mineral density is measured by dual-energy X-ray absorptiometry (DXA). This technique entails placing the subject supine on a bed while a dual-energy X-ray beam passes through the body from a source beneath to a detector on top. The body is scanned along its longitudinal axis, and the bone mineral density is computed. The system uses a three-compartment chemical model of the body, separating it into fat, bone mineral, and lean mass. The machines are expensive but are widely available in sport science laboratories.

Though originally designed for the assessment of skeletal health, DXA has become a prime method for measuring body composition, including fat. It has a high level of precision and can detect small changes in elite athletes within a season. It is convenient for use with wheelchair athletes once access to facilities is secured. The information on fat distribution is particularly relevant, as is the feedback on bone mineral content.

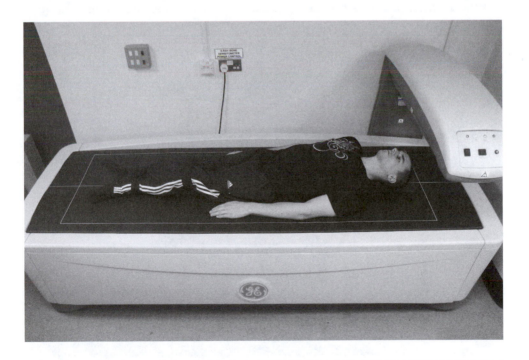

**Participant is in place for assessment using DXA.**
Photo courtesy of John Lenton.

## Skinfold Measurements

Since almost half of all body fat is stored subcutaneously, it is thought that total body fat is predictable if enough representative sites of the body are sampled for skinfold thicknesses. There are over 100 equations in the scientific literature for predicting body fat from skinfold measures. The one mostly used in the European community (Durnin & Wormersley, 1974) adopts four sites for measurement of skinfold thicknesses—the triceps, biceps, suprailiac, and subscapular sites. From these four measurements, percent body fat is predicted, making allowance for the subject's age and sex.

The validity of skinfolds for assessment of body composition was examined in the Brussels Cadaver Study (Clarys, Martin, Drinkwater, & Marfell-Jones, 1987). The researchers had access to a large number of cadavers, and they looked at the relation between external and internal fat deposits, as well as the distribution of fat throughout the body (fat patterning). They found that the best single predictor of total body fat is the skinfold thickness at the anterior thigh, a site not included in most prediction equations.

The use of skinfold callipers requires training for the data to be reliable. It is important also to use a calliper accepted by the International Biological Programme and the International Society for the Advancement of Kinanthropometry. Cheap, plastic devices have a sensitivity of 1 millimetre (versus 0.1 mm on the spring-loaded system), and most are not easy to use. Guidelines for the use of callipers and measurements at anatomical sites are available from Eston and Reilly (2008).

Due to differences in body composition and fat patterning, conventional skinfold equations may not be applicable in wheelchair-dependent popula-

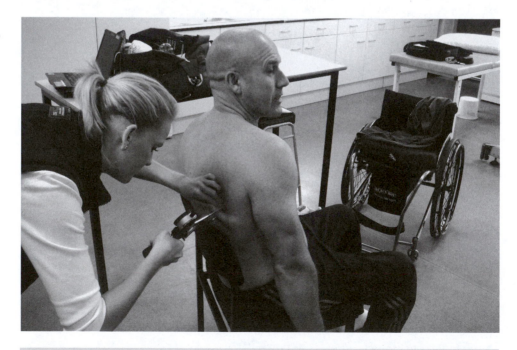

**Use of skinfold callipers requires training to minimize measurement error.**
Photo courtesy of Vicky Goosey-Tolfrey.

tions. Researchers have suggested that the commonly used four-site equation of Durnin and Womersley (1974) does not adequately predict percent body fat in disabled male athletes. Similarly, it has been suggested that the widely-used body mass index (BMI) underestimates body fat in people with disabilities. That said, when skinfold assessments are used for wheelchair athletes, the sum of skinfolds should be reported rather than simply reporting the percentage body fat. The sum of skinfolds can be used in setting targets for the amount of fat mass to be lost and can successfully be used in combination with changes noted in girth measurements. It is especially useful in any input of nutritional advice to wheelchair athletes, particularly if energy requirements are to be tailored to the needs of the individual and help to achieve the necessary goals with regard to the loss of fat mass.

Following are key points to remember about measuring body composition:

- A two-compartment model based on fat and fat-free masses is relevant to athletes and coaches. However, all methods described here have inaccuracies due to the assumptions that have to be made.
- Portable systems that have a large measurement error have limited uses for elite wheelchair athletes.
- DXA has become the reference method, adding information about fat, bone mineral, and lean mass.
- Skinfold thicknesses offer a means of monitoring changes in body composition of wheelchair athletes.

## Conclusion

Sports nutrition is an important factor in enhancing the performance of wheelchair athletes. The specific requirements of wheelchair athletes are currently being investigated, and it is hoped that in the future, more evidence-based guidelines will be available. Each athlete should be considered as an individual when assessing dietary requirements. Advice must be evidence based and applied to training, competition, and lifestyle. It should encompass overall energy balance, the appropriate amount of macronutrients in the diet, and the adequacy of micronutrients. Organized nutritional support so that wheelchair athletes have access to food and drinks when needed is essential. Finally, attention to body composition can complement sound nutritional strategies.

Anthropometric factors such as height are largely determined by genetics, whereas body composition is subject to environmental influences such as diet, training, and lifestyle. Weight control is important for both health and elite performance, and there is likely to be an optimal body composition at which athletes feel best for competition. This value for fat-free mass (muscle mass) and body fat is likely to vary among sports and even among individuals. The technologies available for assessing body composition vary from laboratory-based methods such as DXA to portable devices such as skinfold callipers. The former provide greater precision for detecting small changes in athletes subjected to year-long training programmes. The field methods are of practical use, provided that quality control is applied in data collection and the recorders are formally trained in the techniques.

# References

Clarys, J.P., Martin, A.D., Drinkwater, D.T., & Marfell-Jones, M.J. (1987). The skinfold: Myth and reality. *Journal of Sports Sciences,* 6, 3-33.

Durnin, J.V.G.A., & Womersley, J. (1974). Body fat assessed from total body density and its estimation from skinfold thickness: Measurements on 481 men and women aged from 16 to 72 years. *British Journal of Nutrition, 32,* 77-97.

Eston, R.G., & Reilly, T. (2008). *Kinanthropometry and exercise physiology laboratory manual: Tests, procedures and data.* London: Routledge.

Reilly, T., & Sutton, L. (2008). Methods and applications of body composition analysis. In Ed. P.D. Bust, *Contemporary ergonomics* (pp. 491-495). London: Taylor and Francis.

Siri, W.E. (1956). *Body composition from fluid spaces and density: Analysis of methods.* University of California Radiation Laboratory Report UCRL no. 3349.

# Suggested Reading

Bean, A. (2004). *The complete guide to sports nutrition* (4th ed.). London: A&C Black.

Cardwell, G. *Gold medal nutrition* (4th ed.). Champaign, IL: Human Kinetics.

Griffin, J. (2001). *Food for sport: Eat well, perform better.* Ramsbury, Marlborough, Wiltshire: Crowood.

Steer, S. (2004). *Fuelling fitness for sports performance.* London: Sugar Bureau.

Sutton, L., Wallace, J., Scott, M., Reilly, T., & Goosey-Tolfrey, V.L. (2009). Body composition of female wheelchair athletes. *International Journal of Sports Medicine,* 30(4): 259-265.

Sutton, L., Scott, M., Goosey-Tolfrey, V., Wallace, J., & Reilly, T. (2009). Body composition of highly-trained wheelchair athletes measured by dual-energy x-ray absorptiometry. In Kinanthropometry X1 (edited by P. Hume and A. Stewart). Published electronically on behalf of the International Society for the Advancement of Kinanthropometry. [WWW] Available from: http://www.iskaonline.com.

Wells, C.L., & Hooker, S.P. (1990). The spinal injured athlete. *Adapted Physical Activity Quarterly,* 7, 265-285.

# Suggested Websites

English Institute of Sport (EIS)

www.eis2win.co.uk

ParalympicsGB

www.paralympics.org.uk

Australian Institute of Sport (AIS)

www.ausport.gov.au/ais

International Society for the Advancement of Kinanthropometry (ISAK)

www.isakonline.com

# The Travelling Athlete

Mike Price, Jeanette Crosland,
and Nick Webborn

This chapter examines a number of issues that the travelling athlete may encounter, such as taking care of medical concerns while travelling, maintaining healthy nutrition and hydration abroad, and exercising in the heat. As you will see, many factors overlap, so it is worth reading all aspects even if you think they may not apply to you.

## Medical Issues Related to Travel

The key to safe, healthy travel abroad is to prepare and plan adequately for the country you are visiting and the environmental conditions you are likely to face. This is applicable to any traveller, but for the wheelchair athlete there are additional risk factors to consider.

Consult your family practitioner, or governing-body medical officer if applicable, about any immunizations required for the trip you are planning. Depending on the jabs required, they may cause discomfort at the injection site or flulike symptoms for a couple of days. Therefore, it is advisable to get any immunizations well in advance, preferably during a quieter phase of training. If you are travelling to a malarial zone, you will need to take medication before your departure and after your return. The precise regime will depend on the type of tablets you are advised to take—some are taken weekly and others daily. Also, check with your doctor to see if these might interact with any other medications you're taking. In Britain, antimalarials are not normally prescribed on the NHS, and you will need to pay for them. Unfortunately, the more convenient medications with fewer side effects are more expensive.

Make sure you have enough supplies of your regular prescription medications or other appliances, such as catheters or leg bags, because these may not be available abroad. Divide the supplies between your checked luggage and carry-on luggage so that you have enough to keep you going should one of your bags go missing for a few days.

A letter from your doctor stating your medical condition and medications is recommended, particularly if you need to carry syringes or needles. Discuss this with your airline carrier in advance if you are unsure or speak to the supervisor at the check-in desk. Ensure that your medication is legal in the country you are visiting (e.g., if you use morphine tablets for pain control). Your nation's embassy can advise you, but being arrested at customs is not a good way to start a trip abroad! You will also need to check any visa requirements for the country you are visiting and ensure that your passport is valid for 6 months *after* the date you travel.

Take out appropriate travel insurance that covers all the activities you will undertake while away and will cover you if you become ill. Let your insurer know about your medical condition in advance—the insurance may not cover you for any illness or injury relating to your disability if you have not previously disclosed this information, and the financial consequences could be disastrous. For EU residents travelling within the European Union, make sure you get your European Health Insurance Card (EHIC—formerly E111) to entitle you to free or discounted health care in European countries. Find out in advance what medical services are available at your destination. If you are unable to do this, find out the local emergency services number on arrival.

Many illnesses encountered while travelling can be prevented by taking appropriate care, but it is also advisable to take a small medical kit that includes simple remedies such as paracetamol, rehydrating-solution sachets for diarrhoea, plasters, and so on. Antiseptic hand-cleansing lotions and gels help prevent infections. Use these in preference to the dirty communal hand towel found in some public toilets, for example.

All travellers need to be conscious of good food and hand hygiene. Diarrhoea can be more of a problem for wheelchair users compared with the nondisabled, so you should wash your hands regularly and use hand gels before eating. Certain foods are more likely to cause problems and should be avoided when important training or competitions lie ahead. Avoid shellfish (e.g., prawns, mussels, cockles) since they are likely to carry contamination because of the way they feed. Avoid ice cream served in scoops from open containers because the top layer is exposed to excess heat and to germs; only buy well-frozen, wrapped ices. Use bottled water if there is any doubt over water safety and check that the lid is securely sealed when you buy. If there are doubts about water safety, avoid salads and peel fruit or wash it in bottled water.

Find out about the climate of the region you are visiting and whether you will need to make additional provision for coping with heat, cold, humidity, altitude, or pollution. This may affect what your pack—clothing, hats, small fans, water spray bottles for cooling and so on. People with respiratory conditions, such as asthma, that may worsen upon entering a more polluted environment might need to alter their medication. Ask your doctor for advice on how to manage this.

The risk of developing deep vein thrombosis (DVT) during air travel is well recognized. Some people are particularly at risk, including those with a history of blood disorders, DVT, or pulmonary embolism; those who are taking hormonal medication (including contraceptive pills); those who have cancer or heart problems; and those who have recently had surgery. Although people with SCI frequently have DVT during their initial hospital stay following injury, they do not seem to be particularly at risk thereafter. However, taking the normal precautions to prevent DVT is advisable. This includes wearing compression hosiery during air travel, which reduces the ankle swelling that tends to occur during air travel. There is some debate over whether the use of low-dose (75 mg) aspirin is effective in reducing the incidence of DVT. For those with no history of adverse reactions to aspirin, it is a relatively safe procedure to take one quarter of the normal 300-milligram tablet on the day of the flight. On arrival at your destination,

## revolutions

- Check which immunizations are required for all areas of your trip. Are antimalarials required?
- Obtain a letter from your doctor confirming your medical condition and medications taken.
- Take enough medical supplies for your whole trip.
- Check that your medication is legal in your destination country.
- Check whether you need a visa and how and when it can be obtained.
- Check that your passport is valid for 6 months.
- Check that you have adequate insurance.

check for any abnormal swelling of your ankles and calves. Persistent swelling of one calf in particular should raise the suspicion of DVT, although people without pain sensation would not feel the normal tenderness to palpation of the calf when DVT is present. If in doubt, get this checked out medically after you arrive.

## Practical Concerns Related to Flying

It is important to arrive as healthy as possible, particularly if you are competing. Several things can go wrong during the journey that can be prevented by adequate planning (Webborn, 2000). If you are travelling alone, ensure that any lifting or handling can be carried out by ground staff and give clear instructions on how you would like to be lifted. Make it clear as to what functions you can carry out yourself and what you need help with. Getting your backside scraped across the airline seat arm can lead to skin breakdown and then a pressure sore. If you are travelling with friends or colleagues and they are performing the lifting and handling, make sure they are fully instructed.

Ensure that your wheelchair is properly tagged, and if any parts are disassembled, they should each have their own baggage tag. Take your wheelchair cushion on board with you to use for pressure relief in flight. The risk of developing DVT, a urinary tract infection, or greater travel fatigue is increased by dehydration. Dehydration also seems to increase the frequency of epileptic seizures in those who are susceptible. Remaining hydrated is clearly important for maintaining health. However, more fluid input also generally means more urine output. Some athletes may be put off regular drinking by the difficulties associated with using an aircraft toilet. Having to request a staff person to bring an aisle chair and asking for help to transfer into the cramped aircraft toilet are among the reasons why wheelchair athletes tend to drink less on long journeys. As a result, people commonly arrive feeling unwell, developing a urinary tract infection or even DVT. The hassle of getting to the toilet may not seem worth it at the time, but it is essential to continue to drink during the flight and remain well hydrated.

Sitting in cramped aircraft seats is uncomfortable for most people, and nondisabled people tend to get up and move around at regular intervals to relieve this discomfort. You do not have this option, so you may need pain-relieving medication during the flight. Make sure it is easily reached in your travel bag. People with SCI may have chronic spinal cord neuropathic pain that can be exacerbated by long sitting. It would be advisable to discuss with your doctor in advance what dose of medication you can take if your condition worsens during the journey. The timing of taking regular medication is also important during long-haul travel where there are changes in time zones. To help adaptation to the new time zone set your watch to the destination time as soon as you depart. You therefore may be taking your medication at different intervals than normal on the day of travel. For some painkillers, such as paracetamol, do not take more than eight 500-milligram tablets within 24 hours. You will need to ensure that you do not have an excessive dosage.

Autonomic dysreflexia is a condition that tends to occur in people with a high SCI, usually at the level of T6 or above. It is brought on by painful stimuli applied below the level of the spinal lesion. The pain is not felt, but it produces an exaggerated release of noradrenaline (norepinephrine), resulting in a large rise in blood pressure. The person feels a severe throbbing headache and there may be blotching of the skin above the level of the lesion. If you suffer from dysreflexia make sure that you have any required medication handy in your bag and, preferably, have a printed information sheet that describes the management. Flight attendants have only basic medical training and are unlikely to have come across this condition.

## Accommodations and Adaptations

Hopefully you will have checked that your accommodations are fully accessible prior to travel. You will also need to consider getting around with accessible transportation. The local tourist information office can be helpful in this respect, and also check websites before travelling to find out about accessible transportation. On arrival at your accommodation, check your skin and pressure areas for any sign of breakdown and check your calves for any excessive swelling suggestive of DVT. Check your hydration status by looking at your urine colour. It should not be dark. If it is cloudy and smelly a urinary tract infection may be developing. First, increase your fluid intake to flush the urine through. If cloudy, smelly urine persists, seek medical help to get a urine culture and some antibiotics. If you are prone to urinary tract infections, it probably will be advisable to bring the antibiotics that work best for you.

You will need time to adapt to the new time zone and to get over travel fatigue. In general it takes one day to get over each time zone travelled when this is greater than 3 to 4 hours difference. Avoid training too hard in the early days before you have adapted. Also be aware of the climatic conditions. For example, avoid training in the hottest part of the day, particularly until acclimatization has occurred.

Finally, remember that when you return home, you have to consider all these points again for the return trip. If you develop any illness during the first few weeks after your return from a trip abroad make sure your doctor is aware of which countries you have travelled to and when. Infectious diseases acquired abroad are responsible for a significant number of medical admissions to hospital. Malaria can be fatal, so do not forget to take your antimalarial tablets when you return home even if you are not feeling unwell. Travel means increased risks for everyone, particularly for someone with a disability, but with appropriate planning many of these risks can be minimized.

## Nutrition and Hydration When Travelling

All athletes should carefully plan their strategies for eating and drinking. Even short flights can take many hours considering the total journey time from doorstep to doorstep. Furthermore, you should add in extra time because wheelchair travellers are usually first on and last off planes and because there may be delays along the way. This all means that it is likely the journey will be quite long and a number of meals will be affected. For all athletes this can result in the depletion of glycogen—the vital energy store needed to train or compete. Missing meals can also result in constipation, upsetting bowel management and, for those who are prone, it can cause autonomic dysreflexia. Plan how you will cope with the journey and where and what you will eat, and buy snacks to carry with you to ensure a good eating pattern throughout the journey. You may also find it useful to read chapter 5 regarding nutrition and the recommended further reading.

Ensuring the best hydration status possible is vital. Start your planning in advance of your trip. Begin to increase your fluid intake before you leave home. It takes time for the body to adjust to extra drinking, so give your body the chance to learn to hold on to the extra fluid and adjust bladder management. Toilet access during travel is always an issue but, in addition to potentially affecting sporting performance, dehydration will increase the chances of urinary tract infections. During flights it is usually most effective to drink smaller amounts of fluid regularly, which will increase the chance of the fluid being absorbed into the body and reduce urine losses. Drinking large amounts of caffeinated drinks may increase dehydration. Coffee contains high levels of caffeine, and tea and cola drinks contain some caffeine. If these drinks are part of your normal drinking pattern and you exclude all of them, you may compromise your fluid intake. However, you should avoid excess caffeine and consume other drinks such as water and fruit juice. Avoid alcohol on flights. Include some orange juice if possible because it contains antioxidant vitamins which help fight infection. Plan how you will handle access to toilets and ask for help where needed. If there is a short stop in a long journey and passengers leave the plane, use the opportunity to access toilet facilities either on the plane or in the airport.

## Exercising in the Heat

Temperature regulation is an important concern for everyone. As body temperature increases, whether exercising in cool or hot conditions, the body will increase its sweat rate. Fluids that are not replaced will lead to dehydration, further increases in core temperature, and even heat injury (e.g., heat exhaustion and heatstroke). Losing more than 2 percent of body mass from sweating (i.e., for a 70 kg athlete, this would be 1.4 L of sweat) will affect performance. Therefore, keeping well hydrated and maintaining body temperature is vital. Not only is this of particular importance to elite athletes, who compete in international events often held in hot countries, but also to any athlete exercising or training during the summer months.

### revolutions

- Plan your trip from door to door.
- Request in advance the best seat for accessing toilets and ask for assistance from your team or air staff. If you intermittently catheterize, consider using a bag for the flight.
- On long trips, adapt to the time of your destination and take a snack and a drink to bed for the first couple of nights. Buy fluid after passing through security, where fluids are normally taken away.
- Keep fluid and snacks in your seat. Don't stow them away in the overhead bins.
- Plan where and when you will eat, and carry snacks for emergencies.
- Pack any foods (including sports drink powders) that form part of your competition routine and you may not be able to buy abroad.
- Practise drinking extra fluid before your trip to a hot country. Drinking a little and often could help reduce urine losses.
- Ask for extra drinks during the flight, especially long flights.

SCI results in a reduced ability to sweat and to increase skin blood flow (vasodilation) below the level of injury. Because sweating and skin blood flow are important thermoregulatory mechanisms it stands to reason that body temperature regulation may be affected. As a result, people with SCI are often considered to be at a disadvantage for body temperature regulation. For example, as noted in chapter 3, athletes with tetraplegia have a level of injury above the outflow of the sympathetic nervous system. This system helps to initiate and increase sweating and skin blood flow. Tetraplegic athletes with complete spinal lesions generally have either a greatly reduced or absent sweating response and are therefore at a greater risk of overheating. Athletes with paraplegia will have some use of the sympathetic nervous system and, as a result, will have a sweating response proportional to the level of paralysis. Therefore, an athlete with a low-level injury will have a greater surface area for sweating when compared with an athlete with a high-level injury. Sweat rates of approximately 0.7 to 1.0 litre per hour have been observed for athletes with paraplegia during exercise in cool and hot conditions. Sweat rates at the same relative exercise intensity for nondisabled athletes during arm exercise have been observed to be 0.8 to 1.3 litres per hour (Price and Campbell, 2002, 2003; Price 2006).

## Replacing Fluids

Fluid replacement is important for exercise in both cool (10-15 degrees C) and hot (>25 degrees C) conditions. Athletes sweat in greater amounts as exercise intensity increases, exercise duration increases or environmental temperature increases. As noted previously, if sweat losses are not replaced, the potential for heat injury increases. So how much fluid should be replaced? Numerous studies have shown how fluid replacement improves performance. However, little is known regarding fluid replacement in wheelchair athletes, and most information is taken from research involving nondisabled athletes.

Wherever possible, it is useful if athletes are aware of their own fluid losses (i.e., their sweat rate). The sweat rate values noted earlier may give an estimate for fluid replacement volumes per hour. However, these are average values and there can be large variations from person to person. Therefore, the variations in sweat rate within one sport or team can vary greatly, and one fluid strategy is unlikely to cover all athletes.

An idea of your sweat rate can be obtained during normal training by measuring body weight before and after training (dried down and wearing similar dry clothing if sweat has gathered in sports gear) and taking into account any fluid lost. In other words, sweat losses equal body weight before exercise minus body weight after exercise and considering any fluid volume consumed. If you have gone to the toilet during the exercise session or if you have emptied your leg bag, then you will need to account for this. Some athletes may gain weight during exercise, which is usually due to drinking more than is lost through sweating.

Table 6.1 shows how to calculate sweat losses in a range of exercise scenarios that may relate to your training sessions or competitions. If you use a leg bag, if you have weighed yourself and then emptied your bag, you will need to weigh yourself again or account for the volume of urine emptied. For example, if you have emptied 200 millilitres of urine you have lost 200 g (i.e., 0.2 kilograms). If you weigh yourself after exercise and haven't emptied your leg bag before the end of exercise, it is the same as a nondisabled athlete not going to the toilet and simply having a fuller bladder, so you don't need to adjust your fluid loss calculation.

TABLE 6.1

## Calculation of Sweat Rate in Various Exercise Scenarios

| Scenario | (a) Body weight before (kg) | (b) Body weight after (kg) | (c) = (a) − (b) Weight change (kg) | (d) Fluid intake (L) | (c + d) Total losses (L) |
|---|---|---|---|---|---|
| Weight loss and no fluid intake | 75.4 | 75.0 | 0.4 | 0.0 | 0.4 |
| No weight loss and fluid consumed | 75.4 | 75.4 | 0.0 | 0.5 | 0.5 |
| Weight loss and fluid consumed | 75.4 | 75.0 | 0.4 | 0.5 | 0.9 |

However, if you empty your leg bag between body mass measurements, you will need to account for this loss of fluid by subtracting the volume of the leg bag from the total weight loss. For example, if your body weight change was 1.2 kilograms and your leg bag was emptied in between measures (e.g., 200 ml), you will have an adjusted weight loss (sweat loss) of 1.0 kilograms.

If your sweat rate has been estimated in cooler climates, you will need to adjust this for values expected in the heat. When athletes are able to replace fluid freely (known as *ad libitum drinking*), most will not replace all that they need to—only 50 to 60 percent of sweat losses are routinely and voluntarily replaced. Although athletes should aim to drink during exercise to replace the amount of sweat lost, excess intake above this level is not useful and may be uncomfortable and difficult to tolerate. However, during recovery from exercise, greater volumes can generally be tolerated. The best approach to developing a fluid replacement strategy is to try different amounts and types of fluid during training. This will also help any strategy fit in with the practicalities of your particular sport and your tolerance to fluid ingestion and taste preference. Practicing your strategy before an event is extremely important.

Water ingestion alone has been shown to improve endurance performance, as have a range of carbohydrate drinks. Many research studies refer to sports drinks that are, for example, 6 or 8 percent carbohydrate solutions. This means that in every litre of fluid (1,000 ml), 6 or 8 percent is actually carbohydrate (i.e., 60 or 80 g). As the carbohydrate content of the drink increases, more carbohydrate can be delivered to the body; however, less can be emptied from the stomach. Therefore, there is a relationship between the amount of carbohydrate within a solution, the amount of solution that can be emptied from the stomach, and how much carbohydrate can be transported into the blood. Too much carbohydrate in the solution may cause stomach problems. This is important to note if you are making your own glucose solutions rather than buying bottled sports drinks. Most researchers recommend a solution of between 6 and 8 percent carbohydrate, and many commercially available sports drinks contain around this level of carbohydrate (see table 6.2).

Many commercial sports drinks also contain electrolytes, usually sodium (*Na* on the ingredients list). Because sweat contains electrolytes as well as water, it is important to replace them. Sodium has been shown to aid both carbohydrate and water absorption from the gut. During recovery from exercise, larger amounts of sodium are usually contained in the drink to ensure rehydration.

Fluid replacement is not only important during exercise but also after. This is particularly important if athletes are performing in heats and finals, more than one game on the same day, or more than one training session per day. If athletes are dehydrated before they compete or train, their performance will be reduced. Research with nondisabled athletes has shown that if athletes are acclimated to the heat but are dehydrated, their heat acclimation won't be effective.

Fluid replacement may play dual roles of both fluid and fuel replacement. For the majority of athletes, both are required; however, coaches, officials, and spectators who are also exposed to hot environments may only need the fluid component. Also, sports such as archery may not have large energy expenditures but do involve athletes wearing specialized, often heavy, clothing for prolonged amounts of time, which will increase sweat losses. A 6 percent solution provides 240 calories per litre, so drinking this fluid for sports where less energy is expended could cause weight gain if large amounts are regularly ingested. Instead, consider a 4 or 2 percent (4 or 2 g carbohydrate per 100 ml) sports drink or use a calorie-free drink with salt added at the rate of approximately 1 gram per litre of drink. This will provide the sodium to help water absorption.

An important question often asked is how often athletes should replace fluid. Some people may answer this question with "a little and often". Indeed, ingesting smaller amounts of fluid more regularly may make an athlete feel more comfortable than

## TABLE 6.2

## Sports Drinks and Their Composition

| Type of drink | Amount of carbohydrate | What to look for on label | Sample brands | Effects |
|---|---|---|---|---|
| Isotonic | 6%-8% | 6-8 g carbohydrate per 100 ml | Lucozade Sport (BodyFuel) Powerade Gatorade | • Energy before, during, and after sport<br>• Improved hydration<br>• 240-320 calories per L |
| Hypotonic | 4% | 4 g carbohydrate per 100 ml | Lucozade Hydro Active Plus Powerade Aqua Powerade Pro | • Lower energy level before during and after sport<br>• Improved hydration<br>• 160 calories per L |
| | 2% | 2 g of carbohydrate per 100 ml | Lucozade Hydro Active Plus | • Improved hydration<br>• Much lower calorie content<br>• 80 calories per L |
| Hypertonic | More than 8% | More than 8 g carbohydrate per 100 ml | Lucozade Recovery (11% carbohydrate; also contains protein) | • Extra energy after training for those who need it<br>• Not designed to aid hydration |

> ## revolutions
>
> - Make sure you are hydrated before exercise and maintain a good diet.
> - Sweat rates vary, so you should calculate your own values for typical exercise and environmental conditions.
> - One fluid strategy is unlikely to cover all athletes. Practise different strategies during training and well before any event.
> - Where possible, drink regularly and use every opportunity to drink the amount of fluids you need. Using a drink you like means you are likely to drink more.
> - If you drink more fluid than you lose during exercise, your body weight will increase.

large amounts taken less often. The practical answer is a strategy that allows athletes to take fluid while upholding the rules of the sport in which they are involved, such as drinking during timeouts or breaks in play. In addition to trying different drinks, athletes should practise different drinking patterns well before any important event in order to see what suits them best and what is practical. Being well hydrated and maintaining a good diet before an event is important.

In summary, athletes should know the ideal target fluid intakes to maximize hydration and minimize dehydration for their own situation. People who use intermittent catheterization may need to catheterize more often. Wheelchair athletes may have issues accessing suitable toilet facilities at sport venues. Factors such as these may hinder training and competition therefore, it is important to plan fluid intake in advance and use a drink that will reduce urine losses. A sports drink containing some carbohydrate for fuel and some salt should help this process.

## Preventing Heat Injury

As noted earlier, overexposure to heat can lead to heat injury. This is particularly true if fluids are not replaced and if athletes are not able to sweat or sweat very little, such as tetraplegics. One important consideration is the amount of time spent in the heat prior to exercising or competition. Although a warm-up is an essential component of pre event preparation, it is vital not to overheat before competition. In some instances this may partly be unavoidable, such as where a warm-up track or area is exposed to the environment and offers little shade. There are, however, some simple measures that may be considered. Standard advice of wearing a peaked cap or brimmed hat and wearing a T-shirt to block direct rays from the sun is a good first measure, but other practical methods may also be considered depending upon the facilities available.

Some researchers have examined the effects of wearing cooling vests before and during exercise (Webborn, Price, Castle, & Goosey-Tolfrey, 2005, 2008). Wearing a cooling vest either before or during exercise improved the ability of tetraplegic athletes to repeatedly perform high-intensity sprints. When the vest was not worn, the athletes demonstrated a reduction in the total number of sprints they were able to perform and greater core temperatures (Webborn et al., 2008). However, some cooling is so effective that it may affect skilled performance until the athlete warms up again during the event. An alternative may be to keep a towel or T-shirt in a cool box in order to have access to cool clothes or, at the very least, provide cool fluids.

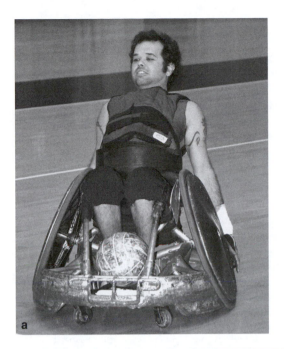 

**Cooling vest (***a***) and spray bottles (***b***) are among the simple means a wheelchair athlete can use to prevent heat injury.**

Photo 6.1a courtesy of Nicholas Diaper. Photo 6.1b courtesy of Jim House.

The use of fans and water sprays may also be considered. For nondisabled athletes, using a fan when sweating increases the rate of evaporation and the skin is cooled more rapidly. Whole-body fanning when sweating removes large quantities of heat from the body. Thin, close-fitting clothing can also be beneficial if the garments absorb water, which can then evaporate when fanned and thus cool the skin. As body temperature decreases, sweat production decreases and the need for cooling is reduced. This is a technique commonly employed by wheelchair athletes; however, remember to use fans sparingly and do not use water-spraying continuously. As it is possible that athletes could cool too much. As with fluid replacement, all cooling techniques should be practised in training to determine how long they should be applied in order to avoid overcooling. This is especially important if you experience any problems with temperature perception due to the nature of your disability. In events with repeated bouts of competition and short rest breaks it is unlikely that there would be sufficient time to fully cool the athlete, and overcooling is unlikely.

## revolutions

- Try to stay in the shade as much as possible to avoid overheating before competition.
- Practise different cooling strategies in training before the event.

# Conclusion

As you can see, there are several factors to consider when travelling, whether competing or not. Most of these can be organized prior to travel. Many people are able to give you advice, such as medical teams, coaches, and fellow athletes. The key point is to determine what works for you and, where possible, practise before you travel. If you do, you should be able to stay healthy and perform well.

# References

Price, M.J. (2006). Thermoregulation during exercise in individuals with spinal cord injuries. *Sports Medicine,* 36(10), 863-879.

Price, M.J., & Campbell I.G. (2003). Effects of spinal cord lesion level upon thermoregulation during exercise in the heat. *Medicine and Science in Sports and Exercise,* 35(7): 1100-1107.

Price, M.J., & Campbell, I.G. (2002). Thermoregulatory responses of able-bodied, upper body trained athletes to prolonged arm crank exercise in cool and hot conditions. *Journal of Sports Sciences,* 20, 519-527.

Webborn, A.D.J. (2000). Medical considerations associated with travelling with athletes with disabilities. *Your Patient and Fitness,* 14 (1), 10-16.

Webborn, N., Price, M.J., Castle, P.C., & Goosey-Tolfrey, V.L. (2005). Effects of two cooling strategies on thermoregulatory responses of tetraplegic athletes during repeated intermittent exercise in the heat. *Journal of Applied Physiology,* 98(6), 2101-2107.

Webborn, N., Price, M.J., Castle, P., & Goosey-Tolfrey, V. (2008). Cooling strategies improve intermittent sprint performance in the heat of athletes with tetraplegia *British Journal of Sports Medicine.* doi:10.1136/bjsm.2007.043687 http://bjsm.bmj.com/content/early/2008/06/14/bjsm.2007.043687. abstract

# chapter 7

# Psychological Aspects of Wheelchair Sport

David Shearer and Elizabeth Bressan

> **❝** I was travelling with a wheelchair basketball team from the UK to the USA for an international tournament. Upon arriving at the airport, I went to check in with one of the athletes who was in his wheelchair. The check-in assistant proceeded to direct a torrent of questions at me. "Can he move through the airport without assistance? Will he need assistance to get onto the aircraft? Has anyone interfered with his bags since he packed them?" The athlete and I looked at each other in disbelief! Did she think he could not answer these questions himself? In my head I began to compose a response, but I was too slow. The athlete provided her with an energetic response aimed at her re-education about his functional capacity. Her red face showed that the desired effect was achieved. Her assumption that people who use wheelchairs are generally incapable was shattered. I doubt that she ever made the same mistake again. **❞**
>
> David Shearer

**M**any people find it difficult to relate to someone who has a physical disability, often because they have not had any personal interaction with anyone with a disability. For example, they might be unsure what to expect from a person who has a mobility impairment and uses a wheelchair because they have never spent any time with wheelchair users. This lack of understanding can create additional challenges for people with disabilities. If society responded more adequately to people who have impairments, they would not experience nearly as many challenges and limitations (LoBianco & Shephard-Jones, 2007). Consider office workers who happen to use wheelchairs. Provided that there is only one level or there are ramps or elevators between levels, they may need no assistance whatsoever in the workplace. In other words, in an adapted work environment, they do not have a disability.

In wheelchair sport, the rules have been designed to ensure that people who have a variety of mobility impairments can play physically demanding and competitive sports in their wheelchairs. They provide adapted sport environments that encourage wheelchair users to become wheelchair athletes. The aim of this chapter is not to convince practitioners that wheelchair athletes deserve equal opportunities to participate in sport. Instead, our goal is to provide practitioners (e.g., coaches, sport science, and sport medicine support staff) with both general and specific psychological considerations for interacting and working with athletes with disabilities. To achieve this goal, we have organized the chapter into three sections:

- Getting Involved in Wheelchair Sport
- Developing Athletes' Sport Commitment
- Understanding Psychological Aspects of Wheelchair Sport

## Getting Involved in Wheelchair Sport

Previous reviews that have compared working with athletes with physical disabilities to working with nondisabled athletes have highlighted more similarities than differences (Hanrahan, 1998, 2005; Martin, 1999). Whether working with a team sport or an individual sport, all practitioners must be prepared to adapt training methods, practice schedules, and communication styles in order to arrive at an optimal approach. This is true when working with any athlete, not just wheelchair athletes. By adopting this professional approach, practitioners will look at all wheelchair athletes as individuals. Although one athlete may have an amputation, another SCI, and another a mobility impairment, these physical disabilities will not be the point of departure when working with them. If practitioners' initial interactions with wheelchair athletes follow the same protocols as their interactions with all other athletes, they are likely to build strong rapport that will enhance the support that they can provide.

## Who Participates in Wheelchair Sport?

From a clinical perspective, people who are eligible to participate in wheelchair sport at the Paralympic level have a variety of physical disabilities, all of which present serious disadvantages in the mobility aspects of sport participation. For example, a person with a below-knee amputation will be at a substantial disadvantage when playing basketball while wearing a prosthetic leg but will be able to participate without any disadvantage in wheelchair basketball.

It can be important to know whether a disability is congenital (present since birth) or acquired (caused by an accident or medical incident). Someone with a congenital disability has never experienced the sudden loss of physical mobility that has changed the life of a person who now uses a wheelchair as a result of paraplegia caused by an accident. On the other hand, the person with a congenital disability may have experienced a lifetime of discrimination. From a practical perspective, the practitioner's commitment to getting to know each athlete as an individual will help the practitioner develop an understanding of how the athlete feels. The realization that each athlete may feel differently about his impairment and the notion of disability will help the practitioner establish effective channels of communication.

**Wheelchair athletes strive for victory and take pride in their achievements just as any other athletes do.**
Photo courtesy of ES Bressan.

When working with wheelchair athletes, remember that in addition to the normal competitive pressures experienced by all athletes, those who use wheelchairs face a number of unique challenges. A wheelchair athlete will encounter disadvantages in nonadapted environments. For example, a gymnasium without an adapted entrance (e.g., a ramp) creates a barrier for fitness training for athletes who use wheelchairs for all their mobility needs, such as someone whose impairment is tetraplegia.

There are other kinds of barriers that present wheelchair athletes with challenges not usually experienced by nondisabled athletes. Researchers have found that elite wheelchair basketball players suffer unique stressors not experienced by nondisabled players (Campbell & Jones, 2002a, 2002b), including worries associated with travelling (e.g., going to the toilet on planes, handling luggage) and a lack of understanding from the general public (e.g., airline staff, support staff). In addition to these general concerns, there may also be sport-specific stressors. For example, research has shown that wheelchair racers experience greater stress about the condition of road surfaces compared with nondisabled racers (Martin, 2005). In our experience, knowledge of the challenges that athletes face is best gained through open and honest communication with them. This knowledge can be enhanced by observing athletes in and out of sporting contexts and noting the challenges faced and the manner in which the person copes with those challenges.

Not all wheelchair athletes use wheelchairs for their day-to-day mobility. Athletes with leg amputations and some athletes with SCI or with cerebral palsy are able to walk. They are wheelchair athletes because they play competitive sport in wheelchairs. There are also people who play wheelchair sport who do not have any mobility impairment at all. They choose to play wheelchair sport based on an inclusive model for recreation or competition. They also may be motivated by a shortage of athletes with mobility impairments needed to form a team. However, athletes without mobility impairments do not meet minimum eligibility requirements for participation in Paralympic wheelchair sport and are not included in our presentation.

## Familiarization With Wheelchair Sport

Beginner and elite wheelchair athletes want support from people who understand their sport. This requires familiarity with their sport. Sport familiarization is a continuous process, and the longer practitioners remain involved in wheelchair sport, the more sophisticated their understanding of how they can contribute.

The simplest way to become familiar with any wheelchair sport is to become immersed in the sport and actively observe the athletes in training and competition. Actively observing is more than just watching; it entails observing with specific objectives. For example, before attending a competition, practitioners could identify specific aspects of the sport on which they intend to focus, such as team tactics in wheelchair basketball or the biomechanics of serving technique and ground strokes in wheelchair tennis.

Often, observation alone is not enough. Using the previous examples, a coach may notice that one basketball team frequently uses the fast break after winning a defensive rebound whereas the other team tends to slow the game down when they get possession in a similar situation. Similarly, one wheelchair tennis player may hit the forehand from a more full-on position than another. Asking questions of people who have specialist knowledge is invaluable in understanding any wheelchair sport. This might include having conversations with existing coaching staff but more importantly speaking with the athletes themselves. Athletes generally enjoy talking about their sport. These conversations will also provide an opportunity to become familiar with the athletes as well as their sport.

You may also consider attempting the sport yourself. For example, a physiotherapist and a sport psychologist for a wheelchair basketball team tried playing one-on-one after the team had finished practice. The physiotherapist thought that this gave him a better understanding of the forces that the athletes' muscles were subjected to and the potential injuries that might occur, and the sport psychologist believed he had a better grasp of the attentional demands of the game. In contrast, the coach of this same team, who was an accomplished basketball coach but was new to wheelchair basketball, decided not to try playing the game. His reasoning was that because his wheelchair skills were poor, he would not have a realistic experience and might unconsciously lower his expectations for the players. For him, sport familiarization did not include actual participation.

In some instances it may be useful to experiment firsthand how athletes' lives are affected by their disability. Hanrahan (1998) suggested trying to complete simple tasks such as getting off and on a chair without the use of leg muscles, a daily ritual for an athlete with paraplegia. It might be helpful to take a trip using a wheelchair to increase awareness of the barriers that wheelchair athletes face on a daily basis. However, the knowledge gained by such exercises should be used for personal insight only. Some athletes may consider such efforts patronizing, so practitioners should not try to use their experiences as a basis for understanding what their lives are like. If you would like to know what any athlete is thinking or feeling, the best advice is to ask her.

Sport-specific knowledge is critical. Learning the rules of the sport as well as the system of athlete classification is central to understanding how the sport is played and how competitions are managed. However, given the various support roles when working with wheelchair athletes, there is some variation in the knowledge required. In some roles, such as coach, sport-specific knowledge must become more and more sophisticated. For the physiotherapist or sport psychologist, developing a good understanding of the sport may be sufficient. Both the coach and the sport psychologist will use an understanding of the areas presented in the next two sections in order to help wheelchair athletes develop their sport commitment and the psychological aspects of their sport.

## Developing Athletes' Sport Commitment

If wheelchair athletes are to gain the benefits of participation in sport and achieve their potential, then they will have to stay involved. In other words, they not only need the desire to participate in sport but also the commitment to continue participation over time. Scanlan, Russell, Wilson, and Scanlan (2003) proposed sport commitment as the central concept that influences a person's choice to participate in a sport in the first place and then to continue participation over a number of years. This sport commitment model (Scanlan et al., 2003) includes the six constructs of sport enjoyment, involvement opportunities, involvement alternatives, personal investments, social constraints, and social support.

## Sport Enjoyment

Sport enjoyment is defined as the positive feelings of pleasure, liking, and satisfaction experienced by an athlete of any age as a result of sport participation (Scanlan, Carpenter, Schmidt, Simons, & Keeler, 1993). The importance of sport enjoyment for both children and adults is supported by research:

- Martin (2006) found that when children with disabilities experience fun in sport, they are more likely to remain in sport.
- Wu and Williams (2001) found that fun was one of the main reasons for sport participation reported by adults with recent SCI who had become recent wheelchair users.

Ryba (2007) confirmed that enjoyment in competitive sport is not only related to winning and achieving public recognition but also to self-perceptions such as "I am getting better" and "I am improving," indicating close links among enjoyment, self-esteem, and self-efficacy. Ryba also found that young athletes enjoyed hard practice sessions in which they worked towards mastery goals, and they gained pleasure in the effort invested to accomplish these goals and the ultimate triumph of success. These findings are consistent with previous research that has found that enjoyment in youth sport is tied to achievement-related factors (Scanlan et al., 1993). Learning new skills, for example, is accompanied by feelings of competence and perceptions of control, both major sources of enjoyment.

If sport enjoyment is found in working hard during practice and learning new skills in order to meet new challenges, then the implications for coaches of wheelchair athletes are clear. As long as the balance between challenge and skills is realistic, athletes will enjoy overloading both their skill level and their fitness. The enjoyment found in real achievement and increased perceptions of competence will be found in physically and mentally demanding practice sessions and tough competitions. Enjoyment from these sources will motivate athletes to continue in sport.

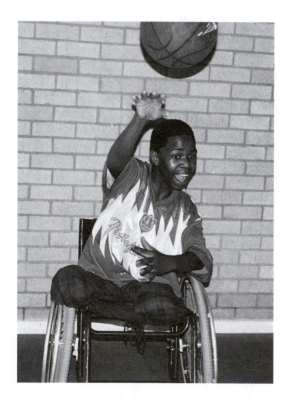

**Enjoyment in skill development is crucial to sustained commitment in sport.**
Photo courtesy of ES Bressan.

## Involvement Opportunities

Involvement opportunities are those opportunities that become available to an athlete because of participation in sport and that will be lost if participation is discontinued (Scanlan et al., 2003). In other words, if the athlete gave up sport participation, other opportunities would also be sacrificed. These opportunities have been described as the added value of playing sport and might include factors such as foreign travel or recognition by the public. Shepherd (1991) pointed out that sport participation often provides opportunities for new experiences, new friendships, and even the chance to counter negative attitudes towards persons with disabilities.

The added value of sport participation is especially evident in the psychological and physical benefits of sport. Researchers have noted that people with SCI who are involved in wheelchair sport or physical recreation report higher satisfaction with life in general when compared with those who do not participate (Tasiemski, Kennedy, Gardner, & Taylor, 2005). Similarly, improvements in physical fitness, opportunities for social interaction, family cohesion, and risk taking have been observed among adolescent wheelchair users who are involved in competitive sport or adventure sport programmes (Johnson & Klass, 1997).

To realize the added value of participation in wheelchair sport, athletes need regular opportunities to practise and compete. Infrequent practice sessions and competitions two or three times a year are insufficient for bringing the full range of benefits to athletes. Travel and the chance to wear a uniform and represent a school, club, region, or even country are important contributions to the added value of sport participation and should not be underestimated when developing wheelchair sport programmes.

## Involvement Alternatives

Involvement alternatives include opportunities that are available to the athlete but are not associated with participation in sport (Scanlan et al., 2003). Some of these alternatives compete for the athlete's energy and attention. If the alternatives are attractive enough, they can weaken the athlete's commitment to sport. The list of possible alternatives that may detract from sport commitment among wheelchair athletes will be influenced by factors such as accessible transportation, discretionary income, and community attitudes towards inclusion of people with disabilities. In some communities, there may be few involvement options for wheelchair athletes. In other communities a wide variety of alternatives may be available, which increases the likelihood that athletes will choose to drop out of their sport in favour of another activity. In these communities, sport participation must be presented in an attractive way so that the athletes choose to stay involved despite other options.

**Sport provides unique opportunities for wheelchair athletes to socialize with each other.**

Photo courtesy of ES Bressan.

In general, people with disabilities have less extensive social networks compared with people without disabilities, often due to mobility issues and negative societal attitudes (Martin, 2006). This means they may have fewer alternatives for social involvement. Allowing wheelchair athletes to experience the social side of sport participation as well as the achievement-oriented side of competitive sport may make a positive contribution to an athlete's sport commitment.

## Personal Investments

Personal investments are the resources that the athlete has put into sport participation that cannot be recovered (Scanlan et al., 1993). For example, the time, energy, and money that have been spent on sport participation are personal investments that cannot be regained when participation stops. Athletes who invest a great deal of their personal resources may be hesitant to give up their sport. An added twist to personal investments might be a player who has spent years playing competitive wheelchair basketball and is expected to retire when a younger player joins the team. If the personal investment has been substantial, the mature player will likely have difficulty accepting the new situation. These athletes need the option to either sustain their involvement in basketball at some level or transfer to another sport. Additionally, they should be provided with support if they enter the process of career termination.

There are some negative aspects of personal investment that affect wheelchair sport. For example, the demand for personal financial investment may be too great for some athletes. A wheelchair tennis player who is selected for the national team may have to make sacrifices in terms of time spent in his job. Since unemployment is a crisis for people with disabilities, any activity that might compromise job performance may be a threat for an athlete with a disability. If that personal investment is perceived to be too great, the commitment to participation at the top level will weaken.

Another personal investment is the financial cost of the sport chair itself. Personal income is a significant predictor that discriminates sport participants with disabilities from nonparticipants (Foreman, Cull, and Kirkby, 1997). If an athlete cannot afford to purchase and maintain a sport wheelchair, and if there are no options for subsidy or sponsorship, then it will not be possible to develop sport commitment.

## Social Constraints

Social constraints are the expectations to remain in sport that are communicated to an athlete by friends, family, community, and so on (Scanlan et al. 1993). If the athlete's social network does not expect sport involvement to continue, countless subtle signals will be sent to the athlete that can detract from his sport commitment. Society in general lacks knowledge about the sport opportunities available for people with disabilities (Williams, 1994). This lack of knowledge can produce low expectations for participation. Williams has suggested that when society holds negative views of disability, many people closest to the athlete tend to regard sport as diversion and a nice time but not a way of life. If this is the case, the athlete may struggle to remain committed.

One can imagine how the expectations of significant others would shape the athlete's approach to sport. If the athlete is surrounded by expectations that training will be hard, that practices will be frequent, and that injuries will occur from time to time, then those expectations become part of the athlete's expectations for what she will experience. If the athlete is surrounded by expectations that striving for excellence will take a long time and require sacrifices, then those expectations also become part of the athlete's expectations.

## Social Support

Social support in the sport commitment model refers to the support that the athlete receives from significant others to continue participating in sport (Carpenter, 1993). Social support includes encouragement as well as reinforcement. It differs from social constraints because it does not focus on expectations but rather on the immediate psychosocial impact of significant others' behaviour on an athlete.

The need for group identification and social interaction is common to all athletes, but it is especially strong during adolescence. Johnson and Klass (1997) studied a group of adolescents who had become wheelchair users as a result of recent injuries. They found that although these young people experienced negative emotions as a result of isolation from their peer group, participation in sport helped promote positive social integration and alleviate the pressure for social acceptance.

Socialization into disability sport is usually dependent on support from family, school, peer group, community, therapists, and peers with disabilities. Many athletes with disabilities have to rely heavily on their parents and family to support their sport participation, at least during their younger years (Martin & Mushett, 1996). The lack of public familiarity with disability sport opportunities is a negative constraint for young people with disabilities (Rudell & Shinew, 2006). For example, elite female wheelchair basketball players noted that the significant others in their lives were often unfamiliar with disability sport. They identified the opportunity to observe wheelchair sport and to chat with participants as key to initiating and sustaining their own sport involvement (Rudell & Shinew, 2006).

**Wheelchair camps for children encourage both young athletes and their families to see sport as a normal part of their lives.**

Photo courtesy of ES Bressan.

Access to participation is severely limited for some athletes because social support is absent. Problems with employment, lack of wheelchair accessibility in fitness and sporting venues, and lack of accessible transport are problem areas that have a negative impact on sustained involvement in sport (Tasiemski, Bergstrom, Savic, & Gardner, 2000). Disability sport programmes and specifically sport camps have been found to have a positive influence on socialization into wheelchair sport (Rudell & Shinew, 2006). For athletes who have acquired their impairment, in-hospital rehabilitation programmes and disability sport clubs also play an important role in introducing sport after SCI occurs (Wu & Williams, 2001).

# Understanding Psychological Aspects of Wheelchair Sport

Working with athletes with disabilities demands an understanding of various psychological considerations that affect individual performers. Vealey's (1988) human development model for psychological skills provides a useful framework for understanding psychological development in all athletes. This model consists of three stages: foundation skills, psychological skills and methods, and facilitative factors. For wheelchair athletes, the development of foundation skills might differ as a function of their disability. Knowledge of these differences will help practitioners make their working practice more effective and get the most from their athletes. Therefore, in this section we shall focus on four specific foundation skills: self-awareness, motivation, self-esteem, and self-efficacy.

## Self-Awareness

Ravizza (1998) described self-awareness as self-knowledge about one's emotions, cognitions, and behaviours. Self-awareness is important because it enables athletes to identify their strengths and weaknesses, which in turn influences the goals they set for training and competition (Butler & Hardy, 1992). Encouraging athletes to become sensitive to the effects of training and competition on their physiological and psychological states is important if they are to develop self-awareness.

The development of self-awareness can be facilitated by keeping training diaries. In these diaries athletes can record specific elements of their training (i.e., type of training session, intensity, volume, and effort) and their physiological and psychological well-being (e.g., hydration status, general health, and mood) each day. Recording this information allows athletes to track their progress over time and reflect on how physiological and psychological well-being interact to affect their performance. For example, if an athlete is in a poor mood before training, how does this affect her effort in training? Or, how does a hard training session affect her hydration status? Reflecting on these interactions can help athletes prepare more effectively for similar occurrences in the future. The diaries can be simple paper or computer-based page-by-day diaries, or they can be one of the athlete diary software packages now available. Training diaries do not need to be complicated. In fact, to encourage adherence, athletes should take no longer than 5 minutes to complete their entries at the end of each day. Therefore, diaries can be completed in short form, perhaps using smiley faces to represent current moods, or 0-to-10 Likert scales for measuring effort during training. Regardless of format, the athletes must be educated regarding the purpose of the diary and how the development of self-awareness will help them regulate their participation.

## Motivation

Helping athletes become more self-aware of what motivates them to participate in sport can lead to personal growth (Martin, 2005). The majority of athletes with disabilities compete in sport for the same reasons as nondisabled athletes. At amateur and recreational levels, these reasons include participation for fun and enjoyment, for health and fitness benefits, and for the social opportunities provided by the sport (Wu & Williams, 2001). At an elite level, many athletes have a strong athletic identity (i.e., they describe themselves as an athlete and clearly identify with this perception) and are motivated by the challenges of competition, including setting task (e.g., skill technique), performance (e.g., personal best times), and outcome goals (e.g., finishing position, winning medals) in a manner similar to nondisabled athletes (Martin, Adams-Mushett, & Smith, 1995).

Despite the general similarities in motivation to nondisabled athlete, the motivation of athletes with disabilities may be affected by disability-related considerations. Research has indicated that athletes with disabilities are driven by a number of unique factors, such as promoting disability sport, demonstrating how "normal" they are, and using sport participation to help them adjust to their disability (Asken, 1991; Wheeler, Malone, VanVlack, Nelson, & Steadward, 1996). Some athletes have reported that sport helps them beat their disability by allowing them to forget that they are in a wheelchair (Wheeler et al., 1996). For wheelchair athletes in particular, improved physical condition and upper-body

### revolutions

1. Adopt a professional approach and look at each wheelchair athlete as simply an athlete.
2. Recognize that athletes who use wheelchairs often experience more stress than other athletes when travelling and interacting with the general public. Communicate with them so you are aware if they are having problems.
3. Be an active observer of wheelchair sport. You can learn a lot just by watching.
4. Develop sport-specific knowledge of the sport rules and classification so that you can help athletes improve their performance.
5. Remember that enjoyment is the key to sustained commitment in sport. Find out what is enjoyable for the athletes in their sport and cultivate it.
6. Wheelchair athletes enjoy putting effort into their sport. Challenge them physically during practice sessions and fitness training.
7. Sport involvement serves an important social function for many wheelchair athletes. Provide opportunities for the wheelchair athletes to socialize with each other as well as do their sport.
8. Have high expectations for the athletes' achievements. Coaches' expectations send clear messages to athletes about their potential.
9. Each wheelchair athlete is an individual and should develop self-awareness and self-knowledge. Encourage athletes to think about their participation and to take responsibility for their actions both in and out of sport.
10. The attitudes of families and friends have a powerful impact on many wheelchair athletes. Find ways to have a positive influence on the ways that significant others perceive participation in wheelchair sport.

strength are the most common reasons identified for sport participation, with improved self-esteem and weight control also identified as important sources of motivation (Tasiemski et al., 2000). It is important for practitioners to understand these factors and how they may influence an athlete's behaviour in training and competition. For example, if an athlete's sole motivation is to prove to others how capable he is, and yet despite his best efforts the attitudes of others remain the same, his motivation is likely to be undermined. By exploring an athlete's motivations through conversations, practitioners will be better positioned to maximize the athlete's chances of success and continued involvement.

## Self-Esteem

Self-esteem is a global measure of people's perception of their self-worth (i.e., how good they feel about themselves), and it is thought to be maintained through success experiences and positive judgements from others (Martin, 2006). In their review of literature, Weiss and Ferrer-Caja (2002) highlighted the following four findings about self-esteem emerging from Susan Harter's research relating to self-perception and self-esteem:

1. Self-esteem is strongly affected by perceptions of competence (in areas valued by the individual) and the opinions of significant others. The impact of these two sources is relatively equal.
2. Perceptions about physical appearance and social acceptance are strong predictors of self-esteem.
3. Social support from one's peer group is the strongest source of social support, with support from family members almost as important.
4. Self-esteem is strongly associated with emotional responses. Therefore, someone with high self-esteem is likely to experience predominantly positive emotions (e.g., happiness, excitement), whereas someone with low self-esteem will experience more negative emotions (e.g., depression, anxiety).

According to these findings, the self-esteem of athletes in wheelchair sport will be affected by the opinions of significant others, the athletes' perception of their physical appearance and social acceptance, peer group support, and the athletes' emotional responses to sport participation. Therefore, we can draw several practical implications for the development of positive self-esteem:

- It appears that the opinions of significant others must be addressed. Parents, coaches, and friends who value wheelchair sport participation and send positive signals to the athlete make a strong contribution to the athlete's self-esteem.
- Finding ways to support the athlete's formulation of a positive body image is a challenge that could be addressed by helping the athlete to develop skills and fitness (positive perceptions of physical competence).
- Social acceptance within the community should not be underestimated. Positive experiences with inclusion in community activities as well as acceptance by community members send powerful messages to a wheelchair athlete.
- Peer group acceptance is not a factor that can be controlled since it is deeply rooted in social and cultural expectations. It is known that wheelchair ath-

letes may regard other wheelchair athletes as their peers. Promoting positive interaction and instilling a tolerant team culture among wheelchair athletes is well worth pursuing. Team-building experiences and cooperative games are strategies that may work.

- Encouraging wheelchair athletes to pay attention to their emotional responses can be facilitated by keeping a training diary, a technique recommended earlier for the development of self-awareness. Learning to identify the sources of positive emotions in order to cultivate them is a step towards gaining self-control, a contributor to self-esteem.

There appears to be little difference in the development of self-esteem and its relationship to sport performance between people with and without physical disabilities (Martin, 2006). Athletes competing at higher levels in any sport tend to display positive self-esteem because their positive feelings of self-worth have been reinforced through their successes (Campbell & Jones, 1994). However, when working with beginners, it is crucial to follow skill progressions that provide opportunities for success and to use positive coaching methods.

## Self-Efficacy

Self-efficacy is a situation-specific form of self-confidence (Bandura, 1997). Athletes experience different strengths of self-efficacy beliefs in relation to different aspects of their sport performance. For example, an elite wheelchair road racer might have high self-efficacy about the ability to perform well during a training push but low self-efficacy about the ability to perform when under the pressure of Paralympic competition, where the challenge is increased. In general, athletes with high levels of self-efficacy across all aspects of performance tend to respond better to pressure, anxiety, and other psychological stressors, and they are able to maintain their efforts even in the face of failure (Bandura, 1997). Consequently, coaches should take steps to increase self-efficacy in their athletes.

The five main sources of self-efficacy have been well-documented (Bandura, 1997; Maddux, 1995), and they provide sound guidelines for athlete development.

1. **Performance accomplishments.** These are past experiences with success in performance situations. If athletes have experienced success in a specific task and believe it was a result of their own efforts and skill, they will be more confident in approaching the same task again (Feltz, Short, & Sullivan, 2008). Therefore, providing opportunities to experience success in training and competition is essential. In training, this might be done by ensuring that the objectives are challenging yet still achievable, whereas for competition, selection of appropriate opponents might allow coaches to strike the balance between challenge and success. As skills, tactical understanding, and fitness improve, the challenges can be increased progressively, thus maintaining self-efficacy.

2. **Verbal persuasion.** Verbal persuasion refers to both internal self-talk and external feedback from significant others, such as the coach or other staff. Athletes should be encouraged to be self-supporters, focusing their thoughts on factors that are positive, helpful, and within their control.

Coaches and support staff should be aware of how they can affect an athlete's levels of self-efficacy. Careless comments, inappropriate feedback, and negative body language following a specific event (e.g., a poor return of service in tennis) can lead to a downward spiral of negative thinking that results in low self-efficacy. In contrast, constructive feedback, positive comments, and gestures may lead to maintenance of or even an increase in existing levels of self-efficacy. In addition, other external influences such as the media, parents, friends, and significant others can have either a positive or negative impact on an athlete's self-efficacy, and therefore they need to be sensibly managed.

   **3. Vicarious (modelling) experiences.** Observing others perform can provide information about a sport that helps athletes form an impression about whether or not the level of challenge is within their capabilities. By watching televised wheelchair basketball games, for example, a wheelchair user begins to get a clear picture of what is involved in the game. Observing others is a good way to give athletes the opportunity to consider getting involved in a sport. It is also a good way to illustrate to athletes how the intensity and skill of the game is raised at the next level, hopefully motivating them to keep involved in the sport.

   The observed models should be competent and perceived as similar to the athlete in question. This is because competent models are more likely to command respect from observing athletes and hold their attention longer (Bandura, 1997). Furthermore, observing models with similar attributes to the observing athlete (e.g., age, gender, disability classification) will have a more powerful effect on self-efficacy beliefs.

**Paralympic medallists such as Ernst van Dyk can provide positive sources for guidance on performance and training, as well as serve as positive role models for aspiring wheelchair athletes.**
Photo courtesy of ES Bressan.

Self-modelling, where athletes watch their own performances on film, can also be used in various forms to increase self-efficacy. For example, DVDs that show the athlete's best performance or a selection of skills rarely achieved by the athlete may provide performance accomplishment information (see point 1) that increases self-efficacy.

**4. Physiological and emotional states.** Physiological states such as fear, excitement, and flow may trigger feelings of either positive or negative self-efficacy and affect a person's judgement about her capabilities. Athletes will benefit from learning how to engage in positive self-talk in order to control their emotional state. By learning to read the signs of excessive tension in their bodies or lack of focus in their mental approach, athletes can respond with self-talk, a self-regulation skill that helps athletes feel more in control of the situation. These feelings of control contribute to self-efficacy.

To maximize self-efficacy, athletes should be aware of their optimal physiological and emotional states. This might include understanding acceptable levels of training fatigue before competition, the distinction between pain and discomfort, their best overall levels of preperformance arousal, or their most successful preperformance emotions. There is no hard and fast rule about what is and is not acceptable; perceptions will differ depending on the person. For example, for some athletes all pregame anxiety is bad, whereas for others, anxiety might be perceived as an essential requirement to perform well. Coaches and support staff should help their athletes to develop an awareness of what works best for them.

**5.** Imagery experiences. The mental images that athletes have regarding their performance can contribute to self-efficacy. If the images are positive and the athletes see themselves coping well with challenges, performing skilfully, and being successful, self-efficacy will increase. These images might be based on previous performances, or they might be images of what the athlete would like to happen in future competitions.

Just as negative self-talk can have a detrimental effect on self-efficacy, so too can negative imagery. Negative mental images may occur automatically. The key is for athletes to take charge of their imagery and make it work with them rather than against them. Rather than imagining scenarios where things go badly, athletes should be guided to imagine situations in which they succeed or overcome difficulties, such as tough opponents. In this way, imagery can be used to build, maintain, and regain self-efficacy (Feltz et al., 2008).

## Conclusion

Working with wheelchair athletes involves the development of both the coaching and support staff and the athletes. Getting involved in wheelchair sport will require a positive attitude towards adaptation and an expansion of one's knowledge base into wheelchair sport. The practitioner's contribution to the athletes can be in terms of their psychological development as well at their sport commitment, and it can be a very rewarding process. Much of what you already know about sport and sport science can be applied to wheelchair sport. Many of the skills used when helping nondisabled athletes develop positive self-esteem and sport commitment will be applied in similar ways when working with wheelchair athletes.

It would be naive to assume that athletes with disabilities are identical to athletes without disabilities. Not only is it possible that an athlete with a disability has experienced a major trauma and loss in life, but most societies still create barriers for people with disabilities. These barriers affect many aspects of life and certainly present wheelchair athletes with challenges that do not affect nondisabled athletes. However, practitioners will discover that if they can create a positive environment that maximizes the motivation, self-efficacy, self-esteem, and commitment of the athletes, they are in for a personally rewarding experience.

# References

Asken, M.J. (1991). The challenge of the physically challenged: Delivering sport psychology services to physically disabled athletes. *Sport Psychologist, 5*, 370–381.

Bandura, A. (1997). *Self-efficacy: The exercise of control.* New York: Freeman.

Butler, R.J., & Hardy, L. (1992). The performance profile: Theory and application. *Sport Psychologist, 6*, 253-264.

Campbell, E., & Jones, G. (1994). Psychological well-being in wheelchair sport participants and non-participants. *Adapted Physical Activity Quarterly, 11*, 404-415.

Campbell, E., & Jones, G. (2002a). Sources of stress experienced by elite male wheelchair basketball players. *Adapted Physical Activity Quarterly, 19*, 82-89.

Campbell, E., & Jones, G. (2002b). Cognitive appraisal of sources of stress experienced by elite male wheelchair basketball players. *Adapted Physical Activity Quarterly, 19*, 100-108.

Carpenter, P. (1993). *Staying in sport: Young athletes' motivations for continued involvement.* Unpublished doctoral dissertation, University of California, Los Angeles.

Feltz, D., Short, S., & Sullivan, P. (2008). *Self-efficacy in sport: Research and strategies for working with athletes, teams, and coaches.* Champaign, IL: Human Kinetics.

Foreman, P., Cull, J., & Kirkby, R. (1997). Sports participation in individuals with spinal cord injury: Demographic and psychological correlates. *International Journal of Rehabilitation Research, 20*(2), 159-168.

Hanrahan, S.J. (1998). Practical considerations for working with athletes with disabilities. *Sport Psychologist, 12*, 346-357.

Hanrahan, S.J. (2005). Able athletes with disabilities: Issues and group work. In M.B. Anderson (Ed.), *Sport psychology in practice.* Champaign, IL: Human Kinetics.

Johnson, E., & Klass, S. (1997). Recreation issues and trends in pediatric spinal cord injury. *Spinal Cord Injury Rehabilitation, 3*(2), 79-84.

LoBianco, A.F., & Shephard-Jones, K. (2007). Perceptions of disability as related to medical and social factors. *Journal of Applied Social Psychology, 37*, 1-13.

Maddux, J.E. (1995). Self-efficacy theory: An introduction. In J.E. Maddux (Ed.), *Self-efficacy, adaptation, and adjustment: Theory, research, and application* (pp. 3-33). New York: Plenum Press.

Martin, J.J. (1999). A personal development model of sport psychology for athletes with disabilities. *Journal of Applied Sport Psychology, 11*, 181-193.

Martin, J.J. (2005). Sport psychology consulting with athletes with disabilities. *Sport and Exercise Psychology Review, 1*, 32-39.

Martin, J. (2006). Psychosocial aspects of youth disability sport. *Adapted Physical Activity Quarterly, 23*, 65-77.

Martin, J.J., Adams-Mushett, C., & Smith, K.L. (1995). Athletic identity and sport orientation of adolescent swimmers with disabilities. *Adapted Physical Activity Quarterly, 12*, 113-123.

Martin, J., & Mushett, C. (1996). Social support mechanisms among athletes with disabilities. *Adapted Physical Activity Quarterly, 13*, 74-83.

Ravizza, K. (1998). Increasing awareness for sport performance. In J.M. Williams (Ed.), *Applied sport psychology: Personal growth to peak performance* (3rd ed., pp. 171-181). Mountain View, CA: Mayfield.

Rudell, J., & Shinew, K. (2006). The socialization process for women with physical disabilities: The impact of agents and agencies in the introduction to an elite sport. *Journal of Leisure Research, 38*(3), 421-444.

Ryba, T. (2007). Cartwheels on ice: A phenomenological exploration of children's enjoyment in competitive figure skating. *Athletic Insight, 9*(2). www.athleticinsight.com/Vol9Iss2/IceCartwheels.htm.

Scanlan, T., Carpenter, P., Schmidt, G., Simons, J.P., and Keeler, B. (1993). An introduction to the sport commitment model. *Journal of Sport & Exercise Psychology, 11*, 54-64.

Scanlan, T., Russell, G., Wilson, N., and Scanlan, L. (2003). Project on elite athlete commitment (PEAK): I. Introduction and methodology. *Journal of Sport and Exercise Psychology, 25*, 360-376.

Shepherd, R. (1991). Benefits of sport and physical activity for the disabled: Implications for the individual and for society. *Scandinavian Journal of Rehabilitation Medicine, 23*(2), 5-19.

Tasiemski, T., Bergstrom, E., Savic, G., & Gardner, B. (2000). Sports, recreation and employment following spinal cord injury—a pilot study. *Spinal Cord, 38*, 173-184.

Tasiemski, T., Kennedy, P., Gardner, B., & Taylor, N. (2005). The association of sports and physical recreation with life satisfaction in a community sample of people with spinal cord injuries. *NeuroRehabilitation, 20*, 253-265.

Vealey, R.S. (1988). Future directions in psychological skills training. *Sport Psychologist, 2*, 318-336.

Weiss, M., & Ferrer-Caja, J. (2002). Motivational orientations and sport behaviour. In T. Horn (Ed.), *Advances in sport psychology* (pp. 101-184). Champaign, IL: Human Kinetics.

Wheeler, G., Malone, L.A., VanVlack, S., Nelson, E.R., & Steadward, R. (1996). Retirement from disability sport: A pilot study. *Adapted Physical Activity Quarterly, 13*, 382-399.

Williams, T. (1994). Disability sport socialization and identify construction. *Adapted Physical Activity Quarterly, 11*, 14-31.

Wu, S.K., & Williams, T. (2001). Factors influencing sport participation among athletes with spinal cord injury. *Medicine and Science in Sport and Exercise, 33*, 177-182.

## Peter Norfolk, OBE

Wheelchair tennis has been an important part of my life for many years, but it has been all consuming since 2001. In 1979 when I was 19 years old, I had my original spinal cord injury as the result of a motorcycle accident. But it was 10 years before I found wheelchair tennis.

On a tennis court I like the fact that I am responsible for what happens. I also hate losing, so I have to develop the skills to be the best and sort out the problems by myself if I want to win. There's no one else to blame for what happens, just me.

The standard of competition has risen enormously. Several current top players had success before their injuries, but better coaching and input from sport science have also influenced the rising standards. Now I always have to look for the extra edge and implement that into my training and lifestyle. It's tough getting to the top, and staying there takes even more effort. Fortunately, I run my own business, Equipment for the Physically Challenged (EPC), which enables me to take time out to train and have access to the best products and technical help.

I have an exceptional team supporting me. The team has grown over several years and adapted as my performance needs have required. I am pretty hard to work with because I require 100 percent commitment to my ideals. You just can't make the grade without total dedication from everyone. I know my team is integral to my success.

The development of the tennis wheelchair has facilitated more skilful play. I began my playing career in a heavy, off-the-peg steel chair; now I play in a custom-built lightweight titanium tennis chair. Speed, turning ability, and balance are hugely affected by chair set-up, so it's crucial to have the wheelchair set-up for your individual ability and skills.

Winning a major event is a great feeling of achievement, but winning a Paralympic Games is awesome because it's the culmination of four years of hard work. I tend to avoid all the fun of the Games and focus completely on the job of playing the tournament. It's a bit sad, but you can't chance taking your eye off the ball after all that preparation. To succeed as a Paralympian, you need to have a drive and commitment to be the best. The effort and sacrifice potentially surpass that of an Olympian when all aspects of life are considered, and yet the rewards and recognition are not equal. There are already some incredible Paralympic athletes in many sports, and hopefully in the years to come there will be many more.

# PART II

# Training for Wheelchair Sports

# Wheelchair Basketball

Mike Frogley

A great deal has been written on basketball skills and how to teach these skills to athletes. Such is not the case in wheelchair basketball. Though wheelchair basketball has been played since shortly after World War II, very little has been presented in the literature specifically for the sport. As a result, most coaches and players of wheelchair basketball have taken what they learned from the running game of basketball and tried to adapt it to wheelchair basketball with varying degrees of success. Some of what is taught in the running game of basketball can be transferred to wheelchair basketball; however, the different levels of muscle function present in wheelchair basketball and the different movements resulting from using a wheelchair present some unique skills. This chapter will focus on some of those differences and emphasize the individual and team skills used in wheelchair basketball.

## Wheelchair Propulsion

The first and most important aspect of wheelchair basketball is the player's ability to move the wheelchair. Very simply, if you cannot move your wheelchair to where it needs to be, it does not matter how well you can perform the other skills of the game. However, players spend little time learning how to maximize their wheelchair mobility. There is a significant difference between the propulsion used in wheelchair basketball and the skills learned in a rehabilitative setting.

Wheelchair movement skills can be broken down into several areas: forward pushing, backward pushing, turning, pivoting, stopping, tilting, and hopping.

■ **Forward pushing.** In order to push forward, the athlete begins with his hands at approximately 12 o'clock on the wheels. This is the position at the top of the wheel. The hand grips the whole wheel, with the thumb on top of the tyre pointing forward and the other fingers gripping the push rim. This position maximizes contact with the wheel and reduces the strain on the wrist when following through in the push. As force is applied forward on the wheel in its arc, the trunk leans forward with the chin over the knees. The stroke finishes with the hands coming off the wheels at approximately 3 o'clock on the wheel. The hands are recovered with the trunk raising back up only slightly as the next push begins.

The push will vary depending on the player's level of muscle function. For most players with full muscle function from the waist up, including some leg function and hip function, the push just described would be accurate. As the muscle function decreases and the athlete has less trunk function, the amount she will be able to lean forward will be reduced. In most instances, the reduced trunk angle results in less force and therefore less speed, but that is not always the case. Athletes can adjust their sitting position in order to provide more stability for pushing by raising their knees above their hips and using a variety of straps to secure their trunk while in propulsion.

■ **Backward pushing.** Similarly, for pushing backwards (i.e., pulling), the player will grip the wheel in a similar way, with the hand position beginning at 3 o'clock, and then lean backwards with the trunk finishing against the backrest of the wheelchair, shoulders slightly past the back posts, and hands coming off the wheels at just past 12 o'clock.

■ **Turning and pivoting.** Turning and pivoting are slightly different movements and are often confused. A turn describes the movement of a wheelchair around a point. In order to turn, the same mechanics for a forward or backward push are applied with one difference—the wheel on the side of the wheelchair in the direction to which the athlete wants to move is kept stationary while the outside wheel is pushed. Conversely, a pivot describes a movement on a point that does not cause a change in location on the court but simply a change in point of view. The athlete still pushes forward on the outside wheel, but while doing so, he pulls back with the opposite wheel.

■ **Stopping.** Stopping the wheelchair is accomplished by locking the arms at the elbows and grabbing the wheels while leaning against the backrest.

■ **Tilting.** Tilting and hopping (discussed a bit later) are relatively new to the sport. In the early 1990s, players began to experiment using straps to keep themselves seated in the wheelchair and, in so doing, prevent physical advantage fouls. An additional benefit is the wheelchair reacting more accurately to the player's body movement. By tilting, players can increase their height and create space or close space on another player. The result is the tilt and hop. Very simply, a quick movement of the player's body while strapped into the wheelchair results in the wheelchair tipping over sideways on two wheels or lifting all four wheels off the ground if the movement is vertical.

The principles of tilting are the same as those used to do a wheelie. The only difference is instead of leaning backwards and finding their balance point, players lean sideways and find their balance point. In order to tilt, players should lean sideways, quickly throwing their weight over the axle on the side to which they intend to tilt. Usually, a player will first lean over the opposite axle and then

**The player creates height to get a rebound by using a tilt.**
Photo courtesy of the University of Illinois, photographers Mark Cowan and Curt Beamer.

quickly lean to the other side. To make the move easier, the player may grab on to the wheel opposite the direction of the tilt and pull up as momentum is transferred from one direction to another.

The keys to tilting and holding the tilt lie in several areas. First, athletes should keep their shoulders aligned with the backrest of the wheelchair. If one shoulder is more forward than another, the athlete will fall out of the tilt. The shoulder on the tilting side should describe a line directly down through the axle and the point of contact on the floor. Athletes should not lean back after getting their weight over the axle; they will lose the tilt and come down. When learning how to tilt, they should keep their hands on the wheels between the backrest and thigh. If the hands slide behind the backrest, the athlete could tip backwards. If the hands slide forward on the wheels, the athlete will carve out and come down forward. As athletes improve their balance, they will remove their hands from the wheels.

An offensive tilt is used to create space and height from the defence. This tilt is done when players tilt away from a defender and lean on the hand on the side to which they are tilting. This is done with the ball in the hand that is free and the player shooting from this position. A defensive tilt pulls up on a wheel and keeps ahold of that wheel as the defensive player leans closer to the offensive player and contests the shot with the free hand.

■ **Hopping.** Players use hopping to move the wheelchair from a position where an opponent is trying to hold them. In some instances, hopping occurs when a player is contesting a rebound. The force of the player's movement in one direction is such that it causes the wheelchair to go up with the rear wheels off the ground. Note that if the player hops the wheelchair off the ground while touching the basketball and doesn't have any hands in contact with a wheel, it is a technical foul.

## Wheelchair Skills

Each of the previously described skills can be practised while doing drills which are similar to the drills that are used in other sports such as soccer, basketball, and American football. The intent of the skills is to isolate these movements to get a lot of repetitions of the movement at an intense level. Following are wheelchair skills that serve as the core of most competitive wheelchair basketball teams, beginning with skills that address the fundamental movements and finish with more complex wheelchair drills and combinations of movements.

### ● POWER START AND STOP

**Purpose**
To develop the first two pushes needed for picking and defence

**Focus Points**
- Hand speed
- Explosive first push
- Complete stop
- Speed of trunk movement
- Speed of recovery to pushing position

## Execution

Each person has a partner, and both people are in wheelchairs. One partner lines up on the baseline of the basketball court, facing the other baseline. The second partner holds on to the back of the first person's wheelchair. The person in front begins by taking two maximal pushes and then immediately comes to a complete stop as quickly as possible. The first person repeats this until the far baseline is reached. The person behind holds on to the wheelchair the entire time. The person holding on should be careful of contact with the first person when the first person leans back to stop. The second person should also keep her arms straight to prevent contact between chairs when the first person stops. The partners switch when they reach the far baseline and then repeat the exercise coming back.

To increase the challenge, increase the size of the person being towed or the number of people being towed.

## ● HALF-COURT TOW

### Purpose

To develop the 10-push sequence, or the number of pushes that a typical player uses when pushing between the 3-point lines during offensive or defensive transition

### Focus Points

- Get to top speed as quickly as possible.
- Maintain high hand speed.
- Push all the way through to the end of the court.
- Stop sharply at the end of the court.

### Execution

Each person has a partner. Both partners are in wheelchairs and lined up on the baseline, facing the opposite baseline. One partner is in front of the other, with the second person holding on to the back of the first person's wheelchair. The first person begins pushing as quickly as possible to half-court. At half-court, the person who is holding on to the wheelchair releases while the first person continues to push as hard as possible, concentrating on maintaining hand speed and power. When both partners reach the baseline, they switch positions and come back.

To increase the challenge, increase the size of the person being towed or the number of people being towed.

## ● FORWARD PARTNER PULLS

### Purpose

To develop pushing ability

### Focus Point

To maintain speed at a high rate

### Execution

Each person has a partner. Both partners are in wheelchairs, lined up on the baseline and facing the same direction. One partner is in front while the other person is behind, holding on to the first person's wheelchair. The first person begins to push around the court as quickly as possible while towing the second person. Once a lap is completed, the partners switch positions.

To increase the challenge, increase the weight being towed or the number of people being towed.

## ● BACKWARD PARTNER PULLS

### Purpose
To develop pushing ability and maintain muscular training balance

### Focus Point
To maintain speed at a high rate

### Execution
This drill is executed in the same manner as forward partner pulls, but the partner who is towing the other pushes himself backwards, with the second person holding on to the front of the wheelchair while being pulled by the first. The partners switch positions once a lap is complete.

To increase the challenge, increase the weight being towed or the number of people being towed.

## ● CLOVERS

### Purpose
To develop motor learning patterns and the power in the movement needed in picking and jump-and-recover defence. Jump and recover is the defensive movement that allows a player on defence to move into proper guarding position (often referred to as *wheel position*) when a player receives the ball. The recover portion of this movement is the action a defensive player does when she collapses off an offensive player when the offensive player passes the ball. The distance a defensive player collapses is determined by a number of factors, including picking angles, offensive threats to score, and the defensive player's need to help other teammates.

### Focus Points
– Explode into the turn with either a push or a pull.
– Stop sharply and go right into the next turn.
– Turns should be one push in length.

### Execution
This drill is done individually. Mark four spots on the floor in the shape of a square. The square should be approximately 2 metres by 2 metres. Mark the centre of the square with a spot.

Beginning at one corner, the athlete pushes to the corner immediately to the right in such a way that the outside rear wheel of the wheelchair rolls over the centre mark of the square (see figure 8.1). This is a simple right turn. Once the opposite corner is reached, the athlete pulls backwards to the corner immediately to the left. In doing this, the player will continue around the square in a counterclockwise fashion, making sure that the outside wheel passes through the centre point of the square. The player will be changing from forward to backwards in order to go around the square. The player continues this manoeuvre until the halfway point of the station time. At the halfway point, change directions.

To increase the challenge, make the clover smaller or change directions during the station.

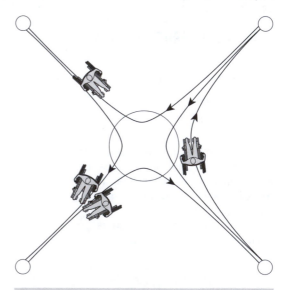

**Figure 8.1** Clovers movement pattern.

## • U-TURNS

### Purpose

To develop wheelchair control and the spatial awareness needed in picking and jump-and-recover defence

### Focus Points

- Focus on the rear-wheel position and not hitting rear wheels.
- Pivot quickly.
- Explode out of the pivot and into the stop.
- Maintain speed.

### Execution

This drill is done individually. Place an empty chair or wheelchair on the baseline of the court. The athlete begins with his wheelchair on the left side of the chair, facing in the same direction as the chair. The two wheelchairs will be side by side (see figure 8.2). The athlete pulls back, clearing the chair with the wheel, turns his chair to the right 360 degrees, pivoting the wheelchair in one spot, and pushes forward so that his wheelchair is on the left side of the empty chair. Repeat this for the left side, beginning by pulling back and clearing the wheel and turning 360 degrees to the left. The athlete should end up where he originally started. Repeat this exercise as quickly as possible for the entire time of the station.

To increase the challenge, add time for any contact with the stationary wheelchair, or move the wheelchair during the drill.

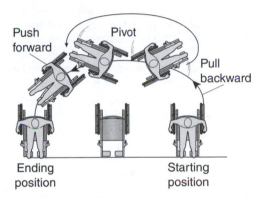

**Figure 8.2** U-Turns starting position and movement pattern.

## • HOPS

### Purpose

To teach transfer of momentum and lateral movement skills

### Focus Point

Quick weight transfer

### Execution

This drill is done individually. While strapped in the wheelchair, the athlete quickly hops both rear wheels or preferably all four wheels off the ground at the same time. The emphasis should be placed on height and distance moved laterally. The athlete should perform this manoeuvre at a developmentally appropriate level, progressing from using two hands on both rear wheels to hopping without any hands on the wheels.

To increase the challenge, do the following:

- Use a line to measure the distance hopped laterally.
- Move from having two hands on the wheels to no hands.
- Have the athlete hold on to a basketball while hopping.
- Jump over objects.

- ## TILTING

### Purpose
To teach transfer of momentum and individual knowledge of the person's centre of gravity in different planes

### Focus Points
- Shoulder should be even with the axle and the point of contact on the floor.
- Keep the weight back.
- Hold the weight over the point of contact.
- Keep head up.
- Keep hands over the axle.

### Execution
This drill is done individually in a wheelchair, and it is best performed while strapped into the wheelchair. The athlete tilts her wheelchair sideways on two wheels and attempts to hold her balance on the two wheels for as long as possible. She should perform this manoeuvre at a developmentally appropriate level, progressing from tilting with two hands, to tilting with one hand, to tilting without any hands. In addition, this drill can be done with a ball being passed by a thrower so that the athlete must tilt in order to catch the ball. The drill can also have the tilting person start with a ball held overhead and then tilting from that position.

To increase the challenge, do the following:

- Move from using two hands to tilt to using no hands to tilt.
- Tilt with a ball in the hands.
- Catch passes and shoot while tilting.
- Take a wheel off while tilting.

- ## CHRISTMAS TREES

### Purpose
To develop the wheelchair skills needed for one-on-one defence

### Focus Points
- Explode out of the pushes, pulls, and pivots.
- Stop sharply.

### Execution
This movement is done individually. It mirrors the movement executed when an athlete is playing one-on-one defence, following the retreat, reading, and readjusting defensive skill patterns. Beginning on the baseline in left corner of the court, the athlete faces the wheelchair toward the corner at a 45-degree angle and begins by pulling straight back twice, maintaining the 45-degree angle. He then stops and pivots right 90 degrees (see figure 8.3). This is a defensive quarter turn. Then he pushes forward once, maintaining the 45-degree angle to the baseline, stops, and pulls backwards twice. Then he pivots back to the left 90 degrees and takes one push forward. All movements are done as quickly and powerfully as possible with the athlete facing the baseline throughout the entire drill. All movements are repeated until the athlete reaches the opposite baseline while traveling backwards. He then begins the process coming back.

To increase the challenge, visualize a defensive matchup.

- ## JUMP AND RECOVER

### Purpose
To develop the mechanics needed for defensive jumping to the ball, contesting the ball, and recovering following the release of the ball

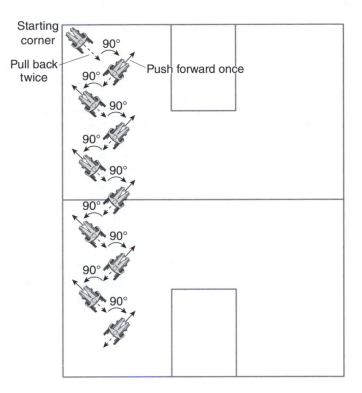

**Figure 8.3** Starting position and initial movement pattern for Christmas Trees.

## Focus Points
- Explosive push to start.
- Take an angle to the stop.
- Sharp stop.
- Get the hand to the passing lane high.
- Shout "Ball, ball, ball" all three times.
- Check shoulders on the recover.
- Stop in the help position.

## Execution
The athlete begins in the help spot in the middle of the key, facing the top of the key (see figure 8.4). At the beginning of the drill, the defensive player jumps to the spot to her right. As the player pushes to the first spot, she takes an angle so that the width of the wheelchair faces the spot. As she comes to a stop at this angle, the hand closest to the spot is raised above the head, as if to contest a ball held by an offensive player, and she shouts, "Ball, ball, ball!"

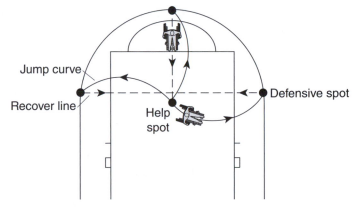

**Figure 8.4** Jump and Recover drill set-up.

as loudly as she can. She then turns the wheelchair and pushes quickly back to the help spot, checking the shoulders as she recovers.

Checking the shoulders refers to a player (it could be either an offensive or defensive player, but usually a defensive player) looking around to see all the players on the basketball court. Seeing all the other players allows the player to make the correct decisions as to the next action to take. The defensive player stops on the help spot and pivots. She then jumps to the middle spot, repeating the actions used during the first jump. The procedure is repeated for the third spot. Once the third spot has been touched, the defensive player begins again by jumping to the first spot and repeating the entire exercise.

Usually, this drill is done with one player to start. As players improve, a second player can be added. If a second player is added, then another help spot should also be added and a greater focus placed on communication between the two athletes.

To increase the challenge, have an offensive player change spots so the jump has to be read, or have a ball to contest in the hands of the offensive player.

# Shooting

There are many ideas on teaching shooting. As related to wheelchair basketball, a great many of these ideas directly carry over from the running game. However, there are significant differences that coaches and players need to be aware of. As we discuss some of these differences, keep in mind two things. First, when teaching shooting to players of wheelchair basketball, apply the principles from the running game and not necessarily the specifics. Second, the running game assumes symmetry of muscle function to a large degree. Because of disability, athletes rarely have symmetry in wheelchair basketball.

Let's use the age-old instructional paradigm of BEEF to discuss some of the differences: balance, eye, elbow, and follow-through.

## Balance

When we talk about balance in wheelchair basketball, we refer to two things. The first is balance in the chair. Proper sitting installation is critical. Strapping at the hips and other appropriate levels is a must to ensure that the body is not moving around unnecessarily. Balance in the chair also applies to functional levels. We want to always maximize the use of whatever function an athlete has. Players with leg function should use their legs as they shoot. A player with leg function should try to jump out of the wheelchair while shooting. This gives stability in the wheelchair by increasing the tightness of the fit, and it gives the person power if timed properly, much like the legs do in the running game.

The next level includes people who have fully or partially functioning back extensors. As the person shoots, we should see back extension. Back extension does several things. First, it gives power to the shot. This allows the muscles in the arms to be used for the fine motor aspects of the shot and not the gross motor aspects. Second, back extension provides more stability to the shooting platform. Third, with back extension comes an opening of the shoulders. By opening up the shoulders, the player can raise the follow-through higher and get the arc necessary to increase the probability of the ball going through the net. Try it—see how high you can follow through while hunched forward in the wheelchair.

As we look at the last group of shooters, those without leg function and back extension, we examine players typically from class 1 and some from class 2. These players should have full contact with the backrest of the chair. From this position, they will get a stable foundation from which to shoot. It's helpful for players of this classification to have a pocket in the back upholstery so that when they lean back, they get lateral stability, too. A slight decline in the backrest is also useful so that the process of leaning back is easier and players are held in contact with the backrest by gravity and not their shoulders. If the backrest is straight at 90 degrees, then players will have to use their shoulders to stay back. The process of raising the shoulder high in a follow-through runs counter to this, and we usually see a flat shot. The advent of the fifth and now sixth wheel has been critical to increased shooting function among players in lower classifications. This has allowed players to lean back without tipping over backwards, providing stability that was denied in the past.

The second aspect of balance is the balance of the ball on the hand. The greatest concern here relates to people who don't have full hand function or wrist flexion. Without full function, the platform from which the ball is shot is significantly unstable and inconsistent. Even with practice, people without full hand function will never be as consistent as those who do have full function. Some principles from the running game still apply. The ball should rest on the finger pads and not the heel of the hand. This will give the ball stability as it leaves for a shot. The wrist should be as close to 90 degrees as possible.

## Eye

There are three main perspectives on this area: Shooters should aim for front rim, back rim, or middle of the basket. My preference is the back rim so that when you get tired, if the ball comes up short it still goes in. Others prefer the front rim and have been very successful with that, as have players who shoot middle of the basket. Regardless of what you believe, you must have a specific target. I like to use the saying, "Aim big, miss big. Aim small, miss small." Narrow the focus point down as much as possible. Particularly with athletes with SCI, a narrow, specific focus point will help with shooting. Many people with SCI have learning difficulties, and providing a small focus point helps overcome that.

An example of this narrow focus point occurs when shooting free throws. I like my players to look at the seam at the back of the rim where the weld joins the two ends of the metal rim. This is a target about 2 centimetres high and .5 centimetres wide. Not only does this give players a very narrow place to aim,

### revolutions

- Practise pushing. A lot of athletes ignore this area of skill development, failing to maximize their mobility and possibly leading to injuries.
- Be creative when practising pushing. Hills make for great resistance when pushing up them, but there are lots of ways to create resistance.
- The goal of any shot in basketball is to get the shot off and get the ball in the basket. If athletes are doing these things, then they have a good shot. The purpose of the different shooting rules is to achieve these goals.
- Develop ball handling with one hand, especially catching. Wheelchair basketball is different from the running game in that one hand is used a lot more than two when handling the ball. Don't forget to work on both the right hand and left hand.

but coaches can check to make sure their players' visual acuity is good. The best shooting mechanics in the world don't matter if players cannot see the basket.

## Elbow

There are two things to keep in mind when looking at the elbow when shooting. First is the elbow starting position. The elbow doesn't need to be perfectly under the ball to start as long as it ends up under the ball. The elbow should start in a comfortable position behind the hand. The sooner the elbow can be under the hand, the better, because it puts the forces being applied to the ball in the same vector. The longer the elbow is moving in a vector that is different from where the player wants the ball to go, the more likely it is going to miss to one side of the basket.

The elbow starting position may vary from one player to another because of disability or sitting installation. Some people may not have normal range of motion in their elbows and that may affect their starting point. Keep in mind what the elbow must do—apply force in the same direction as the player wants the ball to go. As long as it does that, the player will be fine. Some players may sit at such a height or have such a short trunk that their elbow hits the wheel if they start with their elbow under the ball. These players can either adjust their sitting position by changing the wheel size or raising themselves in the wheelchair to allow them to start with their elbow under the ball as the ball moves upward.

## Follow-Through

Several points need to be discussed here. First is elbow position. Following from the previous section, the elbow should finish under the hand but also above the eye. If the elbow finishes above the eye, the arc of the ball for any shot outside the key is generally sufficient to give the shot a good probability that it will go in.

Ideally, the last point of contact on the ball should finish pointing at the target mentioned before in the section on the eye (page 129). For most players, this will be the index finger. The index finger should point at the target with the hand soft and flat and fingers spread. Some people have the middle finger as the last point of contact, and that is fine as long as it points at the target. Because of disability, there may be different points of final contact. The principle is what counts: Whatever is the last point to touch the ball should point at the target.

The drills we use to practise shooting are the same ones I used when I played running basketball. We don't use any special drills specific to wheelchair basketball. We keep in mind the previously mentioned principles as they relate to shooting in general and the unique issues relating to differences in function.

## Passing

When I first starting playing wheelchair basketball, we would spend hours and hours working on chest passes and bounce passes and a little time working on baseball passes and hook passes. This was a direct carryover from the running game. Now I don't have our players spend much time on chest passes or bounce passes at all. I might start by teaching these to younger players as a way of teaching passing principles, but once the principles are understood, we rarely go back to these passes. We do, however, spend a lot of time working on baseball passes and hook passes, especially for distance. This is one of the places where the wheelchair basketball game is different from the running game.

The vast majority of passes in wheelchair basketball are caught and made with one hand. The reason for this is the difficulty in protecting the ball. Our players always keep their body between the ball and the defender. In the running game, this is done by pivoting. In wheelchair basketball, players cannot always pivot because of defensive position, and they cannot always turn their body because of disability. In order to protect the ball, they move the ball instead of the body and chair. The result is one-handed passing and catching.

When we practise passing as a distinct skill, we do a simple drill with three people. One person passes with one hand while a defender contests the pass, and a third player is the catcher. Once the pass is made, the passer goes to the person who caught the pass and defends that person's pass. The catcher waits for the passer to come and defend the pass. The person who was defending becomes the catcher and so on. All passes are made with one hand, either right or left, and all

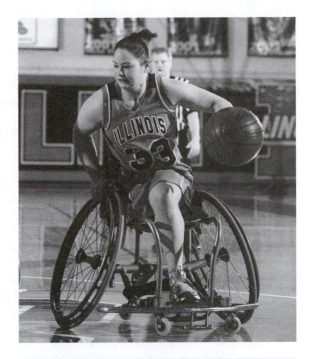

**This player uses one hand to push her wheelchair while using her other hand to dribble.**

Photo courtesy of the University of Illinois, photographers Mark Cowan and Curt Beamer.

passes are caught with one hand, either right or left. It is extremely important to practise all passes and catches with both the right and left hands. Again, because chair position by the defence doesn't always allow players to use their body to protect the ball, they must be able to catch and pass with both hands. As players improve, they move farther apart. As they move apart, even the most talented players will be challenged.

For additional drills, you can again use drills from the running game, but try to make players pass and catch with one hand where applicable.

## Dribbling

There are several thoughts on dribbling. Many people lift the ball from underneath in order to dribble the ball. We always see players spinning the ball sideways as they dribble up the court. I prefer to have players learn how to dribble as they would in the running game, with the hand on top of the ball. The reason for this is that the two functional skills that are unique to wheelchair basketball and used to control the dribble, the bounce stop and the bounce spin, are both done with the hand on top of the ball. If players have to move their hand from the side or underneath the ball to the top to execute a move, then it takes a little longer to execute the move. Often that is time players don't have, and the result is a turnover.

As mentioned previously, one of the distinct skills in wheelchair basketball is the bounce stop. As players move down the court dribbling, they bounce the ball at a 45-degree angle off the front caster, just slightly outside the plane of the rear wheel. This puts the final catch spot of the ball right next the player as momentum carries the player forward after the bounce. We want it just outside of the plane of the rear wheel so that it is easy to catch but the body is between the ball and the defender. To the greatest extent possible, the bounce should be no higher than the rear wheel. This protects the ball from the defence. The farther away from the body the player can catch the ball, the better. However, players in class 1 and some in class 2 will not always have the balance needed to function with power when the ball is farther from the midline of their body and centre of balance. Players in higher classes will be able to lean farther away from the midline as needed in order to protect the ball. Once the ball bounces, the player grabs both wheels at the same time and then catches the ball.

The second skill unique to wheelchair basketball is the bounce spin. This is exactly as it sounds—the ball is bounced and the player spins to change directions. This time, the player should bounce the ball next to the axle of the rear wheel, no higher than the rear wheel, then grab the rear wheels and spin under the ball so the ball is protected with the body, and finally catch the ball with the opposite hand from which the ball started, holding the ball away from the body.

I use two drills to practise dribbling. The first is also a defensive drill. We call it one-on-one shadow with a ball. We have up to five pairs doing this on a court at a time. Each player is matched with another player of approximately the same speed. One player is on defence and the other is on offence with a basketball. The drill begins at one baseline. The offensive player tries to dribble from the starting baseline to the opposite baseline, with the defensive player trying to stop him. If the offensive player beats the defensive player, he stops where he is and lets the defence catch up. The drill then continues. Remember, the point of the drill is dribbling practice and not full-court sprinting. Focus on using both hands in the dribble, protecting the ball with space and movement, and good execution of bounce stops and spins to change direction.

The second drill I use to practise dribbling is one-on-one quarter-court. With matchups of similar skills and ability, one player starts on offence at half-court, the other on defence. The boundaries are the sideline of one half of the court to the midline. The offensive player then attacks the defence, trying to score. There is no shot clock because we want the offence to dribble as much as possible to get in the repetitions needed. Each basket is worth 1 point. The defence can also score in this drill. If a shot is missed and the defence gains possession either by getting the rebound or the ball going out of bounds, the defence gets a point. The offensive player stays on offence until one player gets to 7 or any designated number; then they switch.

## Conclusion

This is a brief introduction to wheelchair basketball and some of the differences between it and the running game. Though there are many similarities between the two games, players and coaches need to be aware of the differences and complete the fundamental skills of the game with these differences in mind.

# chapter 9

# Wheelchair Racing

Tanni Grey-Thompson
and Ian Thompson

Photo courtesy of Nicholas Diaper.

Wheelchair racing is a fast, exciting, dynamic sport that offers opportunities to train and compete at any level, from recreational fun runners to Paralympic-level elite athletes. It is media friendly, with a combination of speed, equipment, colour, passion, and determination; and its now-familiar place within the big city marathons and road races makes it one of the disability sports most widely recognized by the general public.

Wheelchair racers now cover a wide range of distances up to and beyond the marathon, but in the earliest stages of the sport, it was thought that wheelchair racing could be dangerous to the health of competitors, and only races up to 91 metres (or 100 yards as it then was) were allowed, often with doctors and nurses waiting at the finish line. However, this began to change when, with drive from both athletes and organizers, it was recognized that the athletes enjoyed themselves and that they were able to compete over considerably longer distances with no ill effects. Racing was carried out in everyday chairs, even at the early major Games. These chairs were built from chrome steel and weighed in excess of 30 kilograms. They had high backrests, often with push handles, and swing-away footplates. They did not look like sport equipment—a far cry from the current racing chairs with their customized racing functionality, lightweight construction, and components. And training was a far cry from the optimal training regimes used by today's top racers.

## revolutions

### Wheelchair Racing Rules

The rules relating to wheelchair racing generally follow the International Association of Athletics Federations (IAAF) rules for athletics, with the International Wheelchair and Amputee Sport Federation (IWAS) official rules for athletics covering the specific details of the racing chair. A selection of the more important rules is described here.

- The racing chair shall have at least three wheels, with the maximum size of the two rear wheels (including inflated tyres) of 70 centimetres, and of the front wheel 50 centimetres.

- Only manual (hand or arm) propulsion and steering is allowed, with no gears, levers, handles, or chains.

- Only one plain round push rim per rear wheel is allowed.

- Mirrors are not allowed.

- There is no maximum length, but nothing shall extend out of the back of the rear wheels, forward beyond the front wheel hub, or sideways beyond the furthest point of the wheel, tyre, or push rim. (The chair length is limited by the practicalities of turning circle and reaching the steering.)

- Safety: When drafting, the front wheel of the following chair must not cross the vertical plane of the back edge of the rear wheels for the chair ahead. An overtaking athlete must ensure full clearance of the chair being overtaken before cutting across, and the overtaken athlete must not to impede the incoming athlete as soon as that athlete is in sight.

- The front wheel of the racing chair must be behind and not touching the start line. The finish point is the centre of the hub of the front wheel—not the leading edge of the front wheel or the athlete.

Today's racing wheelchair is up to 2 metres in length and has three wheels: 700c or 650c rear wheels, 10- to 14-degree cambered for stability and to better keep the tops of the wheels away from the underarm, plus the 51- or 46-centimetre front wheel. The main frame is made from lightweight, thin-walled aluminium tubing, and the wheels are lightweight spoked, carbon fibre disked, or carbon fibre tri and quad (broad) spoked. The steering is held by a dampner/damper spring, which attaches to the compensator lever on the main frame This rudder-type system points the front wheel where the athlete wants the chair to go (including around the bends of the track) by a mere tap to the lever. The push rims typically measure 35 to 42 centimetres depending on the arm length, strength, and preference of the athlete. Most athletes kneel in the racing chair to improve the air flow under the frame of the chair, aerodynamics, and comfort and function. The athlete leans well forward in the chair, again for aerodynamics and function.

A classification system ensures fair competition between athletes of similar impairment level and functional ability (see chapter 1), and athletes must meet the IPC minimum classification requirements to compete. From 100 to 800 metres, there are four racing classes (T51, T52, T53, T54). The additional trunk function of the T54 athlete over the T53 athlete shows itself principally at the race start. At the start, body movement supplements the arms in delivering force to the push rims, and the abdominal muscles help hold the body down in position, increasing the force delivered to the push rim. Above 800 metres, the contribution of this effect is significantly diminished, so from 1500 metres up to the marathon, the T53 class is dropped and there is only one class, T54. This is sometimes referred to as the *Open* category.

Classification is important for athletes competing at the more elite level. However, especially at lower levels and at smaller competitions, the most important point is that athletes compete. Athletes of different classes can compete against each other to mutual advantage where athletes' speeds and performances are matched. Likewise, women can obtain useful competition by racing against men of similar speed, particularly where the numbers of female racers are fewer.

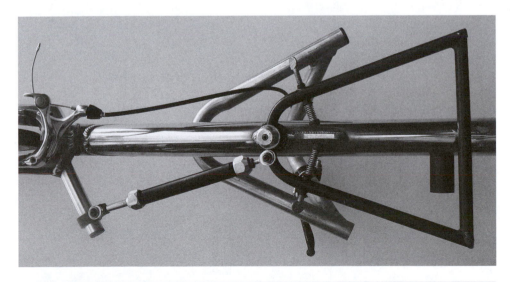

**Steering and compensator systems.**
Photo courtesy of Ian Thompson.

Specialization in events tends to come from body type. Low body weight and high power-to-weight ratio is to the benefit of short-distance sprinters, whereas larger, stronger athletes favour long-distance events. To perform well in endurance events requires athletes to maintain a high percentage of their top-end speed, as well as having a very high top-end speed. But it also requires athletes to accelerate well to get into the leading pack at the start of the race, to cover breaks, and in the final sprint. Sprinters build up significant distance in a pure sprint session as part of their active recovery, and to train at their top-end speed requires a strong endurance base. The requirements for speed in the endurance athlete and a strong endurance base in the sprinter are the reason why sprinters could produce a good distance race, particularly where they can use the slipstreaming (drafting) effect of a large pack of athletes, and an endurance athlete could produce a good sprint performance.

To become an effective wheelchair racer, the first priorities are to establish the correct seating position and to develop effective technique, which fits directly into effective glove design.

## Chair Set-Up

Obtaining the correct seating position to suit one's physical size and level of impairment is all-important to delivering optimum power to the push rim. The three keys to obtaining a good position are (A) horizontal position in relation to the rear axle, (B) seat height, and (C) knee height, aiming to have the gloved hand in contact with the push rim at 7 o'clock, with the arms not quite straight (imagine that the right push rim is the clock—see figure 9.1a-b).

The horizontal position in relation to the rear axle needs to be such that the chair is stable to tipping over backwards (especially on hills) but not so far for-

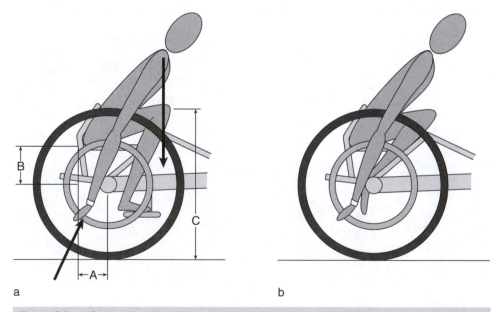

a

b

**Figure 9.1** Conventional position (a) versus kneeling position (b).

ward as to put too much weight on the front wheel. As a guide, while sitting in the most upright position it should not be too difficult to do a wheelie. The knee height should be high enough to provide support while pushing (especially for athletes with little trunk muscle function) but not so high as to be restrictive. With the knee height and position attained, the seat height should be adjusted such that when leaning in the pushing position with the arm very slightly bent at the elbow, the knuckles of the closed fist touch the inside bottom of the push rim at the 7 o'clock position, with the point of the shoulder between the push rim and the tyre. The next step is to determine the position of the legs—kneeling or conventional.

The conventional seating position is similar to that used in the day chair (though lower), and it is a good seating position for beginners and more highly impaired athletes. In this position, the feet are held in front of the rear-wheel axles and placed on a footplate or strap. Further strapping is used to support the legs, usually under the thigh, behind the knee, and around the ankles to prevent the feet from falling off their support. Care should also be taken to ensure that the strapping does not interfere with skin and tissue, possibly using padding between strap and skin (e.g., in the seat itself). Damage to skin and tissue can cause pressure sores and cuts, which can be very dangerous and also take considerable time to heal, resulting in time out of the racing chair.

The kneeling position is now the more popular (and aspirational) position. In this position, the feet are tucked behind the rear-wheel axles, with the support from knee to ankle coming from strapping and padding. This kneeling position can put a good deal of pressure on the knee joint if care is not taken to balance the support and loads. It is obviously a difficult position to reach for those with stiff leg joints and those who are prone to leg cramps, and it may be a difficult position to maintain for those lacking good balance. It is generally considered to be a more aerodynamic position than the conventional position—it was developed in an attempt to reduce the aerodynamic advantage double-leg amputees have over those using the conventional racing position—and for many, it is a more comfortable position. Getting into and out of this position takes practice, however.

## Gloves

Most wheelchair racers use gloves for hand protection, whether they are bought commercially or made by the racer. Making one's own gloves to meet personal requirements tends to be the best option, but it is more time consuming, at least initially. The key requirements are protection of the fingers and thumb, shaping to ensure optimum contact with the push rim, coating to provide good contact with the push rim, and structure to support the hand and ensure that the wrist and forearm are not under tension during the push. The hand needs to be held in a fairly neutral fist position, and the space between fingers and palm is filled with a moulding, some tubing, or tape to keep the hand relatively relaxed. For beginners, the taped gloves offer the best option since they provide protection but are relatively flexible, allowing the athlete to adjust positions slightly. Commercially available gloves tend to require experience of the technique before use, as do solid-type gloves. The technique requires contact with the push rim on the backs of the fingers, with the hand held in a fist—not on the palm of the hand, as with the day chair.

The T51 athlete requires more wrist support to achieve a good technique. A glove that has been used successfully consists of a strong leather glove with a strong wristband with straps that extends a few centimetres along the forearm. This keeps the wrist rigid and protects it from injury. There is padding and support on the thumb and back of hand, and the fingers are held in a fist by tape or strapping (there is no power in the fingers). The thumb is positioned outwards and rigid to aid in pushing.

**Glove types and constructions: traditional tape-padded glove (top row), Harness gloves (middle row), and solid gloves made from thermoplastic and covered with rubber (bottom row).**

Photos courtesy of Ian Thompson.

# Pushing Technique

The pushing technique has developed over the years, and there are now two general types of pushing techniques: the para backhand technique and the T51 technique. Originally the T51 and T52 classes had distinct pushing actions, whereas the T53 and T54 classes had largely similar actions. Thanks to the development of gloves, many T52s now have developed a para-style push.

The movement of the arms during the para backhand technique is shown in figure 9.2.

Contact is made around 1 o'clock with the backs of the fingers around the first joint below the knuckle. The thumb is used as a guide, not to provide force. The wrist becomes slightly cocked and turns inside the push rim as the elbows drive inwards. The hand drives down the inside of the push rim, with the palm of the hand (in a fist) parallel with the wheel—this maintains good shoulder joint positioning. At release, at around 7 o'clock, there is a slight twist at the wrist as it uncocks, and this, along with the momentum of the hands, throws the hand back into follow-through. The hand follows and arches backwards, assisted by a pulling upwards of the elbows. The hand then recovers back towards the next contact. The sweet spot of the technique is from 4 to 7 o'clock, and power (speed of force) is more important than strength—at a top speed around 40 kilometres per hour, there is only 0.1 second to deliver the push stroke.

Some common mistakes in the technique include the following:

- Contact is not sharp and relaxed, resulting in the push rim being slowed and the hand recoiled.
- Wide hand and arm position during recovery result in poor shoulder position (and potentially higher risk of injury).
- Early release from the push rim means not all of the available rim is being used.
- Early release and little follow-through mean that the momentum of the arms is not being used to raise them for the next push—high elbows may

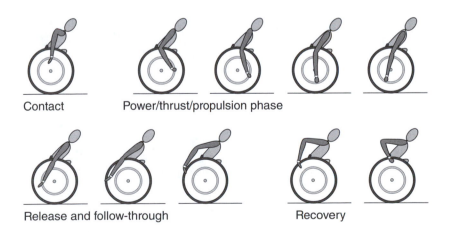

Contact          Power/thrust/propulsion phase

Release and follow-through          Recovery

**Figure 9.2**  Para backhand schematic showing the phases of the push.

be achieved in spite of this, and thus it can be difficult for the less skilled observer to pick this fault up.

- Use of thumb in the stroke puts the fist in a poor position at the bottom of the push.
- Wide elbows should not be maintained after contact strike.
- There may be an overall lack of smoothness or connection between the phases, particularly between release and recovery.

Owing to lack of triceps, the T51 technique may differ significantly from the para backhand technique (see figure 9.3). The hand remains in contact with the rim as much as possible, with the palm mainly perpendicular to the push rim and the thumb on the top outer side of the push rim, as in the contact-and-release diagram shown earlier. The power in the stroke comes from 1 to 5 o'clock using the available shoulder power to push the hand down the push rim (push phase), as well as from 7 to 11 o'clock using the biceps and shoulder to pull the hand up the back of the push rim (pull phase). A smaller, fatter push rim assists the technique.

## Training Programme

To succeed in wheelchair racing, a periodized and progressive approach to training is required. The structure of the wheelchair racing calendar, with the road racing season peaking in the spring and late summer and autumn (the big city marathons) and the track racing season reaching peaks in the late spring and summer (national and international championships), lends itself to single or double periodized training. Wheelchair racers tend to race fairly often, using many of the races to develop fitness and tactics for the major events. Track racers use the early-season events to achieve qualification times for later-season major championships.

The structure of the athlete's annual training programme will reflect periods of preparation, using higher training quantities to build the athlete's capacity to train, and periods of competition and preparation for competition, where the focus

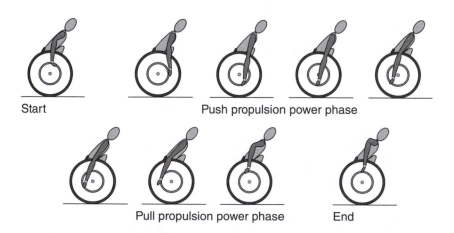

Start

Push propulsion power phase

Pull propulsion power phase

End

**Figure 9.3** T51 pushing schematic showing the phases of the push.

is turned towards quality of training. Regardless, the need to deliver technique effectively should remain a priority, ensuring that training is carried out over a range of speeds, especially work at high speed. The targets for the year should be clear, including time targets, finishing-position targets, and process targets, such as developing particular skills and characteristics.

A typical season programme, including the phases of training and variation in quantity and quality of training, is shown in figure 9.4 (overview) and figure 9.5 (detail).

# Skill and Fitness Training

The wheelchair athlete's training reflects the need to develop and maintain speed, strength, stamina, suppleness, technique, and tactics. Some of the key drills and training sessions are described next.

## Pushing Technique

The key aspects of the pushing techniques are drilled using a combination of low- and high-resistance pushing. Training rollers or treadmills are particularly effective, using the coach, a mirror, or video analysis to provide feedback to the athlete. The full cycle of the technique is carried out, but different phases of the stroke are emphasized: high elbows (at higher speed), contact and drive into the front of the push rim (at low and high resistance), and drive through the bottom and out of the back of the push rim (at lower and higher speeds). This phase emphasis—ideally up to 10 push sets—should be interspersed with full normal technique to ensure that connection between the phases is maintained. One-armed pushing, with the other hand on the steering or frame, is also useful in developing the feeling of the technique.

## Chair Handling

Various degrees of tightness of corner should be used to practise cornering. Using the correct racing line can save time and maintain speed—the less time spent off the push rim, the better. Tight corners should be approached wide and steered around while leaning well into the corner. Less-tight corners can be pushed around with one hand steering and the other pushing, by using the compensator and maintaining pushing, or by hopping the front wheel and maintaining pushing.

Slickness of track compensator hitting should be practised, aiming to hit the compensator with one hand while still pushing with the other. Obviously, this needs to be done on the track for timing accuracy, but the required arm action and coordination can be practised on the rollers or on the track or road by hitting the frame rather than the compensator.

## Drafting

Drafting, or slipstreaming, reduces wind resistance and means that athletes can push faster and longer than they could when pushing alone. When a group, or pack, of athletes shares the leading and drafting, the pack is able to travel faster than any individual in the group—the leading athlete is able to work harder on the front, because after awhile she will be able to drop back into the pack and recover as someone else takes the lead.

Drafting drills require the pack of athletes to take turns at the front of the pack. With the pack travelling at the agreed pace, the lead athlete peels off the front, easing back slightly. When he reaches a position close to the back of the pack, he accelerates slightly, back up to the pace of the pack, and moves in behind the last athlete. As he leaves the front of the pack, the second-place athlete increases his efforts slightly in order to maintain the speed of the previous lead. He holds the pace for 30 to 60 seconds before peeling off the front, and so the cycle continues.

## revolutions

### Wheelchair Racing Innovation and Technology

The quest for perfection in wheelchair racing equipment, training, and coaching continues. Recently, solid gloves have become popular, using the development in thermoplastics to produce effective and durable gloves onto which various materials can be affixed to improve contact (e.g., rubber, abrasives). In the 1980s, German athletes experimented with solid gloves but used cloth tape to build the gloves, which suffered from excessive wear in adverse conditions. Aligned with advances in glove technology, push-rim coatings are being experimented with, such as using rubber or elastomer coatings with a greater degree of compressibility than the more traditional tyre coatings. However, there is not yet a fully reliable method for maintaining strong contact grip in the wet—klisters, pine tars, and ski waxes assist, but are not an ideal solution.

As chairs have become longer, the steering bars have moved farther away, reducing the effectiveness of the steering. To solve this, strongly raked forks and steep sloping have been introduced and the steering and compensator moved to the top of the frame. This has moved the steering closer to the athlete and to a position to improve the aerodynamics of the athlete's tuck.

Aerodynamics has also been improved by the use of helmets, disk wheels, and structural fairing of the racing chair frame—a shell or enclosure of the frame around the lower body of the athlete to improve airflow. To take account of the camber of the wheel, one manufacturer has produced a carbon fibre disc wheel with an angled wheel rim to put the tyre in better contact with the track or road. The jury is still out on this one.

Chair components have continued to follow the developments in cycling, with carbon fibre being the material of choice, particularly for wheels, brake levers, and brakes. However, carbon fibre has yet to be fully embraced as a frame material. The chair seat has been particularly difficult to mould in carbon fibre at a reasonable cost.

Heart rate monitors and cycle computers have been used for a number of years to assist in prescribing and monitoring training. Heart rate monitoring is particularly useful when combined with regular lactate-response testing to determine the most appropriate heart rate training zone. In cycling, the measurement and monitoring of power in training is supplementing or even supplanting heart rate training. Power is the measure of the rate of energy input into the bicycle. Power is an immediate measure of the workload, whereas heart rate is a delayed response—the body responding to the workload. There has been some work to use power measurements in wheelchair racing, more specifically with on-chair devices directly measuring the power delivered to the push rim. Such technology can also provide insights into technique, gathering data on power delivery, distribution of force and power around the push rim, hand contact and release point, and cadence. This would be a significant development in the coaching of top-class performance athletes and novices alike.

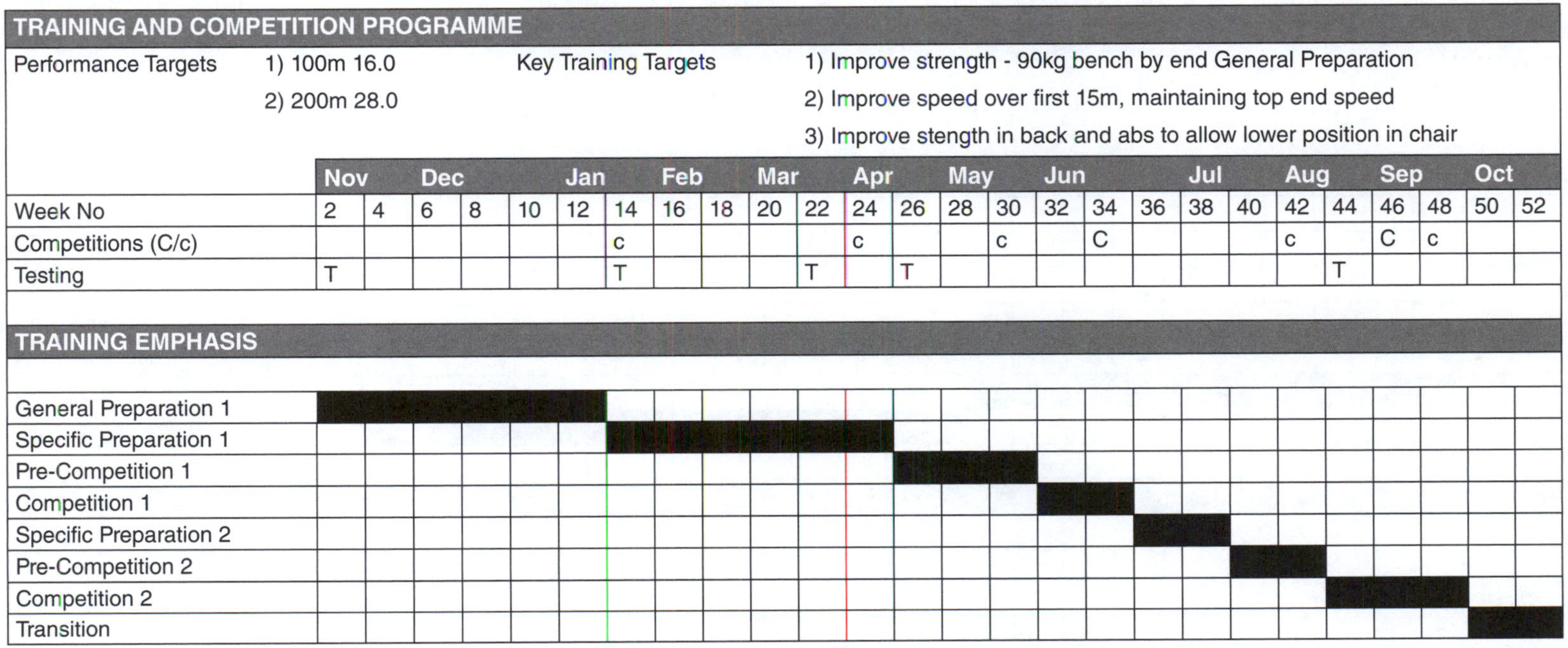

# TRAINING AND COMPETITION PROGRAMME

**Performance Targets**  1) 100m 16.0  2) 200m 28.0

**Key Training Targets**
1) Improve strength - 90kg bench by end General Preparation
2) Improve speed over first 15m, maintaining top end speed
3) Improve stength in back and abs to allow lower position in chair

| | Nov | | Dec | | | Jan | | Feb | | Mar | | Apr | | May | | Jun | | | Jul | | Aug | | Sep | | Oct | |
|---|---|---|---|---|---|---|---|---|---|---|---|---|---|---|---|---|---|---|---|---|---|---|---|---|---|---|
| Week No | 2 | 4 | 6 | 8 | 10 | 12 | 14 | 16 | 18 | 20 | 22 | 24 | 26 | 28 | 30 | 32 | 34 | 36 | 38 | 40 | 42 | 44 | 46 | 48 | 50 | 52 |
| Competitions (C/c) | | | | | | | c | | | | | c | | | c | | C | | | | c | | C | c | | |
| Testing | T | | | | | | T | | | | T | | T | | | | | | | | | T | | | | |

## TRAINING EMPHASIS

| |
|---|
| General Preparation 1 |
| Specific Preparation 1 |
| Pre-Competition 1 |
| Competition 1 |
| Specific Preparation 2 |
| Pre-Competition 2 |
| Competition 2 |
| Transition |

**Figure 9.4**  Typical annual training plan showing training phases (C/c indicate major and minor competitions respectively)

## DETAILED GENERAL AND SPECIFIC PHASES

| | Oct Nov | | | | | Dec | | | | | Jan | | | | Feb | | | | Mar | | | | | Apr |
|---|---|---|---|---|---|---|---|---|---|---|---|---|---|---|---|---|---|---|---|---|---|---|---|---|
| Week beginning | 28 | 4 | 11 | 18 | 25 | 2 | 9 | 16 | 23 | 30 | 6 | 13 | 20 | 27 | 3 | 10 | 17 | 24 | 3 | 10 | 17 | 24 | 31 | 7 |
| Week no. | 1 | 2 | 3 | 4 | 5 | 6 | 7 | 8 | 9 | 10 | 11 | 12 | 13 | 14 | 15 | 16 | 17 | 18 | 19 | 20 | 21 | 22 | 23 | 24 |
| Competitions (C/c) | | | | | | | | | | | | | | | | | | | c | | | | | c |
| Testing | T | | | | | | | | | | | | T | | | | | | | | T | | | |

## TRAINING EMPHASIS

| | Oct Nov | | | | | Dec | | | | | Jan | | | | Feb | | | | Mar | | | | | Apr |
|---|---|---|---|---|---|---|---|---|---|---|---|---|---|---|---|---|---|---|---|---|---|---|---|---|
| General preparation 1 | ■ | ■ | ■ | ■ | ■ | ■ | ■ | ■ | ■ | ■ | ■ | | | | | | | | | | | | | |
| Specific preparation 1 | | | | | | | | | | | | ■ | ■ | ■ | ■ | ■ | ■ | ■ | ■ | ■ | ■ | ■ | ■ | |
| Precompetition 1 | | | | | | | | | | | | | | | | | | | | | | | | |
| Competition 1 | | | | | | | | | | | | | | | | | | | | | | | | |
| Specific preparation 2 | | | | | | | | | | | | | | | | | | | | | | | | |
| Precompetition 2 | | | | | | | | | | | | | | | | | | | | | | | | |
| Competition 2 | | | | | | | | | | | | | | | | | | | | | | | | |
| Transition | | | | | | | | | | | | | | | | | | | | | | | | |
| Training sessions/week | 6 | 6 | 6 | 6 | 9 | 9 | 9 | 9 | 12 | 12 | 12 | 11 | 11 | 11 | 11 | 11 | 11 | 11 | 11 | 11 | 11 | 11 | 11 | 9 |

**Figure 9.5** An expansion of the first two phases of the training plan to show the variation of volume and intensity of training (C/c indicate major and minor competitions respectively)

*(continued)*

## TRAINING LOAD

| Volume x / intensity o | | | | | | |
|---|---|---|---|---|---|---|
| 100% | | | | | | |
| 95% | | | | | | |
| 90% | | | | | | |
| 85% | | | | | | |
| 80% | | | | | | |
| 75% | | | | | | |
| 70% | | | | | | |
| 65% | | | | | | |
| 60% | | | | | | |
| 55% | | | | | | |
| 50% | | | | | | |
| | 3:1 | 3:1 | 3:1 | 3:1 | 3:1 | 3:1 |
| Stamina % | 40 | 40 | 35 | 25 | 25 | 25 |
| Strength % | 30 | 25 | 30 | 30 | 30 | 30 |
| Speed % | 10 | 15 | 15 | 20 | 20 | 20 |
| Skill % | 10 | 10 | 10 | 15 | 15 | 15 |
| Suppleness % | 10 | 10 | 10 | 10 | 10 | 10 |

Ratio of loading to unloading within mesocycle

**Figure 9.5** *(continued)*

## Flexibility and Injury Prevention

Although wheelchair racers are not particularly prone to injury, the shoulder is an area that can suffer in the long term due to impingement in the shoulder joint. Flexibility around the shoulder is key (maintaining the length of the pectorals), as well as strength in the rotator cuff, rear shoulder, and upper back—there should be front and back balance to the shoulder. The rotator cuff and lower trapezius exercises should be done to relatively high reps (15-20) with little or no weight; for example, lying prone, arms straight above head, thumbs up, lifting arms straight up; lying prone, arms by sides, palms up, lifting and externally rotating arms; or prone rowing using light weight, pulling elbows above shoulder height, with elbow positions between shoulder level and side of body. Stretching the pectorals is best carried out with assistance, the extended arms being held at or slightly above shoulder height and pulled straight backwards until a stretch is felt in the chest. It is also important to use stretching to ensure good flexibility in front and rear shoulder, lats, lower back, and legs (even for those with little or no leg function).

## Overspeed

The ability to achieve a high top-end speed (up to 40 kph) and to maintain a high proportion of this for long periods is key to top-level performance in sprints and long-distance events alike. At these speeds, the hand is in contact with the push rim for only 0.1 second, and thus timing is everything. The development of the technique to achieve such speeds is best done using overspeed and reduced loads to allow athletes to push faster than they could do otherwise. Using a strong tailwind; a long, slight decline; and very lightly loaded rollers or drafting behind a bicycle, handcycle, or another athlete are most common. Drafting behind motor vehicles is not recommended.

When using overspeed to increase top-end speed, the target is to get the racing chair moving 2 to 3 kilometres faster than the speed the athlete is currently able to push effectively without slowing down the push rim and the racing chair. This is most conveniently achieved on a long, slight downhill stretch. The athlete coasts up to the appropriate speed and she aims to push at the higher speed, feeling for the push rim and focusing on the drive through and off the bottom of the push rim. It involves relatively low cadence but high hand speed. This is achieved by maintaining relaxed shoulders, chest, and arms and using the feedback from the push rim to match the speed of the push rim to the speed of the hand. Concentration needs to be high, so this type of session is ideally done in a state of low fatigue. Initially, the focus should be on keeping up with the speed of the push rim and then progressing to delivering increased force at that speed. This is an excellent drill to improve athletes' understanding of their technique and to stress the phases of the push. The faster release phase and follow-through lead to higher elbow height and speed of hand drive into the push rim, and the higher elbow lift leads to faster push-rim contact speed and faster follow-through. The athlete should push until the technique starts to fail and then adjust the speed to allow 5 to 30 consecutive quality pushes.

Overspeed is widely used to develop high speed endurance, particularly with long tailwind or paced road interval sessions. Again, this requires a high level of concentration, focusing on the phases of the push. This applies to distance and endurance athletes alike.

## Finishing Sprints and Acceleration

The aim of this drill is to increase speed endurance to maximize performance close to top-end speed, which is particularly useful for the sprint at the end of middle- and long-distance events, as well as in midrace accelerations. The athlete pushes close to top-end speed under reduced load (equivalent of being in the draft of the racing pack), and then aims to accelerate and maintain top-end speed with the load reinstated. The unload–load condition is achieved by slight downhill, easing down to flat; pacing behind another athlete, cyclist, or handcyclist before coming out of slipstream; and a roller system with resistance adjusted through the set. The unload and load periods simulate race conditions, such as 800 metres unloaded, 200 to 400 metres loaded. This training is also used to develop lactate tolerance at the high speeds.

## Cadence Changes

In order to accelerate, there are two options: Increase the force or power, or increase the cadence. Both of these should be within the arsenal of the wheelchair racer. Developing the change in cadence may be preferable, because it relies less on the need to increase force and is more likely to deliver an immediate speed increase. Both the change in cadence and the acceleration with higher cadence need to be developed. Measuring cadence is best done using the stopwatch on the cycle computer, counting pushes over a short time (say, 10 seconds), and doing the math.

On a steady-state push, the athlete is required to push at prescribed cadences for certain periods of time (30 to 120 seconds) before returning to the personally selected cadence. The change in cadence should be fairly rapid but without an associated acceleration. This gets athletes used to pushing at different cadences and helps them to recognize approximate target cadences. The next drill requires the athlete to accelerate using a change in cadence, ideally aiming for some quantifiable change (e.g., standard, higher, high, or very high, or 80, 100, 120, or 150 pushes per minute).

## Starting Sprints and Acceleration

There is a gradual evolution of the push length from the standing start, accelerating up to top speed (see table 9.1).

TABLE 9.1

### Evolution of Speed, Cadence, and Push Length During the Start and Acceleration Phase

| Push number | 1 | 2 | 3 | 4 | 5 | 6 | 7 | 8 | 10 | 12 | 14 | | 50 |
|---|---|---|---|---|---|---|---|---|---|---|---|---|---|
| Push length (°) | 140 | 150 | 160 | 160 | 170 | 160 | 160 | 200 | 180 | 200 | 200 | | 190 |
| Cadence (push/min) | 47 | | | 82 | | 100 | | 112 | | | 120 | | 105 |
| Speed (kph) | | 10 | | | | | | 16 | | | 22 | | 32 |

The initial pushes are relatively short, using shoulder and arm extension to drive the front of the push rim—at low speed, there is little momentum in the arm and hand to make best use of the bottom of the push rim. The stroke gradually lengthens, and the cadence increases in the acceleration phase before the momentum in the arms develops and the cadence falls and settles. Therefore, drills to develop the start and acceleration take account of this: standing starts accelerating up 20 and 30 metres; low-speed rolling acceleration to focus on high-cadence elements (10-30 m); and medium-speed rolling acceleration to focus on the lower cadence power elements (30-80 m). As a technique session, recoveries can be relatively short, but in developing the physiology of the anaerobic alactic system, full (active) recoveries are required. Linking the phases of the sprint together is obviously a must.

A development of the start and acceleration drill is the addition of resistance. A fellow athlete in her day chair holds the back of the racer's chair, or a tyre on a rope can be tied to the back of the racer's chair. The athlete carries out the start or acceleration under this higher load. The load can be released at a predetermined point during the start or acceleration, transferring the strength from the load into speed. Hill starts can also be used to develop strength in the sprint.

## Interval Training

Interval training is bread and butter to the wheelchair racing coach and athlete, with the load and recovery elements being balanced to improve endurance, lactate accumulation, and lactate tolerance. To best use interval training, knowledge of the point at which the athlete starts to accumulate lactic acid (lactate turnpoint or threshold) is required, plus a means to monitor this during training—the best current method is a heart rate monitor. Thus athletes will be working at a target heart rate for many of the sessions and can ideally record and download the session information at the end of training using a suitable heart rate monitor. For sprint intervals, the recoveries tend to be longer and the periods of work more intense, such as 400-metre reps with up to 10 minutes of active recovery. Endurance athletes may work up to 5-minute intervals with shorter recoveries, but care must be taken to maintain the quality of the intervals throughout the session. Figure 9.6 shows some sample interval training programmes.

## Tempo and Fartlek Work

Tempo and fartlek training involve race simulation that is close to but not at race pace. The fartlek elements take the load up to the race situation and generate lactate for removal in the less brisk elements of the session. These sessions can be up to 20 kilometres, but they are not just endurance pushes; the intensity is higher. Figure 9.7 shows some sample training sessions.

## Racing Tactics for Sprints

In developing sprinting technique and strategy, athletes and their coaches need to determine the balance of initial hand position on the rim, initial (and first few strokes) push length, and timing of cadence changes and lengthening of push. Come race day, the conditions will affect these transition points, since the wind speed and direction will affect the speed of the chair. Tactics are particularly important in the 400 metre, where a balance of energy is required—typically, all-out start, hold second 100 metres, kick third 100 metres, and hold and kick the final 100 metres—but again, conditions will affect this.

These intervals follow a 10-minute warm-up of gradually increasing speed, including two to four 15-second flying max efforts, and are followed by a cool-down of 10 minutes of gradually reduced speed. The focus throughout should be on good technique.

***All-out speed intervals (from low pace):***
- 5 × 30 s with 90 s active recovery (AR)
- 5 × 60 s with 120 s AR
- 5 × 30 s with 90 s AR

***Drafting simulation at and below 1500-metre pace (leading and drafting):***
- 3 min on, 2 min off
- 1 min on, 1 min off
- 4 min on, 2 min off × 3-5

***Lactate tolerance at high speed:***
- 15-second sprint to max
- 15-second coast for 5 min on, 3 min AR × 3-5

***Speed and strength endurance—near-max efforts:***
- Tailwind 1 min on, 2 min AR, headwind 1 min on, 2 min AR × 2
- Tailwind 2 min on, 2 min AR, headwind 2 min on, 2 min AR × 2
- Tailwind 1 min on, 2 min AR × 2

***Endurance intervals—race pace, lactate threshold***
- 2 × 5 × 3-5 min on, 1-5 min AR

**Figure 9.6** Sample interval training sessions.

***Tempo:***
- 3 × 15 min just below 1500-metre / 5K pace

***Fartlek:***
- 3 × 15 min at 10K pace with 20-second pickups every 3 min

***Tempo:***
- 2 × 20 min at 10K pace

***Fartlek:***
- 40 min with 10 × 15-second sprints with random timings to simulate race scenarios

**Figure 9.7** Sample tempo and fartlek training sessions.

## Racing Tactics for Endurance

Tactics will obviously depend on the course and the competition, but the key points for athletes are to know and work to their strengths and to know and work to the strengths and weaknesses of others. There is a significant speed advantage of working in a pack, so lone breaks need to be well timed, taking into account the size of the pack and the quality of athletes in the pack. Likewise, once in a pack, all effort should be made to stay in it. A poor hill climber may want to attack before a hill to provide a lead of at least as much time as he would be expecting to have lost should he have been in the pack. There may also be opportunities to break up the pack where it may be appropriate (e.g., to drop someone with a strong sprint who is saving her energies by hiding in the pack).

## Conclusion

Wheelchair racing is a highly developed and technical sport. It offers the opportunity to compete at the highest performance level, to race recreationally and keep fit, and to cross-train when athletes are participants in other wheelchair sports. The key to success in wheelchair racing lies is an appropriate training programme and in optimized seating position and technique to deliver the fitness and power of the athlete through the racing chair. The non-weight-bearing nature of the sport—overcoming wind and rolling resistance rather than gravity—means that training methods draw from a wider range of direction than the standard athletics principles. The sprinter and long-distance wheelchair racer will both need to incorporate a combination of speed and endurance in their training to support their racing and training demands.

# Wheelchair Rugby

Kevin Orr and Laurie A. Malone

Wheelchair rugby is an exciting, fast-paced, dynamic team sport. Also known as *quad rugby,* and previously referred to as *murderball* due to the aggressive and hard-hitting nature of the sport, wheelchair rugby was started in the early 1970s by a group of Canadians with tetraplegia looking for an alternative to wheelchair basketball. Although possessing athletic ability, players with tetraplegia on wheelchair basketball teams were given secondary roles at best due to the loss of function in their upper extremities.

As the sport grew in Canada, wheelchair rugby first appeared in the United States as a demonstration event at a regional multisport competition in the late 1970s. Soon after, the first team in the United States was formed, followed by the first international tournament in 1982, with teams from the United States and Canada. Throughout the 1980s, other local and national tournaments began to take place in various countries. The first international tournament to include a team from outside North America, specifically Great Britain, was held in 1989. As an exhibition event, wheelchair rugby was first played at the World Wheelchair Games in 1990.

The International Wheelchair Rugby Federation (IWRF) was formed in 1993 with 15 charter member teams, and the following year it was officially recognized by the IPC as a Paralympic sport. In 1995 the first Rugby World Championships were held, the next year wheelchair rugby was included as a demonstration sport at the Atlanta Paralympic Games, and finally it was included as a full-medal sport at the 2000 Sydney Paralympic Games. Today, wheelchair rugby is still developing around the world, with play reaching semi-professional levels.

## Game Play and Rules

Wheelchair rugby is a full-contact (chair-on-chair) game played on an indoor court measuring 15 metres in width by 28 metres in length (see figure 10.1). Each team may have up to 12 players with no more than 4 players on the court at any one time. A regulation volleyball is used and must be bounced or passed between teammates at least once every 10 seconds during play. The ball may be thrown, bumped, passed, or dribbled in any direction as outlined in the rules. The court is similar to a basketball court yet has unique features, including penalty boxes adjacent to the court and key area, a portion of the baseline marked with cones to delineate the goal line and key area. In sanctioned play, athletes compete in manual wheelchairs and follow detailed specifications for the wheelchairs to ensure safety and fairness.

The object of the game is to score more points than the opposing team; 1 point is awarded when a player who has possession of the ball passes two wheels over the goal line. The game is played in four 8-minute stop-time quarters with 3-minute overtime periods if necessary. The team with the most points wins.

A number of penalties can occur in wheelchair rugby. If a penalty is granted when a team is on offence, then the play results in a turnover. On defence, players who are penalized are placed in the penalty box and are released when the opposition scores a goal or after 1 minute is served.

Some of the basic rules are as follows:

- Six timeouts are allowed for each team, plus one extra for each overtime played.
- Players must dribble or pass within 10 seconds.

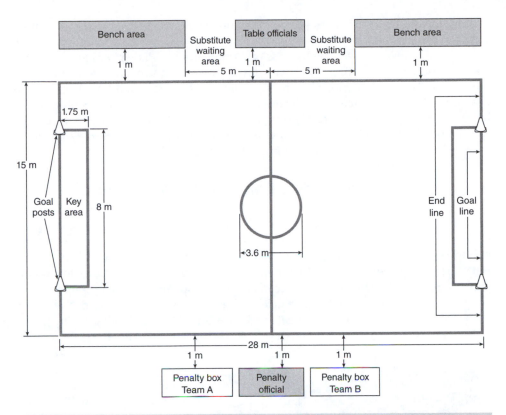

**Figure 10.1**  Wheelchair rugby court set-up.
Courtesy of the International Wheelchair Rugby Federation—www.iwrf.com

- Ball must be advanced over half-court in 12 seconds or less.
- Ball must be inbounded within 10 seconds.
- Teams must score within 40 seconds after the ball is inbounded.
- Offensive players cannot be in the key longer than 10 seconds.
- Only three defenders are allowed in the key at one time.
- Spinning is not allowed (i.e., hitting an opposing player's chair behind the axles, causing the player to turn dramatically).

## Classification

Wheelchair rugby uses a classification system based on levels of function, giving individuals with a wide range of disabilities an opportunity to play in fair and equitable competition. To be eligible, players must have a disability that affects both the arms and the legs, including the following disability types: tetraplegia secondary to SCI (C5-C7), high-level paraplegia with a brachial plexus injury, transverse myelitis, post-polio disability, bilateral upper- and lower-extremity limb loss, and cerebral palsy. Individuals with a neurological diagnosis that affects at least three limbs, or a non-neurological condition that affects all four limbs may be eligible to play. Athletes are classified based on function in their hands, arms, shoulders, and trunk. Further, the classification system is based on physical function, not athletic ability. There are seven player classifications ranging from 0.5 to 3.5, with the lower classes having less functional ability. Players are given a point value corresponding to their functional level. The maximum point value per team allowed on the court at any time during a game is 8.0. For each female player on the court, however, a team is allowed an extra 0.5 points over the 8.0 points. A team can play with fewer than 8.0 points, but strategically aim to maximize the functional ability on the court. Team selection with consideration to varying player point value combinations is a very important task for the coach.

## Equipment Selection and Maintenance

Wheelchair rugby is played in a manual wheelchair, typically custom designed for rugby and adjusted to suit the player's comfort and safety needs. Wheelchair set-up is crucial. Each wheelchair should be specifically measured and custom built for an individual player, fitting like a good pair of shoes—snug, not too big and not too small. The chair also needs to be set up for the player's role on the court, offensive or defensive. The offensive chair is set up with wings between the front bumper and the rear wheels and is designed to avoid being easily picked or held by the opposition. A defensive chair is set up with a big bumper and open space between the rear wheel and the front of the chair to maximize the ability to hit and hold an opponent. Typically, higher-point players (2.0-3.5) play in offensive chairs and lower-point players (0.5-1.5) play in defensive chairs.

The wheelchair is considered to be part of the player. Players are responsible for ensuring that their wheelchair meets all specifications for the duration of the game. A wheelchair cannot be used until it is brought into compliance with these specifications. The rules include detailed specifications for the wheelchair and key design features (e.g., wheelchair height and length, wheel diameter, cushion thickness). All wheelchairs must be equipped with spoke protectors and an anti-tip device at the back. In addition, the wheels are attached at an angle (camber) for greater stability.

**In rugby, the wheelchair is part of the player and custom designed with a player's offensive or defensive role in mind.**
© Paralyzed Veterans of America/Sports 'n Spokes. Photo by Mark Cowan.

Players are allowed to use a variety of other personal equipment, such as gloves, applied adhesives to assist with ball handling, and strapping (trunk, waist, leg, foot) to help the athlete maintain a good sitting position. The strapping used will depend on the player's needs. Gloves and taping at the forearms can also protect against skin abrasions. Players may wear any form of hand protection; however, it cannot include any material that may be hazardous to other players, such as hard or rough material.

## Fundamental Skills

The fundamental skills of wheelchair rugby include wheelchair mobility, ball handling, passing and catching, picking, blocking, and screening. The technique used by each athlete for each skill will vary depending on level of function. Wheelchair mobility depends on use of the available muscles and appropriate wheelchair set-up, including the seating position, type of push rims, and type of spoke guards. Picking the ball off the floor is a skill that must be mastered on both the right and left sides of the wheelchair. Dribbling can be done one-handed, two-handed, or in front of the footrest. Passing and catching require clear communication between teammates and an awareness of each other's ability. Emphasis on passing and catching mechanics from an elementary level is important, with slight modifications based on each player's function. There are many types of passes; the rule of thumb is to consider the role that each athlete will play and develop skills accordingly.

Picking, blocking, and screening are important skills that all players need to develop. A pick is a manoeuvre where one player uses his chair to stop an opponent's chair. Usually a low pointer will use the defensive chair to grab the opponent's chair. A block or screen occurs when a glancing manoeuvre is performed between opponents. The chairs make contact, changing directions or obstructing one player so that the other may advance his position in the direction he was travelling. Picks, blocks, and screens are tools that can be used on offence and defence.

## revolutions

### Emphasizing Fundamentals

Over the years, wheelchair rugby has focused on socializing and play, putting fundamentals on the back burner. Many teams try to teach complex tactics only to be frustrated because their players are unable to execute a simple manoeuvre. How can players learn more complex skills when they can't trap, pass, understand movement, or maintain possession? We emphasize solid fundamentals, teaching the art of possession rugby and the total team concept. Every player should be a threat, and every player should have good defensive skills. Players should be exposed to as many styles of play as possible. This gives players a different perspective on the sport of rugby, which is why we encourage our players to reach out and participate in quality camps. In doing this, players are given the tools to develop into top players, confident players, players who love the game. This wide variety of exposure gives the players confidence, which in turn gives them a chance to develop their own style of play.

# Rugby Offence

Wheelchair rugby is typically a high-scoring game, with international competition averaging between 30 and 50 goals per game. Some games result in scores over 60 points, emphasizing the high level of offensive play in wheelchair rugby. Good offence begins with each player having a specific role, as well as clear communication within the team.

Offensive roles vary from those who have good ball skills and speed to players with less function and less control of the ball. Job responsibilities range from primary ball carrier to the blocker, who is typically a low-point player. All players have a role to make the offence productive (e.g., passing, catching, pushing, blocking), and assuming all team members are performing their set task, the offence is productive.

On offence, the object of the game is to create a lane for the ball carrier to cross two wheels over the goal line while in possession of the ball. This is achieved through a variety of strategies based on the skill and function level of the team. When a team is weak on offence, the opposing team will take advantage of it by dropping into the key on defence, and when in the lead, the defence will do this to slow the game down.

## Half-Court Offence

An integral part of the game, half-court offence can be played as a ground or passing attack. A wide range of plays and strategies can be developed to score.

As in many sports, the passing attack is riskier. Team ball control is essential at all times in order to reduce the risk for a turnover. The decision to make a passing play should be determined by the team's skill level and performance in the game. Players must be familiar with their teammates' catching and passing abilities in addition to their own. Incorporating passing drills into practice is important, and players should experiment with gloves and adhesive to improve their passing and catching ability.

The ground attack creates a greater chance of scoring because it eliminates passing. A ball in a lap is much safer than a ball in the air. To be successful in a ground attack, players must work together in a coordinated fashion with well-timed moves and good spacing on the court.

## Press Break

Because the game is heavy on pressing, teams must be solid in their press break (as in breaking the press in basketball). Full-court press defenders try to get turnovers by pressuring, trapping, and harassing the offence. There are several strategies to beat this pressure.

Spacing, deliberate blocking or screening, and court balance are part of the system. It is important to use the whole court and keep at least one player on the weak side to reverse the ball to the opposite side of the court. The offence needs to inbound the ball quickly, before the defence can set up. When receiving the inbound pass, the receiver needs to know where the defence is positioned, see where available receivers are, and still have the option to bring the ball up the court. Multiple options give teams flexibility when facing pressure. Aggressive attacks on the defence from any spot will stretch the defence and create passing opportunities down the court.

The passer must find the open receiver immediately and make a quick, accurate pass. Passing up the court, creating angles, and avoiding soft lob passes are the secrets to beating the press. The passer should look up the floor and anticipate where to pass the ball. A good offensive player can attack the press and make a long pass up the court to an open receiver for an easy goal. Some teams perform a deep outlet against the press, which is designed to allow for a deep pass and an easy score.

## Rugby Defence

Often the deciding factor in the outcome of a game, defensive play must be an integral part of practice time. Defensive strategy will depend on the opposing team's skill and experience, as well as their speed and stamina. All team members must know their role and have confidence in their teammates to hold up their part of the play. Many variations of both half- and full-court defensive plays should be practised and used in the game.

### Half-Court (Key) Defence

Key or half-court defence is a strategy used to force the offensive team into a turnover or to use up time and slow the game down. In order to be effective, the defensive players must be constantly communicating with each other, and all players must be alert and hold their positions. Key defence is best used when the opponent has more speed or a weak offence. If the defensive team is more than a few points behind, they should not use this strategy since it will run down the clock.

### revolutions

The most valuable players aren't always the players with skill but the players with desire. Many rugby coaches have made coaching complex when the sport is about basics. Coaches only need to remember one thing if they want to be successful: Never give up on the basics. Success is about commitment, desire, teamwork, and fun! Becoming successful in wheelchair rugby requires a long-term commitment, and those who make that commitment will reap rewards.

Here are 10 guidelines for successful coaching in wheelchair rugby:

1. Treat all players as though they are your best player.
2. Everyone must train to his/her potential.
3. Never forget the little things!
4. Bring the developing players up against the experienced players to improve the overall level of play.
5. If you say it, follow through—no matter what!
6. Emphasize fundamentals.
7. Make your athletes believe they are better than they are.
8. Spend the majority of time with the athletes that are not the stars, but don't forget the others!
9. The team needs to be a team, not a group of individuals.
10. Be a teacher—explain how to do something and why you do it.

## Full-Court Press Defence

The full-court press defence tries to get turnovers by pressuring, trapping, and harassing the offence. This strategy is best used to come back late in the game, to capitalize on an advantage in speed and stamina, or to harass an inexperienced opponent. There are two types of full-court press defences, the man-to-man press and the zone press. The objectives are to force a 10-second violation or a timeout during the inbound play, cause a 12-second violation when the offensive team fails to get the ball over half-court, or force a bad pass that will result in a turnover and easy score.

For a successful full-court defence, players must use their chairs for defence and not reach into the backcourt with their hands. The 12-second call requires that players stick to their assignments and have patience. Zone presses require strong communication and trust between teammates. Each configuration will look different to the opponents and force them to a particular area of the court. A variety of presses can be used to trap the opposing team's ball handler or to block an inbounder's pass. In the various zone-press configurations, each player defends a certain area of the court.

# Rugby Season Training Programme

It is crucial to develop the team's training programme before the season begins. This includes finalizing the competition schedule before the first practice begins. The plan should divide the season into pre-season phase, competition phase, and peak phase, with an outline of key activities for each phase. In addition, skill or performance assessment is an important component of each phase. The overall training programme should result in players being at their best during the peak phase.

- **Pre-season.** The main focus of the pre-season should be fitness conditioning and development or refinement of fundamental skills. It is best to begin each new season by reviewing the basics no matter what the experience level of the athletes. Simple drills focused on ball handling (passing, catching, dribbling), wheelchair mobility (pushing, starting, stopping, turning), and basic defence (picking, blocking) are best to begin with. Gradually progressing from 1v1, then 2v1, to 2v2, the game components can be added until the athletes are eventually playing 4v4 full court. Pay attention to ensure that time is spent developing each part of the game.

- **Competition.** During the competition phase, the main focus should be on simulating specific game situations. Special care should be taken to work on and refine plays that will benefit a team during competition. These can be specific plays on offence and defence that allow a team to better match tactical plays with their opponents in various game situations. Physical conditioning and player skill level should still be addressed, but the focus of this phase is tactical execution of skills related to competition. Identifying area gaps in play is essential to continued refinement of competition strategies.

- **Peak.** This phase is geared towards producing peak performance at final competition. Practice time should focus on ultimate refinement of the offence and defence and any specialty plays, with specific strategies developed for each opponent. The overall load is reduced in training while the intensity is maintained or slightly increased. The peak has a short duration and is typically achieved through systematic training.

Each practice session should have a goal with specific objectives for that day. A training session should be a step towards reaching the overall goal for the season. Short-term objectives should be progressive and tie into long-term objectives. The objectives can be applied to specific skills, specialty plays, or game strategies.

Generally speaking, a practice session should consist of a warm-up, conditioning and skill development, strategy work, and a good cool-down. Conditioning can be easily implemented throughout the entire practice. It is important to include a thorough stretching programme in both the warm-up and cool-down. Time must be allotted for breaks that allow for proper hydration and rest but are not too long. A good practice session is typically progressive, with each component tying into the next.

At the end of practice, a controlled scrimmage time can be scheduled, focusing on what was worked on that day. The athletes should focus on what they learned, and the scrimmage needs to reinforce the goals and objectives of the session.

Of particular importance for wheelchair athletes is maintaining a healthy rotator cuff and strengthening the posterior shoulder girdle. Athletes should take time on their own every day to perform appropriate exercises.

# Drills for Rugby Skill Development

Drills are important for skill development in rugby and will ultimately improve the players' overall performance. Critical for new players is development of chair mobility and ball-handling skills, along with cardiorespiratory and muscular endurance training. As players master these fundamentals and become more comfortable on the court, training should begin to include drills geared towards passing, catching, hitting, positioning, and picking, as well as speed. For the more experienced players, drills should become more complex, combining a number of skills to better simulate what happens in the game.

Some sample drills to incorporate into a rugby practice session are presented next.

## Ball Handling

### ● BALL PICKUPS

**Purpose**
This drill helps players pick up the ball while moving.

**Execution**
Players line up on the baseline outside the goal cones. The coach rolls the ball up the court and the first player pushes after the ball to pick it up by trapping the ball against the moving wheel with her hand, causing the ball to climb up the wheel to the player. When the ball reaches the top of the wheel, the player scoops the ball into her lap. This skill requires timing at various speeds and positions and should be practised from both sides of the chair.

**Variation**
A variation of this drill is a game where two players line up and compete for the ball pickup. Players line up at the baseline and a whistle indicates the time for them to chase the ball. Once the player scoops the ball, she advances up the court to score a goal.

## Wheelchair Mobility and Conditioning

### ● WHISTLE DRILL

**Purpose**

This is a simple drill to develop starts, stops, and quick changes in direction.

**Execution**

Players push up and down the court, responding to the coach's whistle blows and hand signals. A single whistle means *stop,* a double whistle means *go* or *accelerate,* and hand signals indicate turns.

**Variations**

Variations for responding to the whistles can be used to focus on direction, speed, or other skills such as pivots or 360s.

### ● FIGURE-EIGHT PUSHING

**Purpose**

This is a simple conditioning drill that encourages conditioning while maintaining court awareness.

**Execution**

The court or pushing pattern is set up with cones in multiples of four. The ideal is to use eight cones and have the athletes weave and intersect with each other frequently during the drill. A set time is determined and athletes push at a constant pace for the duration of the drill. The athletes push in a figure eight and work their way up through the course, crisscrossing with each other while progressing through the course.

**Variations**

Variations include using a ball and playing with the 10-second dribble rule. More cones in multiples of four can be added, the spacing can be changed, and the duration can be adjusted. Penalties for hit cones or dribbling violations can be added.

## Passing

Passing drills should build from simple stationary drills to more intricate drills encompassing passing and pushing. Passing the ball from a stationary position is first. One of the simplest drills is to have players form a circle and have everyone pass the ball to the player on the right. The direction can then be reversed until the players are comfortable passing in both directions. A simple variation of this drill is to skip a player on every pass, thus forcing the players to pass a greater distance and over another player. Another practical drill is Monkey in the Middle, which forces players to complete passes over another person.

The following drills and figures are adapted, by permission, from Blaze Sports America, Inc.

### ● CATERPILLAR PASSING

**Purpose**

This is a dynamic drill to work on all types of passing; it also emphasizes timing and movement.

**Execution**

The players split into two evenly numbered groups and line up facing one another on parallel lines 3.5 metres apart. One ball starts with the player closest to the baseline. After the player passes the ball, he spins to the outside and goes to the end of the line on his side. This works the same for the line on the other side and continues until both lines reach the other end of the court (see figure 10.2).

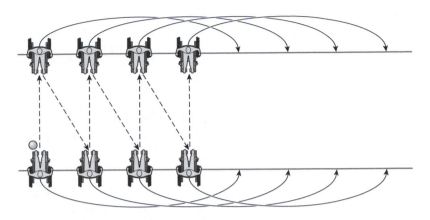

**Figure 10.2** Ball and player movement for Caterpillar Passing.

## Variations

The type of pass (e.g., chest pass, right- and left-hand pass, bounce pass) can be varied. In addition, several balls can be used.

## ● HOT SEAT PASSING

### Purpose

This is a more advanced stationary passing drill. The objective is to pass and prepare to catch another ball. This helps players maximize use of their peripheral vision.

### Execution

Four players line up with a fifth player facing them approximately 1 metre away (see figure 10.3). The first two players in line both start with volleyballs. The first player throws the ball to the player facing him, who then returns it to the third player in line. As soon as the first player releases the ball, the second player throws the other volleyball to the player facing the group, who then passes the ball to the fourth player in line.

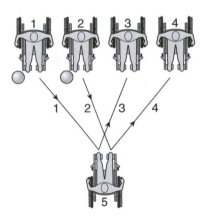

**Figure 10.3** Ball and player movement for Hot Seat Passing.

### Variations

This exercise can also be done in a circle or semi-circle. Depending on the skill level, more than two balls can be used, and the passes do not need to be sequenced.

## ● THREE-PLAYER WEAVE

### Purpose

This drill is used to develop both ball-handling and chair mobility skills.

### Execution

Initially, players line up at three different positions on an end line. One group (A) lines up in the centre, and the other two groups (B) and (C) line up near the sidelines. To begin, the first player in the middle group (A) inbounds the ball to a player in either one of the other groups

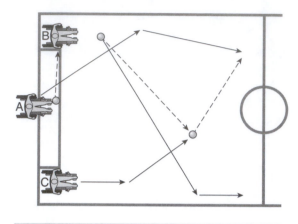

**Figure 10.4**  Ball and player movement for Three-Player Weave.

(e.g., B), then pushes towards her, crossing behind this receiver (B) and attaining the outer position. The current ball handler (B) passes the ball to the third player (C) and then pushes behind that player (C) to attain the outer position. The player from group C becomes the ball handler in the centre and continues this weaving pattern with the player from group A as her receiver. The players execute this drill while generally maintaining their distance apart so they can become more familiar with this positioning, which prepares them for breaking the press. The first group of three players continues this weaving pattern up the court to the other end, after which the next three players in line begin the drill. This continues until all players have participated. (See figure 10.4.)

### Variation

To improve chair mobility and ball-handling skills, this drill can also be run with less distance between the players.

## ● LONG PASSING

### Purpose

As the name implies, this drill works on passing the ball over long distances.

### Execution

This drill is a variation of a basketball layup drill without the basket. The players split into two lines, a passing line and a receiving line. The players start at half-court. As the receiver advances closer to the baseline, the passer throws the ball to the receiver by leading her towards the baseline. After catching the ball, the receiver scores the goal, circles around, and passes the ball to the next passer in line, and then goes to the end of the passing line (figure 10.5).

### Variation

To work on passing from both sides of the court, the passing and receiving lines should switch positions regularly. Different passes can be practised using this drill.

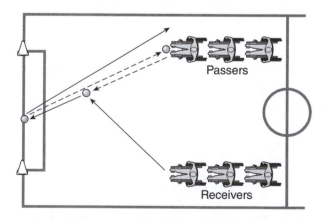

**Figure 10.5**  Ball and player movement for Long Passing.

## ● DIAMOND IN THE ROUGH

### Purpose

This drill is used to practise chair mobility (pivot) with stationary passing.

### Execution

Four players form a circle, and the fifth is in the centre. The players in front and behind the centre player will start the drill with volleyballs. When the centre player faces them, they will throw the ball to him and receive the pass back immediately. Once the centre player has received the ball and returned it, he will turn his chair 180 degrees and receive another pass and return it, then rotate his chair 180 degrees back and repeat this movement. When the centre player turns away from the person with the ball, the ball handler will pass to the player next to him in the circle who will return the pass before the centre is prepared to receive the ball again. The emphasis is on the centre player's execution of quick, efficient turns and quick passes. Chair control is essential at all time. Players take turns being in the centre position. (see figure 10.6)

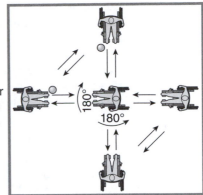

Player in front of center player throws the first pass.

**Figure 10.6** Ball and player movement for Diamond in the Rough.

## ● FOUR CORNERS

### Purpose

This is a dynamic passing drill that coordinates timing, teamwork, and a variety of passes. It is also valuable for working on a give-and-go situation similar to inbounding the ball.

### Execution

A minimum of six players is needed for this drill. Start with one to two balls (as many as four can be used depending on number of players) in opposite corners. Two players should be in the line that starts with the ball, and additional players can fill into the other lines and balance out each corner. To start the drill, the players who start with the ball (players 1 and 3) pass the ball to the adjacent corner (1 to 2 and 3 to 4). After the player passes the ball, that player moves towards the player the ball was thrown to and looks to receive the pass directly back. When player 1 catches the returned pass, she continues to move to the inside (of player 2) and hands off the ball to player 2. Player 1 goes to the end of that line. The drill on the opposite corner occurs simultaneously in the same direction (clockwise or counterclockwise.) After the handoff, players 2 and 4 pivot and continue the drill to the adjacent corner (figure 10.7).

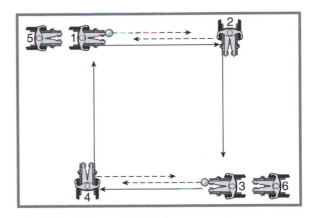

**Figure 10.7** Ball and player movement for Four Corners.

The opposite corners need to function together. All of the action continues from corner to corner. The coach determines the ending point.

### Variation

At any point when the ball is on the corner, the ball can be reversed using the simple cue, "Reverse".

Additional drills should be incorporated into practice to develop defensive skills such as back picking and containment. Hitting to bump an opponent off the play is another important skill that must be practised. Stations are an effective way to practise fundamental skills and work on fitness conditioning. The number of stations and time at each station can vary depending on the condition of the athletes and time in season. The deeper in the season the more conditioned the athletes are, so the volume is increased.

# Skills Testing

To assess an athlete's performance level as part of the training programme, a variety of skills should be assessed on a regular basis, including passing, sprint speed, agility, and endurance.

Skills testing should be conducted at the beginning of the season, halfway through, and when the athletes are at their peak. Such testing is beneficial for all players, from novice to expert. The skills assessment should be used to monitor progress and can be used for comparison to other athletes with similar classification. Subjective skills are also important to assess and include communication, playing one's role properly, positioning, transitioning, attitude, contribution to team chemistry, coachability, leadership, and other intangibles (e.g., desire, heart, determination). Some sample skills tests are presented next.

## Passing

Players pass to a target from various locations.

- Throw the ball at a target from three positions (left, straight, right) and two distances (long, short).
- Low classes (0.5-1.5) throw or bump from 3 and 4.5 metres; high classes (2.0-3.5) throw or bump from 4.5 and 6 metres.
- Do right and left passes 2 metres from centre, using hand on respective side. When passing from a left position, the players uses his left hand and when on the right uses his right hand. The player uses both hands when passing from the centre.

Players should try five passes from each location for a total of 30 throws. The score is calculated according to the location hit on the target (centre = 3 points, middle section = 2 points, outer sections = 1 point; total possible score = 90 points). (See figure 10.8.)

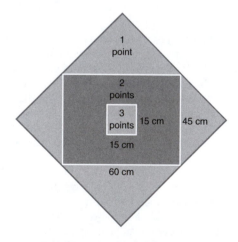

**Figure 10.8** Target for passing skill assessment.

### 20-Metre Sprint

Players sprint from a stationary position through 20 metres.

- The stopwatch starts upon initial movement and stops when front casters cross the 20-metre line.
- Do three trials, best time and average score calculated.

### Endurance Sprint

Players sprint from a stationary position starting at half-court.

- Their path should take them around cones at the baseline down to other end of court, finishing at half-court.
- Do three trials clockwise and three trials counterclockwise, calculating the best time and average score using all six trials.

### Up and Back

Players start from a stationary position at the baseline, then sprint to each of seven lines measured 90 centimetres. The first line is 100 centimetres from the baseline.

- The athlete must pass two wheels over the line each time and then reverse direction back to the baseline.
- Time stops after the final baseline crossing.
- Do three trials, best time and average score calculated.

### Slalom

Players start from a stationary position at the baseline on the left side of the cones, then weave through seven cones measured 122 centimetres apart.

- Conduct one trial with the ball and one without, starting from both right and left sides, for a total of four trials.
- For each cone hit, add 1 second to the time.
- The ball must be dribbled every 10 seconds; if a violation occurs, add 5 seconds to the time.

# Conclusion

Wheelchair rugby is a relatively new sport with no nondisabled equivalent. It provides athletes with tetraplegia the opportunity to take part in an exciting competitive team sport that combines speed, power, and tactics. In addition, participation provides athletes with many health and fitness benefits, including muscle strength, cardiorespiratory endurance, and increased mobility skills.

Wheelchair rugby continues to grow, with teams scattered across many countries in North and South America, Europe, Asia, Africa, and Australia. It gained wide exposure when it was featured in the Oscar-nominated documentary *Murderball,* and it has drawn a lot of worldwide interest and is rapidly advancing at the international level. The future is bright for this intense, fast-paced, strategic game.

Chapter acknowledgements: Evolution of the game and drills of wheelchair rugby are attributed to the hard work of many, including Ed Suhr, Terry Vinyard, Reggie Richner, James Gumbert, Kevin Orr, and Wendy Gumbert.

# chapter 11

# Wheelchair Tennis

Dawn Newbery, Geraint Richards,
Stephanie Trill, and Martyn Whait

Photo courtesy of John Lenton.

Since 1976, the sport of wheelchair tennis has undergone phenomenal growth. Today at the international level it can be seen at all four of the major tennis Grand Slams. The ITF World Champions Dinner each year at Roland Garros honours not just the top professional players, such as Roger Federer, Andy Roddick, Lleyton Hewitt, Justine Henin, Kim Clijsters, and Serena Williams, but also the end-of-year wheelchair world champions, such as Esther Vergeer, Robin Ammerlaan, Shingo Kunieda, Michael Jeremiasz, David Hall, and Daniela Di Toro. At the Paralympic level, the 2008 finals in Beijing took place in front of 10,000 spectators with full television coverage and broadcasting rights being sold round the world. The game is truly worldwide, now enthralling spectators in all five continents.

The game follows the same rules as nondisabled tennis, except that the ball can bounce twice so long as the first bounce is in the court. The court is the same size, the surface is the same, the net is the same height, and the rackets and balls are the same. To play competitively, a player must have a mobility-related physical disability that is permanent and that has been medically diagnosed. Players initially start the game in their day chair, but if resources allow and they wish to play competitively, they start to use a tennis-specific wheelchair that is customized to their specific disability and personal preferences.

## Ten Steps to the Top

Within each 4-year Paralympic cycle, it is possible for players to begin playing wheelchair tennis and achieve a top-four world ranking if they already had a strong tennis background before an accident or illness. There are no age restrictions and both men and women enjoy the game at all levels, playing both singles and doubles. Here are some progressions for a new player wishing to get into the sport from grass roots to world class.

**1.** Have a game of wheelchair tennis with some friends. Because the rules are the same, wheelchair tennis can easily be integrated on the same court. You could also try the game out at a spinal unit, introductory camp, "have a go" day, or school.

**2.** Find out if there are other players in your area and meet up with them for a game. Join in some group coaching sessions. Enter a couple of low-key tournaments.

**3.** Decide if you wish to play recreationally or train a little more and compete at more events. Have some one-on-one lessons to look at technical and tactical changes. Check whether your disability will allow you to play competitively on the ITF Wheelchair Tour.

**4.** Tennis lessons now have more of a purpose and are closely linked to your strengths and weaknesses both technically and tactically. Look at getting a tennis chair and see if you need some new rackets, too.

**5.** Start to set performance goals for each tournament. After each event, your training is adjusted depending on how you played. Tournaments increase by number and standard; depending on where you live, you could be travelling farther afield and playing in Europe.

**6.** Your training programme is now consistent across the whole year. You may be drug tested, so become aware of all medication contents to ensure no performance-enhancing drugs are involved.

**7.** Your coaching team starts to include a physiotherapist, a strength and conditioning coach, and maybe some sports psychology. You look carefully at what you are eating to maximize your training (refer to the previous discipline sections of the book for guidance).

**8.** The tennis programme involves all facets of performance sport and starts to be periodized with phases of training. Each week starts to look different. Phases include general, precompetition, competition, recovery, and so on.

**9.** Your world ranking starts to improve, travel could be far and wide around the world, draws get larger and tougher, and prize money starts to increase.

**10.** Training gets professional and you start to look at where marginal gains can be made (e.g., acclimatization, jet lag, cooling methods, biomechanics, video analysis). You start to look for sponsors to support your programmes and travel.

## Taping

Many of the players in the quad division of wheelchair tennis use taping as a way to get a better grip on the racket and then a better push. For some players, the racket would not remain in their hand without the tape. Numerous methods can be used to achieve this; some may use a glove and then tape the glove to the racket, others start with a sweatband or wrist support taped on to the racket, some stick the tape directly to their wrists and hands, some use a combination of tapes, and others look to mould the grip of the racket to the shape of their hand. All are striving to get the best grip to allow them to play their best tennis.

The method players choose may be dictated by their grip strength. Also, the choice of grip they use to play their shots can influence how they tape. Once taped, there is little chance the grip can be changed dramatically, so it is basically one grip for all shots. This means they have to adapt their shots to fit the grip that they choose.

Other factors that influence the position and taping of the grip include how the player chooses to push. Quad players can push off the palm or grip of the racket, and some also push off their knuckles. Players may also try to reverse the tape on the outside so as to acquire better purchase when pushing. A tacky outer grip is better than a smooth tape finish.

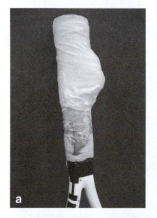 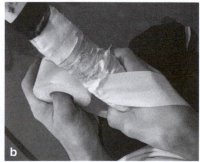 

*(a)* **An example of a taping method.** *(b)* **The tape holds the hand in position.** *(c)* **The reversed tape adds more power when pushing or stopping.**

Photos courtesy of John Lenton.

**The tennis player on the left is using the taping method wheras the tennis player on the right is not.**
Photos courtesy of Dawn Newbery.

# Attack and Defence Drills

Within a player's development, a coach will introduce many exercises to train a specific skill. All drills should be realistic to wheelchair tennis and be working towards a movement pattern and skill seen in match play. Drills can be closed (with balls fed by a coach) or open (involving decision making). A good drill is one where the intensity and degree of difficulty can be adjusted. All drills should have a purpose of developing the player's technical, tactical, physical, or mental attributes.

As a player improves, the drills become more challenging. This may involve reducing the size of target areas, hitting off one bounce rather than two, and moving faster around the court. Drills that simulate match play and pressure are used in precompetition and competition training phases. These will revolve around serve and return routines, patterns, and score lines. Conditioned sets can support a player's development here (e.g., one set serving from advantage court, best of three sets starting at 3–3 each set, best of three tie breaks).

The following drills cover the two main tactical skills of attacking and defending. Players may also benefit from the drills described in the other sport chapters of this book—it is important that tennis training involves physical conditioning in the wheelchair in addition to hitting practice.

## ● RETURNING SECOND SERVE

### Purpose
To take advantage of receiving a second serve

### Execution
The coach serves a second serve and the player hits to the target area. The player should achieve a set number on each side of the court. Over time, increase the number of shots on target to be achieved and decrease the size of the target area (ideally 1 metre from inside tramline).

**Focus Points**
- Rolling into the court to receive the serve
- Looking for clues from the server as to the type and direction of serve being hit
- Early decision on taking it on one bounce or two

**Variations**
- Practice off all types of spin (e.g. slice and top), together with all types of direction (e.g. into the body, forehand and backhand sides).
- Practice from both sides of the court but in particular the advantage side.
- Condition the return so the player has to make it on one bounce.
- Integrate this drill into receiving the first serve.

## ● HIGH FOREHAND

**Purpose**
To take advantage of a strong attacking position and put the ball away

**Execution**
The player starts at M1. The coach feeds in a medium-high ball and then moves to one side of court, thereby providing a visual stimulus. The player pushes in and hits a high attacking forehand to opposite side of court from where the coach is standing. The player then recovers behind M1. Repeat as a set of 10 to 15 shots. Repeat the same drill starting from M2 and recovering behind M2 after each shot (see figure 11.1).

**Focus Points**
- Quick movement to the ball
- Good chair set-up by getting into position early, allowing for good stroke production
- Ball taken at shoulder height either at its highest point or just beginning to fall, not rising
- Racket taken back high

**Variations**
- Vary target areas on court.
- Introduce recovery after each shot.
- Adopt a similar technique when attacking a short second serve.

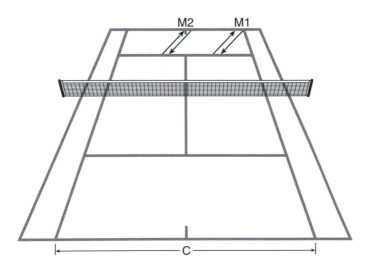

**Figure 11.1** Player movement and positions for High Forehand.

### ● DEEP, SHORT, DEEP, SHORT

**Purpose**
To learn how to create an attacking opportunity from a defensive position

**Execution**
The player hits a shot from a deep position and then pushes into court and plays a second ball from around the service line. Then the player pushes at an angle back to the baseline and plays a third shot from a deep position, finishing the sequence with a final shot from the service line. If all four shots are completed, the player goes 15–love up. If the player makes a mistake, the coach goes 15–love up. Play a set in this way (see figure 11.2).

**Focus Points**
- Fast explosive pushing off the ball
- Efficient court coverage and turning
- Strong shot technique maintained as the player tires

**Variations**
- Mix up one bounce and two.
- The better the player, the faster the drill.
- The first ball hit could be the player serving, and then the coach feeds.

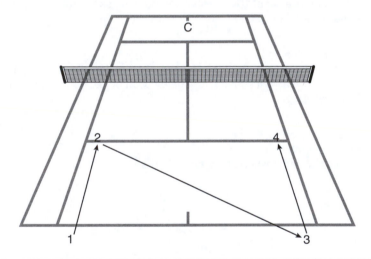

**Figure 11.2** Player movement for Deep, Short, Deep, Short.

### ● DEEP, MID, SHORT

**Purpose**
To develop movement up the court and increase confidence at the net

**Execution**
The player starts with a deep ball, then turns and pushes into court diagonally to play a second ball around the service line, and then turns and pushes into court diagonally to play a volley. If all three shots are completed, the player goes 15–love up; if the player makes a mistake, the coach goes 15 love–up. Play a set in this way. This exercise can also be done on both forehand and backhand sides for more variation. (See figure 11.3.)

**Focus Points**
- Early preparation for each shot
- Good balance

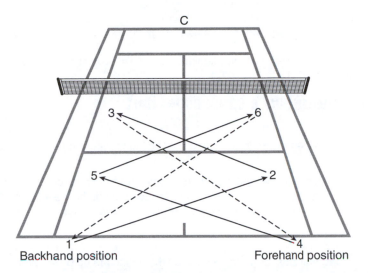

**Figure 11.3**  Player movement and position for Deep, Mid, Short.

- Smooth transition from hitting phase through to pushing phase
- Efficient turning

**Variations**
- Play a set starting on the opposite side of the court.
- The drill can be made harder by setting a specific target for the final shot.

## ● BOUNCE–SMASH

**Purpose**
To develop confidence in taking a high midcourt ball off one bounce above the head

**Execution**
The player starts behind M1 (figure 11.4). The coach feeds in a midcourt high ball to bounce before service line. Player pushes in and hits a bounce–smash, then pushes behind M2 and the coach feeds in the next ball. Repeat as a set of 10 to 12 shots.

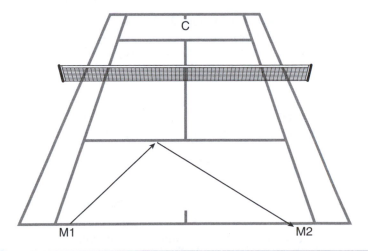

**Figure 11.4**  Player movement from M1 to M2.

### Focus Points
- See the opportunity early and move quickly to get in a strong balanced position.
- Serving grip used.
- A player who serves underarm may find this exercise difficult and may choose to practise the high forehand drill.

## ● HIT DOWN THE LINE OFF A CROSSCOURT BALL

### Purpose
To learn when it is the right time to go from a rally ball to an attacking one

### Execution
The player hits the first and second balls back crosscourt to the coach. The third ball is hit down the line to the target area. If all three shots are completed, the player goes 15–love up. If the player makes a mistake, the coach goes 15–love up. Play a set in this way.

### Focus Points
- Patience
- Hitting a strong ball crosscourt to help set up the chance to go down the line
- Being in a strong court position and in control when going down the line

### Variations
- Play a set hitting crosscourt shots from the advantage side of the court.
- Play alternate points from the deuce and advantage sides of the court. Play a set in this way.
- Play alternate games from the deuce and advantage sides of the court. Play a set in this way.

## ● HIT CROSSCOURT OFF A DOWN-THE-LINE BALL

### Purpose
Changing the direction of the ball after movement to it

### Execution
The player hits all the balls crosscourt back to the coach. The coach goes down the line, and the player hits crosscourt. The player must make the ball cross the sideline after the first bounce before it crosses the baseline. If the final ball is completed, the player goes 15–love up. If the player makes a mistake, the coach goes 15–love up. Play a set in this way.

### Focus Points
- Maintaining good technique for the first shot
- Fast and efficient movement off the ball
- Great drill for left-handed players or right-handed players with a strong backhand that they want their opponent to hit to

### Variations
- Play a set from the advantage side of the court.
- Players set a target of so many complete sets out of 10 or 20.
- After shot 3 by the coach, hit a slice backhand back down the line.

## ● TWENTY SHOTS

### Purpose
To develop consistency and make the opponent play another ball

### Execution
The player rallies 20 shots back to the coach, who remains on the same side (ad or deuce) during the rally. The player has to alternate from side to side and return the ball to the

coach's side of the court. If the 30-shot rally is achieved, the player goes 15–love up. If the rally breaks down, the coach goes 15–love up. Play the next rally with the coach staying on the opposite side of the court. Play a set in this way. If 20-shot rallies become too easy, set a target of 30 shots.

### Focus Points
- Concentrate on each individual shot
- Full and correct technique; not playing safe when the total gets close to the end rally target
- Allowing sufficient recovery time

### Variation
Play each game with the coach on one side (deuce or advantage), alternating the coach's side from game to game.

## ● RABBIT EARS

### Purpose
To develop a robust serving technique

### Execution
The player serves two balls from each marker (figure 11.5). If the player fails to get the ball in at any point, she must return to the starting point of the drill. The player stops when she has successfully hit all 18 serves into the correct service box. Note that the starting point can vary, but all 18 serves must go in to complete the drill.

### Focus Points
- Maintain serving routines throughout. If the ball toss is not in the right place, don't hit the serve.
- Beginners should take their time, whereas advanced players should serve at the same tempo as they would in a match.

### Variation
Bias the advantage side.

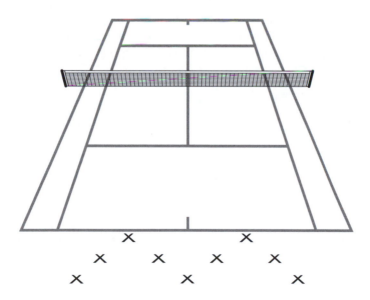

**Figure 11.5** In Rabbit Ears, a player serves twice from each of the markers.

## ● HUSTLE

**Purpose**
To be able to defend from all areas of the court

**Execution**
The coach feeds six random balls. The player must get all six in court between the service line and baseline. If the player makes all six shots, he gets a point. If he makes a mistake, the coach gets a point. Play a tiebreaker in this way.

**Focus Points**
- Fast hands, quick reactions, always looking for the next feed from the coach
- Good recovery between each set of six feeds
- Maintaining high technical standards

# Mobility Drills

Technological advances are always sought by wheelchair manufacturers, and the best players are always fine-tuning their chairs to search for that added extra in their game. Players initially will spend considerable time trying out designs and set-ups. Costs are high, so time invested at this stage is extremely beneficial.

Pushing and mobility around the court is one of the most crucial skills for a player to learn. It is also difficult for a nondisabled tennis coach to teach. All strokes should be learned technically and tactically, with mobility integrated into all areas of the player's game. Players should strive for an effective first push with the racket held in the hand at all times. Drills should be created to develop the skills of turning in, turning out, and reverse mobility, and these are linked closely to court positions and the attacking–defending flow of the game.

Players and coaches also need to develop on-court mobility drills without hitting. These would be done in a tennis chair and could be with or without a racket. The following examples show a wide variety for beginners through to tour players. At the highest level, working with a strength and conditioning coach and a physiologist can help tailor these drills, making them an integral part of a player's training programme. Many of the drills can take place at the start or end of an on-court session.

## ● DOWN THE MOUNTAIN

**Purpose**
To develop turn of speed and pushing tempo

**Execution**
The player gently pushes along the baseline from A to B. The player then increases speed gradually as she pushes up the tramline towards C. She turns at C and sprints back down to A. Repeat in sets of three or five.

**Variation**
Start at B, gently push along baseline to A, increase speed up to D, and sprint back down to B (figure 11.6).

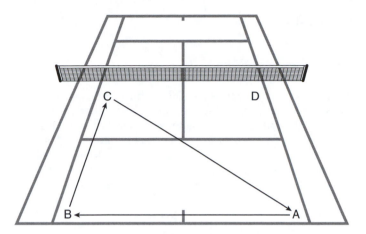

**Figure 11.6** Player movement and variation position D for Down the Mountain.

## ● PARK THE CAR

**Purpose**

To develop basic chair skills—start, stop, and turn

**Execution**

The player starts at A and sprints just behind the baseline. He then turns 90 degrees and parks his chair in area P, braking sharply. The player then reverses his chair out of the marked area beyond the baseline, turns 90 degrees, and sprints along baseline before turning the chair 90 degrees and parking the chair in the area Q. The player reverses out of area Q, turns 90 degrees, and sprints along the baseline back to area P. Repeat for 60 seconds or 90 seconds. (See figure 11.7.)

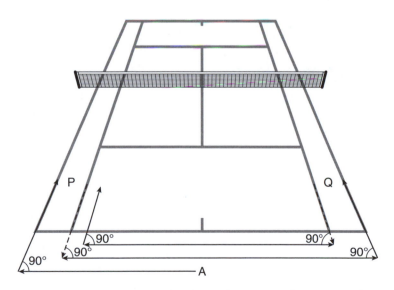

**Figure 11.7** Player movement for Park the Car.

## ● THROUGH THE GATE

### Purpose
To enhance change-of-direction skills

### Execution
The player starts at point S, pushes through gate G, and then pushes around any marker (A, B, C, or D). Having gone around a marker, the player must push through the gate again and then pushes around a different marker, but not one directly in a straight line with the marker they have just pushed around (e.g., if the player pushes around A first, then they cannot push around C next; likewise, if B is first, D cannot be next). The player must push around all markers, followed by passing through the gate. Each time, the next marker cannot be straight in line with the one just passed. Finish back at S. (See figure 11.8.)

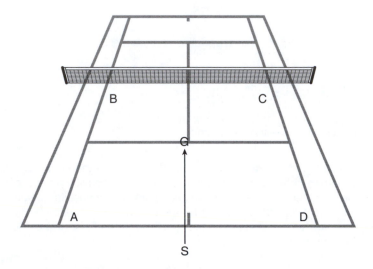

**Figure 11.8**  Through the Gate markers set-up.

## ● SPRINT, SLALOM, REVERSE

### Purpose
To develop chair-handling skills at top speeds

### Execution
The player starts at A and sprints to B, turns and sprints up to C, slaloms through markers to D, reverses the chair backwards to E, and turns and sprints to A (figure 11.9).

### Variations
- If two players are present, they can race on opposite sides of the net.
- If more than two players are present, this drill can be done as a team relay race.
- Complete the drill in the opposite direction.

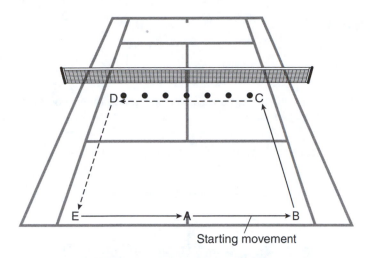

**Figure 11.9** Sprint, Slalom, Reverse player movement.

## ● TWO-PUSH SLALOM

### Purpose

To develop first two pushes, acceleration, and turning

### Execution

The first player starts in position A, the second player in position B. On the coach's command, each player completes the slalom course but is restricted to two pushes between cones. After the first slalom run, players switch positions and repeat the drill. (See figure 11.10.)

### Variation

An individual player can perform the drill in repeat sets separated by timed recovery periods to work on speed and endurance.

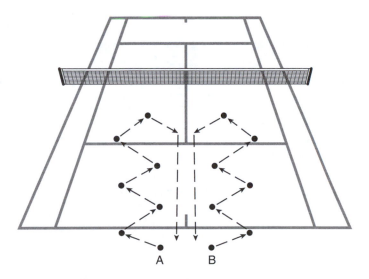

**Figure 11.10** Push pattern for two players in Two-Push Slalom.

## ● HALF-COURT MAP

**Purpose**
To develop forward and reverse pushing and speed endurance

**Execution**
The player begins the drill in the start position facing the net. Tennis court markings outline the course to be taken (figure 11.11).

**Variation**
If two players are present, they can race on opposite sides of the net.

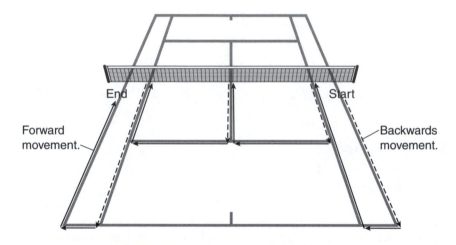

**Figure 11.11** Players follow court markings for Half-Court Map.

## ● FAN DRILL

**Purpose**
To develop sprint performance, quick turns, and recovery to the hub

**Execution**
The player begins at the hub, which is a marker cone 2.75 metres behind the baseline in line with the centre T. The player sprints to 1, turns and sprints back to the hub, turns and sprints to 2, and turns and returns to the hub. Player continues the same for points 3 and 4, finishing with a sprint through the gate on the service box line. The solid lines in figure 11.12 show the route taken when pushing to the outer markers, and the dashed lines indicate the route taken when returning to the hub.

**Variation**
If two players are present, they can race on opposite sides of the net.

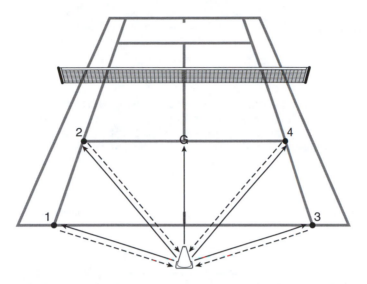

**Figure 11.12** Travel path for Fan Drill.

## ● AGILITY DRILL

### Purpose
To develop speed, reaction, agility, and endurance

### Execution
The player begins parked in area P, facing the net. As the coach shouts positions 1 through 8, the player must react, turn and sprint to the command number, and turn and return to the parked position in P. The player must work as quickly as possible for 60 seconds followed by 60 seconds recovery (figure 11.13).

### Variations
  – Work and recovery times can be manipulated to accommodate training goals.
  – Reverse pushing can be included in the recovery to the parking box.

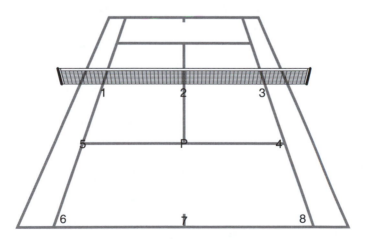

**Figure 11.13** Positions for Agility Drill.

## ● BOX-COMMAND DRILL

### Purpose
To develop first-push power and stopping

### Execution
The player begins parked in position P, facing the coach (figure 11.14). As the coach shouts the instructions, "Volley," "Lob," "Backhand", or "Forehand", the player must turn towards the command and make one powerful push to leave the parking box. Immediately on leaving the box, the player must then apply the brakes, stop the chair, and reverse into the box, parking his chair facing the direction he reversed from. The drill duration is 60 seconds followed by 60 seconds recovery.

### Variation
Work and recovery times can be manipulated to accommodate training goals.

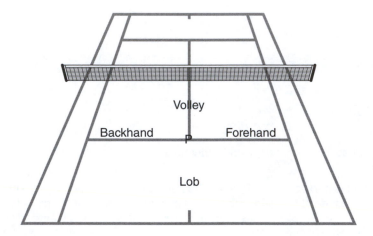

**Figure 11.14** Positions for Box-Command Drill.

## ● SPEED PLAY

### Purpose
To develop speed and endurance

### Execution
The player pushes clockwise around the outside of the half-court markings and performs six circuits to complete one set, with the number of sets varied to manipulate the intensity of the session (figure 11.15).

**Circuit 1:** Recovery pace, recovery pace, recovery pace, recovery pace
**Circuit 2:** Sprint, recovery pace, recovery pace, recovery pace
**Circuit 3:** Sprint, sprint, recovery pace, recovery pace
**Circuit 4:** Sprint, sprint, sprint, recovery pace
**Circuit 5:** Sprint, sprint, sprint, sprint
**Circuit 6:** Recovery pace, recovery pace, recovery pace, recovery pace

### Variations
– Perform the drill counterclockwise to work right turns.
– Perform the circuit order in reverse.
– Randomize the order of the circuits.

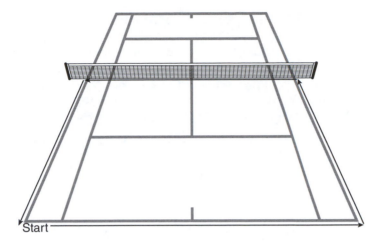

Start

**Figure 11.15** Player movement for Speed Play.

## revolutions

- Coaches should incorporate agility drills with the tennis racket at all times.
- Players who do not use the wheelchair for daily activities must spend additional time in a wheelchair other than specific wheelchair tennis training in order to gain the skills of turning in, turning out, reverse mobility, and so on.
- Tennis is often played in warm environmental conditions. However, if you choose to use head and neck cooling strategies then these methods may not provide you with sufficient cooling power. Please refer to chapter 6 for further information.
- If you do use cooling methods during tennis match play, then there may be a need to adapt your fluid intake strategy accordingly and not just rely on feelings of thirst.

# Tennis Serve Comparison

In wheelchair tennis, the serving technique can vary depending on the ability and disability level of a player. For example, a player with a high spinal cord injury will have a different technique compared to an amputee. In the observational comparision that follows, the wheelchair player has full use of his trunk.

At the prestretch position in the wheelchair, the player has

- reduced inclination of his shoulders due to the inability to push his hips forward, and
- reduced rotation of the upper body.

**Prestretch position.**
Photos courtesy of John Lenton.

As the hitting phase starts, the following occurs:

- The moment of maximum external rotation of the shoulder is reduced when in the chair due to the lack of leg drive.
- When standing, the player rotates his hips to face the courts, whereas in the chair he does not. Some wheelchair players pull back on the wheel with their nondominant hand to simulate this action.
- At contact point, due to the lack of leg drive, the ball is between the shoulders when in the chair but out in front of the body when standing. This allows efficient use of the internal rotation of the shoulders to produce power.

**Beginning of hitting phase.**
Photos courtesy of John Lenton.

**Contact point.**
Photos courtesy of John Lenton.

- Use of momentum and body weight to produce power is reduced when serving from the wheelchair. When standing, the player follows the serve forward into the court. Some wheelchair players try to simulate this by pushing the chair forward before serving (one push allowed).

- A wheelchair player's serving technique depends crucially on the level of disability. A single amputee, for example, will have a different technique compared with, say, a player with complete paraplegia or tetraplegia.

**Follow-through.**

Photos courtesy of John Lenton.

# Conclusion

The growth of wheelchair tennis has been phenomenal, and it is now played in many countries around the world. From a research perspective, it is a young sport, and we are only beginning to scratch the surface into applied sports science research. It is an exciting time for wheelchair tennis as new innovations, discoveries, and limits are found within the game. These will in turn help players, coaches, and scientists gain a greater understanding of how wheelchair tennis players can push the boundaries and play to ever-increasing standards that once were inconceivable.

Chapter acknowledgments: Special thanks go to Dr. Vicky Goosey-Tolfrey and John Lenton (Peter Harrison Centre for Disability Sport).

# Handcycling

Thomas Abel, Yves Vanlandewijck, and Joeri Verellen

Handcycling is primarily a sport for people with impairments of the lower extremities (e.g., persons with SCI or amputation). It involves the propulsion of two crank handles that are connected over a chain or belt transmission with the front wheel of a three-wheeled cycle. The cranks can be arranged synchronously (parallel) or asynchronously (180-degree shift), which is the same arrangement as in nondisabled cycling. Athletes prefer the synchronous arrangement of the cranks, mainly because it results in better steering performance.

Two major handcycle categories can be distinguished according to their main purpose, competitive versus all-round. All-round bikes, also called *adaptive bikes,* consist of an extra wheel connected to the wheelchair and equipped with a cranking device. The all-round set-up is mainly used for activities in daily living and recreational purposes. The main characteristic of the competitive bike is its solid frame, reducing internal friction forces to a minimum. Also, air drag is minimized through handcycle configuration and optimal positioning of the athlete.

Modern handcycles have an enormous impact on the freedom of movement of those who use wheelchairs for mobility. In contrast to conventional wheelchairs, handcycles perfectly serve the purpose of wheeling longer distances and overcoming inclinations without exerting enormous forces. Handcycles allow wheelchair users to go on trips or to complete training sessions with their nondisabled counterparts (e.g., cyclists, in-line skaters, runners) depending on their level of fitness. Handcycles are ideal in particular for untrained people because they offer a significantly higher mechanical efficiency compared with daily wheelchairs. Moreover, overexertion, pain along the pectoral girdle, humpback posture, and problems with the wrists, all related to hand-rim wheelchair propulsion, have not been reported as a consequence of handcycling.

The first modern handcycles were developed in the United States in the 1980s. In Europe, the first bikes were put on the market 10 years later. In the summer of 1999 in Blois, France, at an extraordinary IPC convention of sports, handcycling was officially accepted as a new cycling discipline. At the Paralympics in Athens 2004, individual time-trial and road race competitions were held for the first time. In the same year in October, the first World Cup in Lausanne, Switzerland, took place. Nowadays numerous city marathons in Europe integrate competition for handcycling, which enjoys increasing popularity.

Within these competitions, athletes can also choose to cover shorter distances, such as the 10K sprint races, or longer distances, such as the race around the lake of Geneva (Tour du Lac Léman) with a distance of 174 kilometres. In general, the association of handcycling with cycling is increasing. Hence, handcycle races are taking place within road-bike criteria. Recently, multiday events with a combination of road races and time trials or team relays completed the handcycling agenda. At the Paralympics, stage distances vary from 5 to 30 kilometres for the individual time trial and from 20 to 70 kilometres for the road race, depending on the classification (division) of the athletes.

In the early years of handcycling, participants came from other sport disciplines such as wheelchair racing or Nordic skiing. Today, more and more novice wheelchair users first access sport through handcycling. The popularity of the sport is documented by the continuously growing numbers of participants at various events. In addition to the number of active athletes, the quality of performance has increased significantly. In 1998 the average speed of a top athlete during a marathon race was 28.8 kilometres per hour, whereas a winner nowadays reaches an average speed of more than 40.0 kilometres per hour. However, the boundaries of maximal performance are not reached yet, and further improvement is expected in training regimens, handcycle configurations, and adjustments of the handcycle to athletes' physical potential. Also, handcycling is progressively evolving from amateurship to semiprofessionalism, with athletes spending more time in training and race preparation thanks to grants and sponsorship.

The participation of athletes with various impairments and levels of abilities demands an adequate classification system to minimize the impact of impairment on the outcome of competition. Currently the UCI classifies handcycling athletes into four divisions, as well as two subdivisions. Please refer to chapter 1 for the classification according to UCI (page 12). To demonstrate the complexity of classification in handcycling, the following paragraph will compare arm-trunk-powered handcycling (ATP; figure 12.1a) with arm-powered handcycling (AP; fig 12.1b).

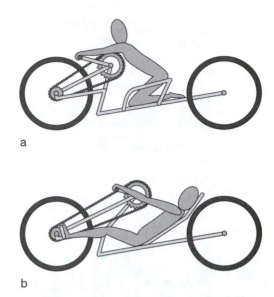

**Figure 12.1** Handcycling in kneeling, or ATP, position (a) and lying, or AP, position (b).

At first sight, ATP handcycling has the advantage over AP handcycling. In ATP handcycling, both the trunk and upper extremities can generate force on the cranks. Furthermore, downward force generation is supported by gravitational forces. However, ATP has many disadvantages. First, athletes need almost full trunk control to overcome the kneeled position. Moreover, this position is uncomfortable over a long period of time. Second, in ATP the front of the handcycle and athlete is significant, resulting in extreme air drag. Third, the use of low gears (high cadence) in ATP is mechanically more inefficient, almost not feasible, because of extreme trunk muscle activity. In conclusion, ATP is beneficial for short exercise bouts of high power generation such as sprinting, but AP is recommended for long stages where fluency and economy of movement are most important. Each stage has different challenges, and the best handcycle–athlete interface is athlete and task determined.

## Training Programmes

Optimal performance in sport is the result of optimal preparation. One of the key determinants in the preparation of an athlete is training. An optimal training programme is a key to success in high-intensity sports such as handcycling and nowadays requires an individualized sport- and task-specific approach. Knowledge of basic exercise physiology to accurately determine the training zones for each athlete allows a well-balanced training programme. In this section, the key exercise physiological thresholds (figure 12.2) and the demarcation of training zones based on these thresholds will be discussed.

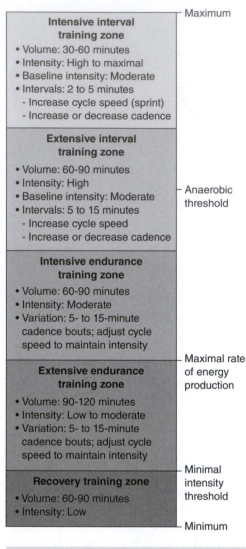

**Figure 12.2** Exercise physiological thresholds and training zones.

The minimal intensity threshold is the exercise level that is minimally required to achieve a training effect, typically an exercise intensity eliciting 50 percent of the peak $VO_2$. In elite nondisabled cyclists, this corresponds to 60 percent of the heart rate reserve (HRR = maximal heart rate − resting heart rate). Although it has not yet been investigated, it can be assumed that the corresponding HRR percentage in handcyclists is lower.

At lower exercise intensities, muscles get a huge amount of the energy supply from fat metabolism. This system can provide energy for longer times but has limited power. At moderate exercise intensities, fat oxidation has reached its maximal rate of energy production. Above this intensity, the extra energy is supplied by the oxidation of carbohydrate, and fat oxidation is even suppressed. However, the carbohydrate reserve in the body is limited, therefore limiting the duration of exercise at this intensity. This intensity mainly determines the performance level in endurance sport.

The anaerobic threshold is the highest exercise level without the accumulation of lactic acid. Above this exercise intensity the lactate production in the muscles exceeds elimination and the blood lactate concentration gradually increases. This point is critical because exercise intensities below this level can be sustained for longer durations without the onset of muscle fatigue. The anaerobic threshold represents the transition point from predominantly aerobic to an increasingly anaerobic energy supply. At exercise levels above this threshold, the extra energy supply is generated in absence of oxygen, leading to extra accumulation of lactate and causing muscles to fatigue.

Based on these thresholds, the following training zones can be differentiated:

■ **Recovery training zone:** The purpose of training in this zone is to recover from a heavy training or competition phase. The intensity is lower than the minimal intensity threshold, with a very low heart rate and short training duration. Training in this zone stimulates recovery but has no training effect.

■ **Extensive endurance training zone:** Exercise in this zone serves as the basis of each training schedule, and it stimulates fat metabolism. Extensive endurance training allows the energy supply from mainly fat oxidation to be maintained at higher cycling speeds during training and competition. Such training therefore prepares athletes for more intensive training efforts and is very suitable in long-duration sports. The intensity during this type of training is rather moderate; the duration, however, is long (longer than competition duration).

■ **Intensive endurance training zone:** During intensive endurance training, the energy supply is mainly generated through the oxidation of carbohydrate. The lactate concentration in the muscles is higher, but the balance between production and elimination remains stable. Since a fair amount of carbohydrate is oxidized during this type of training, the training duration is limited. The intensity during this type of training, however, is high.

■ **Extensive interval training zone:** The intensity in this type of training is close to the anaerobic threshold ($\pm 4$ percent). Exercises in this zone can be sustained for 30 to 60 minutes. The aerobic energy supply (fat and carbohydrate metabolism) reaches the maximal intensity that allows a balance between lactate production and elimination. Extensive interval training should be conducted in the immediate build-up to competition.

■ **Intensive interval training zone:** This is the anaerobic training zone. The purpose of anaerobic training is to increase an athlete's tolerance to lactate accumulation. It is a very strenuous type of training; the intensity is nearly maximal and requires lots of recovery.

## Assessment

Athletes often use cycling speed to determine their training intensity. However, an athlete's response to a certain cycling speed may vary depending on a number of external and internal factors such as air resistance, crank cadence, the athlete's mental and physical health, and so on. Therefore, it is recommended for athletes with a normal cardiovascular response to exercise to use heart rate as an indicator of training intensity instead. Athletes with a lesion level above T4, however, often have a dysfunction of the sympathetic nervous system. As a consequence, heart rate reaches lower maximal values. People with complete tetraplegia will reach maximal heart rates of 110 to 120 beats per minute during exercise. Thus, heart rate should not be used as an indicator of training intensity for this group (as discussed in chapter 3). Such athletes should use power output rather than cycling speed to set the training intensity because it excludes external factors, influencing the intensity indication. Power output during handcycling can be registered through systems such as the SRM crank system or the PowerTap. Regular assessments under lab or field conditions as described in chapter 3 are therefore necessary.

In addition, the influence of several sport-specific factors needs to be considered. In handcycling, the influence of the crank cadence has been well documented and should be implemented in the training schedule. It is recommended to increase and decrease the cadence on a regular basis during all training types and intensities. For example, during extensive interval training, the interval blocks can be achieved by increasing or decreasing the crank cadence to train cycling rhythm or cycling power. Higher cadences to maintain a certain cycling speed will result in a later onset of muscle fatigue since athletes often have a tendency to adopt a cadence that is lower than the optimal. In combination with a higher capacity for power generation, this will result in a significant improvement in performance. However, cadence training should be restricted to the preparation phase because it takes time for training effects to occur.

# Training Activities

Success in handcycling is mainly a product of well-organized training. Several aspects must be considered to reach a well-balanced, systematic training programme. In the following text, the main contents of handcycling training are discussed. Obviously the training schedule has to focus on expected specific training outcomes and the athlete's physical capacity.

**Training well is the key to success in handcycling.**
Photo courtesy of Thomas Abel.

### ● HIGH-VOLUME TRAINING

**Purpose**
To develop a solid baseline endurance capacity

**Focus Points**
High volumes at the extensive endurance training zone are needed during preparation for the next season of competition.

**Execution**
Mileages between 300 and 400 kilometres a week are not unusual for the top competitors of division H4. Beginners or cyclists interested in leisure should aim for at least three units a week

with moderate training intensities. Short anaerobic bouts should complement each aerobic training unit to keep the anaerobic system awake. For example, in a 90-minute extensive endurance stage, a 2-minute high-intensity bout is implied every 30 minutes. High intensity is achieved through shifting to lower gears (higher cadence), keeping the velocity constant.

## ● RECOVERY

**Purpose**
To avoid over- or undertraining

**Focus Points**
Find a good balance among extensive, intensive, and recovery training.

**Examples**
After 3 to 4 days of intensive training, there should be 1 day to recover. After 2 to 3 intensive weeks of training, a week of reduced volume and intensity should follow.

## ● POSITION

**Purpose**
To optimize ergonomic position

**Focus Points**
Because of the increased force generation or the increased movement speed, cyclists will find out soon how their handcycle has to be adjusted. They should try to find better support via changes of the backrest (inclination and distance) and upholstery.

**Examples**
Try to reach a high velocity with both a high gear (low cadence, i.e., <50 rpm) and a low gear (high cadence, i.e., >90 rpm) and hold it for a longer time (3 to 5 minutes).

## ● STRENGTH FOR LONG AND INTENSIVE ROUTES

**Purpose**
To optimize climbing capacity

**Focus Points**
On hilly routes, cyclists will have to generate high power over a longer amount of time. To prepare for this kind of power generation, strength endurance training is necessary.

**Examples**
Select a medium to high gear transmission ratio and ride with a low frequency (40-60 rpm). Ideally look out for a long and moderate climb. Begin the climb with a low cadence and a high gear transmission ratio and hold this cadence without changing gears. It is vital to recover well after each bout of intensive effort. Extensive, intensive interval training would be best (ride the climb, U-turn, next load).

## ● VELOCITY

**Purpose**
To increase peak power and velocity

**Focus Points**
Try to find maximum velocity on flat terrain and different slopes. Remember, maximal exercises require a long recovery and demand high motivation and concentration.

**Examples**
Perform a maximal sprint of 200 to 300 metres using different gear transmission ratios. Include a long, active recovery (recovery training zone) after each sprint.

## ● MECHANICAL EFFICIENCY

**Purpose**

To increase strength in function of movement directions during handcycling

**Focus Points**

Develop strength within the circular path in each case only via pulling or pushing movements. For athletes of divisions H1 and H2, the pushing movement in particular provides a high potential for development.

**Examples**

Good results can be achieved through nonspecific strength training.

## ● CADENCE VERSUS POWER

**Purpose**

To increase cycling cadence to postpone muscle fatigue

**Focus Points**

High-cadence training is important because athletes often have a tendency to shift to higher gears, which are less efficient. High gears (low cadence) demand high power generation and recruit more type II fibres, leading to rising lactic acidosis and muscle damage.

**Examples**

When implementing cadence bouts in training sessions, adjust cycle speed to maintain or increase training intensity. For example, in an extensive interval training session, build in 5-minute cadence bouts. Maintain cycle speed and shift to a lower gear transmission ratio until the desired intensity is achieved.

## ● NONSPECIFIC TRAINING

**Purpose**

To optimize the training programme by including nonspecific training

**Focus Points**

Specific training in the handcycle should be completed with general methods. Therefore, training contents from the domain of strength training are particularly important. Exercises can be chosen that use body weight, equipment, or dumbbells.

**Examples**

Depending on the goals and the period of competition, athletes should plan two to three strength training sessions per week. It is particularly important to train the agonists and antagonists in all degrees of freedom to keep the joint musculature well balanced and to avoid repetitive strain injuries. Strength training should always be immediately followed by stretching exercises.

## ● STEERING, BRAKING, AND ACCELERATING

**Purpose**

To train in realistic conditions

**Focus Points**

There are many stages of competitions with various inclinations, curves, U-turns, and so on. Passing quickly and safely through these points should be the aim of this training.

**Examples**

Learn to pass through curves without losing cycle speed, to brake effectively, and to accelerate fast.

## ● RIDING IN GROUPS

**Purpose**
To ride in groups

**Focus Points**
During road races it will be necessary to ride along with a group. Athletes should work on this with their training group as in a team pursuit or time trial.

**Examples**
Ride in team and follow each other closely in line to minimize total drag. After a certain amount of time, the lead rider (who works the hardest) peels off the front and rejoins the team at the rear.

# Racing Tactics

There are two main competition forms in handcycling: road races and time trials. During a road race, competing riders start simultaneously, whereas in a time trial, athletes race alone against the clock and are sent out in intervals. Both forms require specific skills and tactics.

## Road Races

Besides the physiological premises and the used cycle as well as cycle components, racing strategy plays an essential role in completing a competition as successfully as possible. In principle, there are no differences between race tactics in handcycling and cycling. Masking fatigue, intimidating the opponent through repetitive short accelerations, taking the lead or staying in the slipstream, and collaborating with other athletes to get rid of a sprinter are just a few examples of the tactical game. Of course, the better an athlete is physically prepared for competition, the more strategic options are available during the race.

**Race tactics are similar for cycling and handcycling.**
Photo courtesy of Arno Becker.

The athlete's anaerobic capacity, which is developed through extensive and intensive interval training, makes a big difference during the race. To successfully break away from the peloton or to accelerate uphill, athletes need to be able to resist the rising lactic acidosis. Athletes need to know how their bodies react and adapt their racing strategy accordingly. Heart rate monitoring is the first step in learning how the body reacts in different external conditions.

If the external conditions are extreme (headwind or side wind), the peloton is easily fragmented. In these conditions, it is critical to use the aerodynamic advantage gained by slipstreaming. In handcycling, slipstreaming can reduce the overall work up to 25 percent. Slipstreaming is a skill that should be practised in different external conditions during training.

Due to the increasing numbers of participants in races, team tactics start to dominate strategy development. As a consequence, new tactical skills have to be incorporated in team training (e.g., the front runner's teammates slowing the pack down).

## Time Trials

The individual time trial (ITT) is highly demanding of the athlete's physical and psychological capacity. For ITTs above 15 to 20 kilometres, the exercise intensity is continuously near maximum (at or above the anaerobic threshold). As a consequence, training units in preparation of ITTs include repetitive workouts in the extensive and intensive interval training zones. Economy of movement (mechanical efficiency) is of highest importance at these workload levels. Workloads should be achieved through a combination of medium-high resistance (e.g., continuous slope of 6 percent) and high pedalling cadence. The latter is the absolute priority because high cadence recruits fewer type II fibres and therefore avoids rising lactic acidosis. Furthermore, muscle damage is minimized through high cadence. Finally, air resistance is the main force handcyclists encounter during ITT. Thus, aerodynamic factors such as the athlete's riding posture and handcycle configuration play a major role.

A prerequisite for adequate performance control during ITTs and training for competition is analysis of the athlete's condition and the demand during the race. Although the evaluation of personal capacities can be done in a laboratory or field setting, it is difficult to collect race data because that requires testing during competition. Understandably athletes are not interested in being exposed to invasive and distracting test procedures during a competition. Nevertheless, if an athlete is collaborating, data registration can be realized using portable spirometric systems, heart rate monitors, or systems measuring the workload. Even collection of blood samples is possible in short resting phases.

The value of such tests is enormous. A precise description of energy-delivering systems and their limitations as well as verification of cardiorespiratory function are possible. The previously described setting, for example, allows the calculation of mechanical efficiency during competition, which can provide information about working economy during a prolonged competition. Physical capacities can be evaluated to enhance the athlete's performance and may lead to optimized training. Needless to say, such tests also claim relevance for less competition-orientated concerns, such as prevention of arteriosclerotic diseases due to increased energy expenditure. Although these aspects have a limited impact on performance, they have a considerable influence on the athlete's life.

From a tactical viewpoint, there are only a few guidelines. Athletes should use the environment (walls, hedges, parked cars, trees) to minimize air resistance during the time trial. They should pay attention to follow the optimal racing line, because in a time trial the full extension of the road can be used. Due to particularities of the route, such as slopes, trees, bumps in the street, and road markings, the optimal racing line is not necessarily the shortest route from start to finish. In either case, the track should be examined in detail before the race starts. Pass through narrow curves with racing speed to guarantee an ideal racing line. Surface coverings show significant differences regarding the rolling frictions that every athlete has experienced during training. Lanes from cars or continuous and wide road markings show a seriously reduced rolling friction. Look out for these advantages especially because there is a lesser risk to slip with the three-wheeled handcycle compared with the two-wheeled bicycle.

## Conclusion

Handcycling is an attractive and popular worldwide sport. Due to systematic training and improvements of the handcycle itself, the quality of performance has increased significantly. Beside the fascination of a competitive performance-orientated activity, handcycles have an enormous impact on the freedom of movement of those who use a wheelchair for mobility.

# The Baroness Grey-Thompson

My international competitive career spanned five Paralympic Games, but sport was always something that was just there. I don't remember a time when it wasn't a passion.

I was born with spina bifida and could walk in my early years, but by the age of seven I was paralysed and became a wheelchair user. It's hard to remember precisely, because it didn't make that much difference to me; perhaps it mattered more to others. I do remember a few times when walking was difficult, and I fell a lot, but at six years old you don't question things. Having my first chair changed my life and gave me the freedom I craved, but watching the London Marathon on TV had the biggest impact on me: I knew that one day I would do it.

At my first Games in Seoul in 1988, there was limited coverage in the media, and many people in the UK didn't know about the Paralympics. The momentum in the UK changed leading up to the 1992 Barcelona Paralympics. There was daily coverage in the written press, highlights programmes on TV, and the beginning of an understanding of what the Paralympic Games were.

In wheelchair racing we were also lucky because we had road races that were covered on television. That was a great base, but there are still challenges in terms of getting more mainstream coverage.

After the 1996 Olympics (where the team won only one gold medal), changes in the administration of sport had a huge impact on the Paralympic team. Through the lottery to fund national governing bodies, it became possible to achieve excellence in sport.

It has been by no means an easy ride. Inclusion was encouraged but has been handled very differently by various governing bodies, and there is still a long way to go. I know that in many cases we are in a better position than most other countries. The support, sponsorship, and media coverage we receive are fantastic, but as always I am ambitious about moving forward and improving for the next generation. There are so many more opportunities for athletes, from the grassroots level to the elite level, that we can't stop working to make it better.

I retired from competitive sport in 2007 and am involved in many other things now. In Beijing I worked in the media and got to sit on the other side. I am actively involved in the athletics governing body and sit on several other panels, not all related to sport. The challenges of changing attitudes remain, and the goalposts move, but those are what make the work interesting.

Photo courtesy of Tanni Grey-Thompson.

# Index

**PLEASE NOTE:** Page numbers followed by an italicized *f* or *t* indicate that there is a figure or table on that page, respectively. If there is an italicized *ff* or *tt*, following page numbers, there are multiple figures or tables to be found on those pages, respectively.

# About the Editor

**Vicky Goosey-Tolfrey, PhD,** is a senior lecturer in exercise physiology and director of the Peter Harrison Centre for Disability Sport at Loughborough University in Leicestershire, UK. Her work in 1994 with Prof. Ian Campbell and the Baroness Grey-Thompson sparked her interest in disability sport, and she went on to earn her PhD in sport science from Manchester Metropolitan University five years later.

Dr. Goosey-Tolfrey attended the Atlanta 1996 and Sydney 2000 Paralympic Games with the Great Britain wheelchair racing and wheelchair basketball teams, respectively, and was the lead physiology consultant for the British Paralympic Association for the Athens 2004 and Beijing 2008 Games. In her leisure time, she enjoys being with her family, golfing, and watching films.

# About the Contributors

**Thomas Abel, PhD,** has degrees in sport sciences and special education from the German Sport University in Cologne and is on the faculty of rehabilitation pedagogy at the University of Cologne. His doctorate is in sports medicine and rehabilitation. From 2001 to 2003 he was a lecturer at the Institute of Cardiology and Sports Medicine at the German Sport University. Since 2003 Abel has been a senior lecturer at the Institute of Movement Science at the German Sport University. From 2007 to 2009 he was head of the department of motor function and neuroscience, and in 2009 he became vice head of the institute. Dr. Abel has been responsible for adapted physical activity at the university, where his research focuses on exercise physiology.

**Andy Allford** is the lead strength and conditioning coach for badminton at the English Institute of Sport. After graduating in 1996 from the University of Brighton with a sport science degree, Andy has spent his time exclusively in the fields of health, fitness, and performance. Before joining the EIS full time in 2006, Andy worked for the University of Hertfordshire as head of health, fitness, and performance while working for the EIS part time and serving as the lead strength and conditioning coach with the British Paralympic Association.

**Mike Boninger, MD,** is professor and chair of the department of physical medicine and rehabilitation at the University of Pittsburgh School of Medicine, where he serves as associate dean for medical student research. Dr. Boninger is a physician researcher for the Department of Veterans Affairs and is medical director of the Human Engineering Research Laboratories, a VA Rehabilitation, Research, and Development Center of Excellence. Dr. Boninger is also a professor of bioengineering and rehabilitation science and technology and director of the UPMC Institute for Rehabilitation and Research. He has published over 150 papers on spinal cord injury and assistive technology.

**Elizabeth Bressan, PhD,** completed her BS and MS degrees at the University of North Carolina and her PhD at the University of Southern California. She joined Stellenbosch University in 1990. She coordinated the sport science services for the 2000 and 2004 South African Paralympic teams and was a member of the Scientific Committee of the International Paralympic Committee from 2003 to 2009. She is currently the director of the Centre for Human Performance Sciences at Stellenbosch and is responsible for developing academic networks with African and other international institutions in the areas of disability sport, youth sport, and sport for girls and women.

**Rory A. Cooper, PhD,** is the FISA and Paralyzed Veterans of America chair at the University of Pittsburgh and director of VA Human Engineering Research Laboratories. He has received the Olin Teague Award, U.S. Army Outstanding Civilian Service Medal, James Peters Award, Maxwell J. Schleifer Award, and DaVinci Lifetime Achievement Award. He was also inducted into the SCI Hall of Fame. Dr. Cooper has over 225 peer-reviewed journal publications and is a fellow of RESNA, IEEE, AIMBE, and BMES. He was a bronze medallist at the 1988 Paralympic Games, on the steering committee for the 1996 Paralympic Scientific Congress, and a sport scientist for the 2008 U.S. Paralympic team. Cooper was featured on a Cheerios cereal box for his achievements.

**Rosemarie Cooper, MPT,** received her BA in international business from California State University at Sacramento in 1994. She received her master of physical therapy degree from the University of Pittsburgh in 1998. Rosemarie is the director of the Center for Assistive Technology and a clinical instructor in the department of rehabilitation science and technology at the University of Pittsburgh.

**Jeanette Crosland, MSc, RD, SENr,** is a registered dietitian and a registered sport nutritionist. She began working in Paralympic sports in 2001 and since 2002 has worked with ParalympicsGB. During this time she has gained extensive knowledge of the nutritional needs of wheelchair athletes, helping to prepare teams for the Athens and Beijing Paralympics. She has written and contributed to several books on sport nutrition and is a regular contributor to medical and nursing journals on diet, exercise, and health. She also contributes regularly to nutrition and sporting publications.

**Nicholas Diaper, MS,** has been working in elite Paralympic sport since receiving his master's degree in exercise physiology from Manchester Metropolitan University in 2002. He is currently the lead Paralympic talent identification scientist working for the English Institute of Sport. His role involves supporting British national governing bodies in their quest to identify medal-winning athletes for the London 2012 Paralympic Games and beyond. Nicholas' previous roles include physiologist for the Great Britain wheelchair tennis team and performance profiler for Paralympic sport within the English Institute of Sport.

Injured in 1986, **Mike Frogley** started coaching high school basketball before starting to play wheelchair basketball in 1988. He played four years of college wheelchair basketball at the University of Wisconsin at Whitewater before beginning his coaching career at UW-Whitewater. After four years at UW-Whitewater, he moved to the University of Illinois, where he still coaches. He was a member of the Canadian national team, competing in the 1992 Paralympics. He was an assistant coach with the Canadian women's national team at the 1996 Paralympics and served as the head coach of the Canadian men's national team at the 2000, 2004, and 2008 Paralympics.

**Tanni Grey-Thompson** was born in Cardiff and educated at Loughborough University. She competed at five Paralympic Games (winning 11 gold medals) and retired from international athletics in 2007. She has coached athletes up to Paralympic level. As well as working in the development side of the sport, she has been a board member of UK Sport and vice chair of the UK Lottery awards panel. In 2005 she was named Dame Commander of the Order of the British Empire, and in 2010 she was elevated to the House of Lords as a Crossbench Peer.

**Justin Z. Laferrier, MSPT, OCS, SCS, ATP, CSCS,** received his master of science degree in physical therapy from the University of Rhode Island. Before pursuing his PhD, he served in both the U.S. Marine Corps (enlisted) and U.S. Army (officer). During his time with the army he was the officer in charge of amputee physical therapy for Walter Reed Army Medical Center in Washington, DC, and the Center for the Intrepid in San Antonio, Texas, as well as officer in charge of physical therapy for the 31st Combat Support Hospital deployed to Baghdad, Iraq. He is currently employed as a physical therapist and researcher at the Pittsburgh VA and Human Engineering Research Laboratories.

**Hsin-yi Liu, MS,** studied physical therapy at the National Taiwan University and worked as a certified physical therapist for five years in Taiwan. She received her MS degree in rehabilitation science and technology from the University of Pittsburgh in 2008 and is currently a PhD student in the same program. Hsin-yi's research interests include optimization and use of human machine interface of mobility devices for people with disabilities.

**Laurie A. Malone, PhD,** has served as director of research and education at Lakeshore Foundation since 2002. In 1999 she received her doctorate degree from the University of Alberta, Canada, with an emphasis in sport biomechanics and adapted physical activity. Dr. Malone's research uses a multi-disciplinary approach to examine the impact of physical activity and sport on the lives of people with disabilities. Lakeshore Foundation is designated as a U.S. Olympic and Paralympic training site, where Dr. Malone is responsible for providing sport science services to national team athletes training at the facility. She has worked closely with the U.S. wheelchair rugby team since 2002.

**Linda Mitchell-Norfolk, MSc, MCSP,** is a freelance consultant in disability sport. She qualified as a chartered physiotherapist and has held posts as a consulting physiotherapist to the British Paralympic Association and a squad physiotherapist to the Great Britain disability shooting team. She is also a partner in EPC (Equipment for the Physically Challenged), a company that specializes in the provision of lightweight and sport wheelchairs. She is married to Paralympian tennis player Peter Norfolk.

**Dawn Newbery** took the Great Britain wheelchair programme from its infancy in 1992 and developed it into an internationally recognized programme leading teams at 5 Paralympic Games and 17 World Team Cups to gold, silver, and bronze medals. Dawn held many key positions, including national coach, performance coordinator, and team manager. She introduced and developed a multi-disciplinary support programme that placed the British wheelchair players among the best in the world. Dawn was a member of the ITF Coaches Commission and has been selected to vote as a member of the International Wheelchair Tennis Panel for the election of individuals to the International Tennis Hall of Fame.

**Kevin Orr** is the head coach of the Canadian national wheelchair rugby team. He has 20 years of wheelchair rugby experience from the club level to the international level. At Lakeshore Foundation in Birmingham, Alabama, Kevin developed a rugby team, the Demolition, which is one of the top clubs in the world. He coached the U.S. High Performance team and Paralympic team from 2001 to 2004. From 2005 to 2008 Kevin was the national team coach for U.S. wheelchair track. Kevin and his wife, Stephanie, are the proud parents of Allysa and Kaylee.

**Mike Price, PhD,** obtained his first degree in human movement science at the University of Liverpool in 1992. He went on to attain his MSc in biomedical engineering at the University of Dundee and then completed his PhD at Manchester Metropolitan University in 1997. His thesis examined the thermoregulatory responses of able-bodied athletes and athletes with spinal cord injuries to prolonged upper-body exercise and thermal stress. Since then he has been involved with several studies examining cooling strategies and thermal responses of both wheelchair athletes and nondisabled athletes.

**Thomas Reilly, PhD,** was universally respected and admired. His work spanned the disciplines of ergonomics, chronobiology, sport science, football, and research methods. Having completed his MSc in ergonomics, Tom always remained true to his roots in that all of his research had an applied focus. His PhD, an evaluation of the demands of soccer, allowed him to combine his emerging academic focus (science and football) with his passion for the Everton football club. One of his last collaborations was with Laura Sutton, Vicky Goosey-Tolfrey, and Jeanette Crosland, which involved the measurement of body composition in wheelchair athletes. Tom passed away on June 11, 2009.

**Ian Rice, MS,** is a doctoral student in the School of Health and Rehabilitation Science at the University of Pittsburgh. He received his MS in occupational therapy from Washington University. As a doctoral student, Ian was awarded the Integrative Graduate Education and Research Traineeship (IGERT) and Pre-Doctoral Associated Health Rehabilitation Research Fellowship. Ian's research interests include rehabilitation biomechanics, assistive technology, injury prevention, and wheelchair propulsion training methodologies. Ian also completed more than 45 marathons and was a member of the 2000 and 2004 Paralympic racing teams.

Named 2009 Coach of the Year by the International Wheelchair Tennis Association, **Geraint Richards** began coaching wheelchair tennis in the late 1990s as general manager of the Welsh National Tennis Centre. He was appointed national junior coach in 2006 and twice guided British players to a sweep of all four titles at the Junior Masters in Tarbes, France, as well as to victory in the junior event at the 2007 Invacare World Team Cup. He also coached Great Britain's women to the final of the 2009 Invacare World Team Cup and has travelled extensively on behalf of the ITF to help establish sustainable wheelchair tennis programmes in many developing countries.

**David Shearer, PhD,** was employed by the Great Britain Wheelchair Basketball Association to provide match analysis for the British men's team while working on his master's degree in sport and exercise science (psychology) at Manchester Metropolitan University. Between 2000 and 2007, his initial role as match analyst developed into team sport psychologist, providing psychological support at both the 2000 and 2004 Paralympic Games and the World and European Championships. In 2007, David completed his PhD in sport psychology at Swansea University, where he now holds a lecturing post. David is a BPS chartered psychologist and a BASES accredited sport and exercise scientist (psychology).

Born in Hull, England, **Ian Thompson, PhD,** was educated at Manchester University. Until 2008 he worked in research and product development in the chemical industry and is now a consultant in coaching wheelchair racing and in sport science and disability sport. After a spinal cord injury in 1984, he became involved in wheelchair racing as an athlete (he is Great Britain's record holder at two Paralympics) and as a coach and programme leader at two Olympics and Paralympics. He has been involved in the science of wheelchair racing since the 1990s and has had particular interest in pushing technique and ergonomics. He is married and has a daughter, Carys.

**Stephanie Trill** has more than 10 years of coaching experience in wheelchair tennis. She was the coach to national champion and Sydney 2000 Paralympic semi-finalist Kimberly Blake (nee Dell) and was Great Britain's national quad coach from 2005 to 2009. At the 2008 Beijing Paralympics, she saw Peter Norfolk win his second Paralympic quad singles gold medal before pairing up with Jamie Burdekin to win bronze in the quad doubles. In 2009 Steph was named Coach of the Year by WheelPower (British wheelchair sport) after captaining the three-strong Great Britain quad team's victory in the Invacare World Team Cup, the Davis Cup, and Fed Cup of wheelchair tennis.

**Sean Tweedy** is the MAIC research fellow of physical activity and disability in the School of Human Movement Studies at the University of Queensland. He is chief investigator on the IPC Athletics Classification project, which aims to develop an evidence-based system of classification for Paralympic sport. Sean has been an international classifier since 1993 and has classified at the Beijing, Athens, and Sydney Paralympic Games. He has been a member of the IPC Classification Committee since 2009.

**Yves C. Vanlandewijck, PhD,** is a full professor on the faculty of kinesiology and rehabilitation sciences of the Catholic University of Leuven, where he obtained his PhD in 1992. His research interests are exercise physiology, biomechanics, and ergonomics for people with disabilities in a continuum of rehabilitation to elite sport. Main research applications focus on the development of evidence-based classification systems in disability sports, with a particular interest in the relationship of intellectual functioning and performance of athletes with intellectual disabilities. Since 1995 he has been a member of the IPC Sport Science Committee of the International Paralympic Committee and has been the chairperson since 2004.

**Joeri Verellen, MSc,** is a scientific assistant on the faculty of kinesiology and rehabilitation sciences at the Catholic University of Leuven, where he obtained his master of science degree in motor rehabilitation and physiotherapy and completed the European master's program in adapted physical activity. Currently he is in his final phase of completing a PhD in ergonomic aspects of handcycling at Leuven University under the supervision of Prof. Yves Vanlandewijck. His main research interests are exercise physiology, biomechanics, and ergonomics, particularly in wheelchair sports. He is also a member of the Committee of Top Sport and the Committee of Adapted Tennis in the Flemish League of Disabled Sports.

**Nick Webborn, MB, BS, FFSEM, FACSM, FISM, MSc,** is medical director of the Sussex Centre for Sport and Exercise Medicine at the University of Brighton and an honorary clinical senior lecturer in sport and exercise medicine, Queen Mary, University of London. He is chief medical officer to the British Paralympic Association and a member of the IPC Sport Science Committee. Nick has been a medical officer with the British team at the Paralympic Games in Atlanta, Nagano, and Sydney and later joined the anti-doping committee of the International Paralympic Medical Commission attending the Salt Lake, Athens, and Torino Paralympics. He leads the IPC sport injury surveillance programme. He was a member of the London 2012 health advisory group presenting to the IOC evaluation commission; subsequently he was a member of the LOCOG Medical Advisory Group advising on the health care planning for the 2012 Games.

**Martyn Whait** has coached British players at the Sydney, Athens, and Beijing Paralympic Games during his time as Great Britain national men's coach. He has also worked as personal coach to several British players, including seventh-ranked Jayant Mistry and David Phillipson, one of Mistry's recent successors to the British No. 1 ranking. He has guided Great Britain men's teams to the semi-finals of World Group 1 in the Invacare World Team Cup as well as to victory in World Group 2 in 2008. Martyn has also worked extensively on behalf of the ITF and has made presentations on wheelchair tennis at coaches' workshops throughout the world.